# The Politics of Empire

The Transnational Institute is an independent fellowship of researchers and activists living in different parts of the world, who develop innovative analyses of world affairs. It serves no government, political party or interest group.

# The Politics of Empire

## Globalisation in Crisis

Edited by
Alan Freeman and Boris Kagarlitsky

Pluto Press

LONDON • ANN ARBOR, MI

*in association with*

**Transnational Institute (TNI)**

First published 2004 by Pluto Press
345 Archway Road, London N6 5AA
and 839 Greene Street, Ann Arbor, MI 48106

www.plutobooks.com

British Library Cataloguing in Publication Data
A catalogue record for this book is available from the British Library

ISBN    0 7453 2184 4 hardback
ISBN    0 7453 2183 6 paperback

Library of Congress Cataloging in Publication Data applied for

10   9   8   7   6   5   4   3   2   1

Designed and produced for Pluto Press by
Chase Publishing Services, Fortescue, Sidmouth, EX10 9QG, England
Typeset from disk by Stanford DTP Services, Northampton, England
Printed and bound in the European Union by
Antony Rowe Ltd, Chippenham and Eastbourne, England

# Contents

# Introduction
# World Empire – or a World of Empires?

*Alan Freeman and Boris Kagarlitsky*

On 17 February 2002, the Transnational Institute (TNI) called a weekend seminar in Amsterdam to discuss perspectives for what is variously known as the movement for global justice, the movement against anti-corporate globalisation or simply the anti-globalisation movement.[1] The result is this unique synthesis, the product of two years of collective work and discussion between prominent writers and activists in global justice and peace movements spanning five continents.

From a refreshingly wide range of views two clear points of consensus emerged. First, 'globalisation', as commonly understood, had entered a phase of crisis. A two-decade-long process of expansion of the world market, marked by accelerated financial deregulation and multilateral agreements overseen by supranational organisations, notably the International Monetary Fund (IMF), the World Bank and the World Trade Organisation (WTO), was in deep trouble.

Second, this crisis was structural. It was not temporary and did not appear reversible. It stemmed, participants agreed, from deep-seated problems within the globalisation process itself. At the very least, globalisation had run up against some fairly heavy difficulties. More significantly, there was no clear indication that its supporters could resolve these difficulties.

Here was a new message: globalisation, as we know it, might not just be unjust: it might also be unsustainable. Doubts were surfacing, no longer about whether it was desirable but whether, as originally proposed, it was even possible. Many argued that new events augured the end of globalisation, some that it had never really existed. Wherever the actual truth lay, global justice movements and peace movements clearly faced a new stage of history and needed to make an in-depth appraisal of the tasks facing them.

The discussion gave rise to this work. We want to express three debts of gratitude: to the Economic Research Centre of the Middle East Technical University in Ankara, which funded two joint sessions at its Sixth International Conference; to the Global Studies Association and University of California, Santa Barbara, who co-organised the Critical Globalisation Studies conference in May 2003, and to the organisers of a unique conference in June 2003 on the initiative of the Moscow Institute for Globalisation Studies, which witnessed a path-breaking dialogue between Russian and Eurasian activists and writers, and the Communist Party of the Federation of Russia.

The result is unique: a contribution to understanding that has arisen from engagement. The writers set out to dissect what is actually going on in the world today; to understand 'where globalisation is at' – why and to what extent it has failed, what its results have been, where the whole process is now leading, and what prospects and challenges this implies for all who seek global justice.

It is therefore no activists' manual; it contains no instructions or manifestos. It was, however, produced neither in an armchair nor a bank. Its authors are active in movements across the world against the impact of corporate globalisation. This is the authentic voice of a confident and experienced movement for change.

## THE WORLD AFTER 9/11

To understand the issues the authors attempted to grapple with, it is useful to remember what was going on at the time. In February 2002 evidence of crisis was not hard to find. As Bello and Malig testify, globalisation's early triumphalism was already in retreat.[2] The 1997 Asian crisis was only five years past, and the aftershocks of Argentina's financial and political collapse were roiling round the world. The dotcom bubble had burst, and Standard & Poor's 500 index of US stock market prices was already down 26 per cent from its August 2001 peak.[3]

Corporate globalisation's supermodels had woken up with uglier faces than they took to the party: on 9 January 2002, four months after Enron filed for Chapter 11 bankruptcy, the US Justice Department launched a formal criminal investigation into the conduct of Enron directors, and on 19 January the White House formally acknowledged that Dick Cheney had helped Enron secure payment on a $64 million debt arising from an Indian energy project. Two months later Arthur Andersen officials were to be formally indicted for having 'knowingly, intentionally and corruptly' persuaded employees to shred Enron-related documents.

Globalisation was in trouble on another front, unforeseen in Fukuyama's rosy vision of the end of history. The war in Afghanistan was under way and the axis of evil had been named. By the time of our Ankara conference it was clear that the US was going to invade Iraq come what may. A new, uncertain and warlike world was emerging from the ashes of 9/11.

The Bush administration's bellicose stance was raising ever bigger question marks about the USA's true relation to the international institutions in whose name it had so far acted. Whether it had ever subordinated itself to supranational institutions is a question that has provoked hot debates reflected in this book. With the Iraq War it literally crossed the Rubicon. It became clear that the US government would pursue the policies it had decided on, with or without a coalition, and with or without the international institutions. If multilateralism was not dead in the water, it was certainly closer to drowning than waving.

When the world backed the USA, as it did in 2002, then the semblance of multilateral action persisted. When it did not, as in 2003, not even the semblance remained. Moreover the USA had shown, in the unilateral protection given to its steel producers, that it was prepared to be just as partisan in the economic sphere. Given its enormous political, military and economic weight, what real power did this leave in the hands of the IMF, WTO and the World Bank – not to mention the United Nations and its myriad satellites?

### Multilateralism in question

The extent of multilateralism has been in hot dispute ever since globalisation began. This matters: throughout its short intellectual history the concept of globalisation has straddled two domains, the political and economic. At the economic level it is almost indisputable that the 'extent of the market' has got bigger with time. But although it is often convenient for the proponents of 'globalisation' to reduce it to the economic level when defending it, the idea usually includes another and more contestable assertion: that the national state is no longer a sustainable or viable vehicle for the world market economy.[4] Therefore, it is argued, the growing powers of the IMF, World Bank and WTO are not the result of a conscious choice, but are an inevitable consequence of underlying economic developments. Consequently, it matters 'who really decides'. If the IMF dictates the policy of the US state, then we have at least prototypically true multilateralism. But if in practice the US state dictates the policy of the IMF, we have unilateralism in multilateral clothing.

At least two interpretations of the relevant events have co-existed for some time, and still do. One standpoint is what we will here call formal globalisation theory – the body of academic writings, whether supportive or critical of the outcome – which has sought or claim to provide a new analytical framework to explain the changes in world governance of the past three decades.[5] From this viewpoint, these changes expressed long-term processes that have made it increasingly difficult for nation-states to act alone or in defiance of international institutions. True multilateralism is from this standpoint an economic *fait accompli*; the new world political and financial institutions are merely a recognition of necessity.

National states in this view were either losing their power or operating more and more as vehicles for stateless multinationals or international classes. As Held and McGrew[6] put it:

> At the heart of the globalist thesis is the conviction that globalization is transforming the nature and form of political power today. Globalists argue that the right of most states to rule within circumscribed territories – their sovereignty – is on the edge of transformation, as is the practical nature of this entitlement – the actual capacity of states to rule.

From this viewpoint, from 1980 onwards capital had simply recognised the necessity underlying the impotence of the national state in the face of the world market, by creating the appropriate international political institutions.

Robinson in this book thus argues that in the 1970s capital accumulation had already entered a crisis, which it could only solve by 'going global'; by creating a transnational state apparatus, a 'loose but increasingly coherent network comprised of supranational political and economic institutions and national state apparatuses that have been penetrated and transformed by transnational forces'. The nation-state system is therefore 'no longer the organizing principle of capitalism. National states as components of a larger [transnational state] structure now tend to serve the interests of global over national accumulation processes.'

### The USA – agent or agency?

The alternative view, coming from within what we will call the classical anti-imperialist left, was cogently expressed by Gowan:

[globalisation] has been not in the least a spontaneous outcome of organic economic or technological processes, but a deeply political result of political choices made by successive governments of one state: the United States.[7]

From this standpoint the new international institutions were from the outset created by, shaped by, and subordinate to a conscious alliance between Washington, the world's most powerful political entity, and Wall Street, the world's most powerful economic entity. Following what Todaro[8] has called the 'neo-classical counterrevolution' the World Bank, the IMF and subsequently the WTO fell under the control of a specific political bloc animated from within the state apparatus of the United States of America. The weakness of 'the nation-state' observed by the globalisation theorists was merely a weakness of all other existing states vis-à-vis the enormous and unprecedented concentration of power and wealth in this one particular state.

Neither view is entirely incompatible either with the process that preceded 9/11, nor with the events that unfolded after it. On the one hand, the fact that international institutions exist does not prove the globalisation thesis, and neither does the fact some nation-states have weakened relative to these institutions. This could equally happen because other nations have become stronger. Multilateral or transnational governmental systems may function as nothing but a transmission belt for national ambitions, and have often done so. If a nation complies with an international directive – as interwar Germany did for several years after the Versailles Treaty – this may only signify that other nations have imposed these directives on them. This does not change if the powerful nations choose to exercise their power in the name of an international agency. Despite its present ambiguity, the United States – which created the League of Nations – has a long history of promoting its aims through international institutions. Not least, it found this a convenient way to rein in the imperial ambitions of its older European rivals.

On the other hand, one may accept that the US state has ceased to function under the direction of the international institutions, and at the same time argue that it is really just a convenient agent for the international interests it represents. During the whole period of the 'Plan Cavallo', while the peso was pegged to the dollar, the whole sum of international lending to Argentina was equal and opposite to the outflow of dollars held by Argentine nationals whose allegiance to world financial markets clearly outweighed any national commitment.[9] Financial deregulation brought about an extraordinary rise in international liquidity. This has made it much easier for wealthy nationals to liberate themselves from the fortunes of their country of residence and operate on a truly world scale. These dollar capitalists need an international order that can defend their interests as much as any burger-munching mid-Westerner, and in countries such as Colombia – not to mention Venezuela – they have every interest in both encouraging and shaping unilateral US actions. Ghosh documents the important role played by 'non-resident Indians' in the formation of Indian state policy, and the contribution of writers such as Bhagwati to the globalising agenda itself is well known.

That said, what really matters is not where things are, but in what direction they are going. There is not really much evidence that the United States is becoming *less* sovereign than it was, say, 30 years ago. What can be learned from this fact? The issue is not the past but the future. Can the nation-state be abolished, or substantively undermined, either through the complete supersession of class – in liberal variants – or by the capitalist class itself, in the more Marxist-influenced variants? Or can it only be accomplished by a working-class agency as the classical Marxists believed – or is a world freed of national barriers simply impossible?

## Can capital dispense with the territorial state?

This in turn boils down to the question: are there functions of the nation-state that are actually indispensable to capital? Savran, in this volume, argues that under capitalism

> traits that derive from the very essence of statehood such as a national currency, the existence of a public finance system, a specific labour relations regime and an overall economic structure distinguish the economic territory of each nation-state from the others.

From this standpoint, no matter how much capital would prefer to function independent of nation-states, the national state provides things it cannot do without. Transnational governance under capitalism is therefore ultimately impossible.

Can such conflicting interpretations co-exist within a single response to globalisation? Is there any real consensus, or is the opposition to corporate globalisation nothing more than a coalition of the grumpy, papering over its differences to unite by throwing sand in the wheels of progress? We would argue that both the consensus and the differences are essential to a truly coherent understanding, because both analyses recognise essential aspects of today's reality. It is *both* true that existing national states cannot function as before, *and* that the international institutions have failed to replace them. This is what we mean by structural crisis: a set of problems to which there is no immediate stable solution.

The past thirty years have stretched the capacity of existing nation-states to function in world markets as an adequate agent of capital beyond tolerable limits, and this is the primary source of political instability in the world today. But, as post-9/11 events have shown, the new international institutions are equally incapable of serving as adequate instruments either of national capital or of world capital.

What we face, therefore, is a general crisis of all political relations including not just the nation but the international order that was supposed to replace or supplant it. We cannot know the outcome by appealing to abstract schemas, to visions of how a new capitalist order might function, if only the dreams of the globalisers were fulfilled and if only the Seattle and Genoa activists abandoned their obscurantist opposition. Nor can we know it by appealing either to a mythical pre-modern polity of independent small nations, or to a just but utopian alternative world order, regardless of the actual possibilities inherent in the world we now inhabit and independent of the real relation of forces. We can only know the future concretely, analysing the actual dynamic and direction of motion of events. If we do this right, we can also shape it.

The policies of the globalisers rest on an unproven doctrinal assertion: that globalisation, at least in its present form, offers a stable solution to the governance of the planet. As this book shows, this doctrine simply does not fit the facts. Whether or not the international institutions have strengthened in relation to the national ones, the fact of the matter is that they have not produced a stable political alternative. On the contrary, the accumulated evidence is that they are busily undermining the conditions for their own existence.

The decisive agreement between the contributors, born of long experience of the results of corporate globalisation, is that the present solutions on offer neither solve the problem, nor offer any comfort to humanity. Another world, therefore, is not just possible: it is necessary.

## THE GLOBALISATION OF DIVERGENCE

This book opens a necessary debate by insisting that the discontents of globalisation are neither wilful, external, nor the result of bad management, but are produced by it and intrinsic to it. The problems of globalisation stem from globalisation itself: it is, in a word, unsustainable. The most basic reason for not buying into it is that it simply does not work. This does not mean it is an empty concept, simply that it is not going where everyone thinks it is.

So where is it in fact going? In trying to assess this the next question is: where does its crisis come from? At the top of the list offered by the authors of this book, and perhaps at the root of the problems of globalisation, is that it is making the world more unequal. As Kagarlitsky puts it, 'It is a myth that free markets lead to homogenisation. In fact they lead to polarisation – between social classes, between countries, between regions.'

There is, *prima facie*, a fundamental contradiction between the idea that globalisation has no limits, and the fact that it is polarising the world. Polarisation – above all territorial polarisation – *is* the most basic limit on globalisation. When we talked about it, none of us could see how an unequal world could be a global one. In a way, this is the sticking point of the movement for global justice as a whole, and this is why we think this volume reflects and respects the experience of the movement.

What unites the very disparate movement against globalisation, as so far seen, is the old-fashioned Jacobin nostrum that freedom without equality is a nonsense. Not just because it is wrong, but because it is impossible. It is hard to see how any social process that mercilessly segregates the poor from the rich without limit can sustain itself as an integrated totality. The problem is not that globalisation is in some sense 'at war' with alien tendencies towards fragmentation, as some writers express it, but that it produces fragmentation as it develops, as a part of its contradictory essence, setting up an organic internal limit that it is now running up against.[10]

This is not just a theoretical question. It is practical and immediate. There is a tight relation between territorial inequality and political instability, both in space and in time. Looking at a map of the world today, there is an almost one-to-one correlation between those regions in which territorial extremes are sharpest – beginning with the Middle East itself, the nemesis of globalisation and the cockpit of its self-destruction – and those in which military and civil conflicts are the most endemic and liberal democracy the most remote. The number of military conflicts recognised as wars by the United Nations follows a rising curve, which tracks, year by year, the rising curve of inequality on a world scale. The idea that territories whose average wealth is separated by factors of 20, 40, 80, and lately well over 100 will submit calmly, indefinitely and without conflict to a single rule of law is breathtakingly utopian.

Region by region and case by case, the contributors to this volume chart how the globalisation process *itself* generated the instabilities at every level – social, regional, geopolitical; military, commercial, financial – which rendered global governance impossible.

### Is global justice possible?

Does this mean that the authors of this book, and the movement for global justice in general, have given up or should give up on the idea of a just international order? The slogan 'another world is possible' has real content. It signifies that a just international order is an attainable goal, which cannot be achieved by present means. The conclusion of the analysis above is that it cannot be achieved through the market, and above all, through the market in capital. In short, if you want a just global order, it cannot be a capitalist one.

Growing economic inequality, above all territorial inequality, is not imposed on the free market: it is a result of it. As documented in Pritchett's[11] seminal article, it has been a secular tendency throughout the growth of the world market. It has also been going on for a very long time. At the dawn of the twentieth century (and the high tide of classical imperialism) the gap between the GDP per capita of the poorest and richest nation was in the ratio of just 22 to 1. By 1970 this had widened to 88 to 1. By 2000 – that is, after the market had reached its greatest extent in history – it reached 267.[12] It is inconceivable that this process has any source other than the market itself.

Inequality has grown fastest where the market has advanced or the state has receded. Freeman, Robinson and Ghosh document statistically, and all contributors recognise, how globalisation's most universal product is inequality. This sharply accelerated after 1980, and moreover its acceleration was most pronounced where existing state structures were dissolved, with the fall of the USSR. Notably it was most reduced within the European Community, precisely where a nascent territorial state is in formation.

Growing inequality is moreover quite unlike any other tendency in capitalism in that it is by and large not reversible. The ten-year business cycle, in terminology first introduced by Kondratieff,[13] is a reversible process so that slump follows boom follows slump. Consequently, although slumps introduce many serious problems, these problems are usually eradicated or transformed in the boom phase.

Kondratieff, as Bello and Malig note, also argued that the long 40–70 year movements of the world market economy, in which periods of prolonged stagnation alternated with periods of accelerated *Belle Époque* growth, were reversible in this sense. A significant unstated assumption in Greenspan's economic strategy is the idea that the USA can kick-start a new Kondratieff expansion and so jerk the world out of its economic torpor, solving the crisis of globalisation.

Even if this turns out to be true – and so far all evidence is to the contrary – inequality has never shown significant signs of reversing in either the upswing or the downswing of the Kondratieffs, and so a new Kondratieff is not a solution to the discontents of globalisation.[14] On the contrary, the *Belle Époque* of the third Kondratieff upswing (1873–93) actually coincided with the high tide of classical imperialism and culminated in the First World War. Divergence may accelerate and decelerate at times (although these seem to have not much relation to the timing of the Kondratieffs); the material basis for the relative stability of the 'golden age' from 1947 to 1968 was a rapid rate of world growth combined with a slow rate of divergence. However, unlike overall growth, divergence may slow but never stops.

The accelerated extension of the world market has proceeded at one and the same time as a parallel acceleration in the rate of divergence, without solving the basic problem of world growth. Globalisation has been busily digging its own grave. This does not mean that globalisation can never happen, or that the nation-state must last forever. It does mean, however, that market-driven or corporate globalisation is a contradiction in terms. There may well be powerful historical tendencies towards the dissolution of national barriers, and the market has functioned as one of them. The issue, however, is whether the market can finish what it has started. The experience of the last 20 years suggests that it cannot.

## ORIGINS OF THE AGE OF WAR

If there is such a thing as a globalisers' consensus, it goes something like this: globalisation is a long-standing and almost inevitable result of deep-rooted historical and technical processes – the compression of space and time, the information revolution, the worldwide organisation of production, the formation of the world market – which may be muted and modified, but which can only be stopped, in effect, by throwing history into reverse. Only one post-modern world, it seems, is possible.

From within this oddly teleological[15] perspective there are only two basic policy options. One is to stand in its path, and, in the words of Kurt Tucholsky, 'clearly say no'. But few globalising accounts really indicate how saying 'no' can lead anywhere. Indeed, if calling a halt to globalisation could lead anywhere, it would seem to vitiate most of the globalist argument. The only course is therefore to act on the assumption that globalisation is inevitable, with or without reservations, and try to direct it into something mildly better, perhaps offsetting its most glaring social defects with Third Way policies and poverty-eradication programmes.

This stark vision has a mesmerising influence on political debates in the Third World, as the chapters in this book testify. However the evidence is stark. The actual net effect of opening capital markets to the North has been to drain them. Out of 28 emerging country stock markets listed by the *Wall Street Journal*, in dollar terms only three – Hungary, Brazil and China – stood higher by the year 2000 than they were in 1992.[16] Even the simple arithmetic does not add up to a practical method of staying afloat: in 1992, debt service payments by the developing countries totalled $179 billion and net financial inflows were $128 billion. By 2000, debt service payments had reached $330 billion while net financial inflows had dwindled to $86 billion.[17] The function of financial liberalisation was never to send capital from the North to the South, but quite the reverse: the US economy, with a balance of payments deficit running, as of February 2004, at an annual rate of $517 billion and rising, has run like a vacuum-cleaner through the savings of the world.

Those success stories that can be found are nearly always exceptions that prove the rule. The runaway success of the Chinese economy, as Freeman points out, has precious little to do with globalisation and far more to do with policies that place China squarely outside the standard IMF framework. The much-maligned Malaysian response to the 1997 crisis, in clamping down on capital movements and reverting to strict controls, proved a far more effective rescue package than any IMF prescription. Russia's 1997 debt default in fact laid the basis for a substantive if temporary economic recovery. As Ghosh points out, even the qualified successes of Indian capital flowed from India's good fortune in failing to become a major target of international capital movements. With little capital flowing in, fortunately, little flowed out.

The evidence is that on present terms and conditions, globalisation is injurious to health. So why have so many Third World governments gone along with it? The ideology of the globalisers has played a role, and the authors of this book display a justified scepticism towards it. Academic globalisation theory also bears a measure of responsibility for unleashing, *de facto*, a deterministic and unilateral account of world development offering few alternative choices for Third World nations except to lie back and make the best of it.

This idea that there is no alternative is clearly false even under present circumstances, as China and Cuba demonstrate in different ways. Nevertheless, with the collapse of the Soviet Union, many protective mechanisms previously available to Third World countries vanished, and they stood alone and exposed both to the world market and the political offensive of the globalisers. There is thus an underlying material basis for the globalist argument. The alternatives were always there, but they involved hard choices and exposed the country concerned to great risks, both internal and external, as the case of Venezuela shows. However, the globalisation argument has always lacked somewhat in the historical specificity department. The dilemma facing Third World countries was not eternal. If, as we believe, a new historical situation is emerging, then although the challenges may be harsh – probably even harsher than before – the range of options is also far wider.

No ideology takes root without a material basis. Two historically specific factors operated to batter down Third World resistance to the globalising political offensive. The first was plain economic terror: debt and the threat of economic destabilisation. This was in turn preceded by a phase of direct political terror which is often conveniently omitted from bowdlerised accounts: the coup in Chile, the dictatorships of Argentina, Brazil, the Philippines, Turkey and countless others created a social and political environment in which the IMF option appeared as the only alternative to ruthless military extinction.

These were the initial, and remain the most potent, weapons of mass persuasion. Many a government has co-operated not so much out of confidence that things would get better, as in the certainty that they could be made a lot worse.

## The Third World bourgeoisie – transnational or comprador?

The second factor is that there is strong evidence that a 'transnational bourgeoisie' of some kind has real material existence, regardless of the framework in which one chooses to analyse it. The category of 'comprador bourgeoisie', which dependency theorists of the 1970s used to describe those of their own capitalists who accepted the subordination of their own country to foreign economic domination, no longer adequately captures the status of a new Third World layer integrated into world capitalism directly through the circuits of financial capital. Globalisation has fostered, and rapidly enriched, a corruptible minority that populates the political elites of most Third World countries, and has elevated itself into prosperity independent of the fate of its country of origin.

This elite has played a substantive role in securing Third World backing for IMF policies. It does not necessarily occupy stage-centre, as the career of the evanescent Kemal Dervish testifies in Turkish politics – but it can always create a social base within the Third World middle classes by promising special access to the favours of the capital-rich. It can offer alliances to keep a beleaguered party in power. It can summon new populists from the vasty deep of anonymity at breakneck speed, just in time, and just for long enough, to reconstitute a pro-globalisation bloc when all seems lost – as Alberto Fujimori's chequered career testifies. It can hold the ring between national and international institutions. It enjoys the classic status of the intermediary, which is to be courted by both sides, and so it adopts the ideology that both sides listen to. Academic globalisation theory, combining inexhaustibly ambiguous discourse with inexorably unambiguous conclusions, has filled the gap to perfection.

## The Third World state as transmission belt for external power

Yet, paradoxically, the outcome of the whole process is that the power of the international institutions was never in fact a power over Third World governments but always only through them. It worked, in the last analysis, by securing their consent. Of course, the consent of the government is by no means the same as the consent of the people, and so this power always worked only as a power of co-option. In this sense the globalisers' analysis seems to holds good. On a world scale this is a *differentia specifica* of the Third World state; it is much more like an agency than an agent.

But the last two decades have seen this power erode to the point of non-existence. During 2001–02 Argentina, the prototypical graveyard of IMF hegemony, worked its way through four presidents in fewer months, and when a president who appeared willing to stand up to the IMF was finally elected, he recorded opinion polls of 85 per cent and upwards in his support.

Freeman therefore argues that world governance has actually consisted not of a transnational polity but a world governing bloc: an alliance with Washington and Wall Street at its head and Europe and Japan as supporting cast, accompanied by a train of more or less reluctant subordinate Third World governments. At every decisive juncture when a nation has set its own policies in defiance of international strictures – the Russian debt default, Malaysia's response to the Asian crisis, China's ongoing strategy, Cuba's dogged independence or Argentina's robust response to the IMF and its creditors alike – the nation has in fact prevailed over the international institutions, and no way has been found to bring a determined nation to heel except direct political intervention by destabilisation, or by war. Indeed, in large measure this lies behind the United States' frustration with the institutions and the resolve of the Bush administration to impose by force what the institutions have failed to secure by other means.

### The erosion of the social basis for governmental consent

Consent, in a nutshell, has evaporated. Country by country and people by people, it is becoming impossible to establish stable governments that implement IMF policies. The ability to do this has been eroded by the corrosive and grinding social impact of the relentless rise in inequality provoked by market-led globalisation itself.

Argentina, for years a darling of the international financial community, was in many ways a classic case. A discredited political elite found that it no longer possessed the social base to form a government. Nevertheless, and significantly, popular opposition was expressed at least initially as an inchoate rejection of each and every politician. Political stability, of a kind, came only when dark-horse President Nestor Kirchner stood up to the IMF and said no, Argentina will place its own growth first, and will pay the debt only out of this growth.

The failure of consent does not necessarily take the form of coherent, stable or indeed pleasant alternatives. In Central Asia or Central Africa, descent into political barbarity has merely followed in the wake of the economic barbarisation of the global economy, which has simply dissolved the social fabric that any civilised order demands. With supreme irony, this is precisely what creates the excuse for external intervention.

All this simply illustrates how dangerous it is to substitute a utopian vision for a concrete analysis of reality. What earthly reason is there to suppose that if the nation-state falls, it must be replaced by anything at all other than chaos and old night, let alone a new international order? It should not be forgotten that the nation-state is more than just a sovereign body; it is an integrated one. It holds the social fabric together. It sits at all the levers: from money and guns, through policing and education, down to social provision, traffic and even pest control. It can deploy any of these instruments in support of any other. It places them in such an intimate relation with each other that their connections persist long after central direction is removed or changed. One of the forgotten functions of bureaucracy, when all is said and done, however badly and with whatever corrupt self-interest, is that it makes things work. It provides indispensable conditions for the reproduction of the whole of society, not just bank accounts and academic reputations.

The IMF, the World Bank and the WTO – or for that matter, the transnational corporation – have no such integrated capability. They are narrowly focused and single-function bodies, specialised and professional (and frequently, therefore, very wrong) in what they do and they neither take responsibility for, nor involve themselves in administering, anything not directly related to their immediate job.

### The continental imperative

This is precisely why the Europeans are so busily engaged in constructing all the apparatus of a nation-state at the European level, including a pan-European military capacity. *Simply* controlling money or trade, or for that matter *simply* controlling social policy, is no way to run a society. The EEC is not 'another' international institution like the WTO; it is an exercise in constructing a new nation-state with an integrated capability to make laws, execute them and enforce them. The fact that European capital seeks a new nation, and not a strengthened non-national transnational polity, speaks volumes for the limits of the existing transnational organisations.

Hence the only functional political mechanism actually available to the IMF and the WTO was to secure territorial governments of some kind that, no matter how weak or coerced they were, consented to and implemented what the international organisations wanted of them. And this was their limitation. A.J.P. Taylor once remarked, in discussing the diplomatic history of nineteenth-century Europe, that a puppet state always has ultimate power over the puppeteer, because it can always threaten to collapse. Generations of English politicians found this to their cost in Northern Ireland. In the same way, the fate of the international organisations is far more intertwined with the stability of national governments that the globalisers seem to recognise, which accounts for some of the World Bank's more agonised recent discussions.

Without a territorial basis in national governments that translate their instructions into living policies that maintain and reproduce society day by day, the writ of these international bodies simply does not run. A law from which an entire territory can secede is not a law at all, which accounts for the paradoxical fact that nation-states the world over are the most vehement opponents of self-determination.[18]

At the end of the day all these issues, at least as far as capital is concerned, reduce to one: the international organisations do not dispose of means of enforcement. In particular, they do not dispose of force itself. The IMF does not have an army: the IMF's army is called the United States of America.

History until now shows that whatever capital cannot obtain by consent, it will secure by force. The imperative of force arises from the dissolution of consent. This goes to the heart of the contradictions of globalisation. In the last analysis, just as it is because globalisation has destabilised the nation-state that force is becoming the primary instrument for world capital, it is because it must resort to force that world capital needs the nation-state to deliver it.

Hudson's chapter on the US nuclear war drive therefore constitutes the key link in an anti-globalist understanding adequate to respond to the next stage of the offensive. The movements for peace and global justice are from now on twins. On the one hand, the only lasting basis for economic justice is if the USA is unable to impose its objectives by force. On the other hand, it is the economic injustice in the world that is fuelling the drive to war. It will be very important to understand the mutual nature of this relation.

The US war drive, going well beyond what it is now doing in Iraq, up to and including its clear and announced intention to deploy nuclear weapons, is not the deluded fantasy of a Strangelove but a considered and well-prepared response to the emerging new world situation. It is a part of a concerted strategic drive to ensure that whatever the international institutions fail to deliver by jaw, the Pentagon can secure by war.

But for this very reason, it is not a product of strength but of weakness: it has come about because globalisation has failed to secure territorial governments that can impose the policies on which the US's existence depends. With the failure of consent, the curtain falls on the age of globalisation, and opens on the age of war.

## ENTER THE NEW IMPERIALISM

War, Clausewitz tells us, is politics pursued by other means. What are the political objectives of the Bush administration? What does the USA hope to gain from it?

Early in 2002 few used the word 'imperialism' to describe the modern world, even in the movement for global justice, let alone the world of respectable academic publication. The language of Lenin – literally common coin when English pennies bore the legend 'Queen Victoria, Empress of India' – was frowned on in most academic disciplines, and foreign to a generation of activists separated by 80 years from the first 'war to end wars', from the overt colonialism of the great powers, and from the experience of revolutionary Russia.

In 2004, it is already commonplace to speculate that we might return to those times. When the European Stability Initiative (ESI) produced a report likening Bosnia to a European Raj, and its 'high representative', Liberal Democrat former leader Paddy Ashdown, to a 'liberal imperialist Indian Viceroy', there was only a minor scandal.[19] By 2002 the emerging doctrine of 'failed states' had already sanctioned the idea of a new imperial mission, implying that a growing range of countries – how many is never stated – were not fit to govern themselves and, implicitly, should be governed by someone else. Serious attempts to float this mission as the underpinning of a new world policy were already filtering through into the media from such as Robert Cooper, Tony Blair's respected adviser, and from the now better-known websites of the New American Century. As the *Wall Street Journal* reported on 15 July 2003:

A decade ago, being against empire would have been like being against rape. To all but the perverse few who cheered for the wrong side in Star Wars movies, 'empire' was a dirty word. Today, it has re-emerged, newly laundered. The most aggressive advocates are 'neoconservatives' such as William Kristol, publisher of *The Weekly Standard*, who said on Fox television recently that 'if people want to say we're an imperial power, fine.' Or Max Boot, a veteran of this paper's editorial page, who wrote shortly after Sept. 11, 2001, that 'Afghanistan and other troubled lands today cry out for the sort of enlightened foreign administration once provided by self-confident Englishmen in jodhpurs and pith helmets.'

Left-leaning foreign-policy thinkers have taken up the battle cry as well, saying they disagree less with the ends of the neoconservatives than their means. They want empire, but administered through multilateral institutions. Robert Cooper, director-general for external affairs at the European Union and a senior adviser to British Prime Minister Tony Blair, calls for a 'new kind of imperialism' by which Western states, perhaps acting under the guidance of the United Nations, take political responsibility for zones of disorder. Ivo Daalder and James Lindsay at the Brookings Institution, a more-liberal leaning think tank here, write: 'The real debate is not whether to have an empire, but what kind.'

We are all, it seems, imperialists now.

The global justice movement is more and more receptive to the idea that the world is entering a new, overtly conflictual, and possibly overtly colonial, stage. More problematic is whether the concept of globalisation was always, in fact, nothing more than a form of concealment for a reality better described as, simply, imperialism.

In this book Sungur Savran, dealing with the pivotal relation between Europe and the Middle East, and Jayati Ghosh, dealing with the Asian continent, directly refer to globalisation as an imperialist project. At the Santa Barbara conference Tariq Ali spelled out in even stronger terms a view that many delegates shared:

I have a confession to make to this conference. I loathe the word globalisation and always have done because I have always felt it is a mask. David Harvey spelt that out this morning and I must say I agree with him. What is this globalisation? It's a new form of capitalist exploitation which has been with us for some time, disrupted in the twentieth century for seventy years and it's back to business – of course in a totally different way.[20]

A reversal has occurred. Only five years ago it was revanchist, doctrinaire or downright quirky to inject the word 'imperialism' into a serious conversation about the present state of the world. So rapidly has the intellectual crisis unfolded that – not for the first time – an idea that five years ago was marginalised and often ridiculed, which was placed on the agenda by radicals of the left and the right, has moved to centre-stage, so that the radicals are in advance of the mainstream intelligentsia in discussion and assessing it.

### Empire – return or continuity?

It is always a relief to use the language one prefers, and it makes for clarity. However, just because a word has come back into usage, it cannot be assumed that everyone uses it to mean the same thing, or that it validly describes a reality that may in fact have moved on. The different meanings assigned to the word 'imperialism' need to be teased out, not only to ensure a fruitful dialogue, but much more importantly, to get at the truth.

From the standpoint of the radical right and the liberal left, imperialism is a reversion to a previous state of affairs, which existed in the heyday of the great powers but came to an abrupt end, or at least started petering out, in 1918. The nations of the Third World are part of a now free and independent polity in which while they may be economic inferiors, they are at least political equals.

As far as the right are concerned this independence is excessive and must be curtailed, because a growing list of these nations are delinquent and have lost the right to freedom. They are acquiring weapons of mass destruction, fostering dictators, harbouring terrorists and generally threatening the American way of life. Therefore, the civilised nations should rein in, or override, this freedom because it is a threat to the freedom of everyone else. As far as the liberal left are concerned this should not be done because it means finishing with the basic rule of international law, which is rooted in the sovereignty of nations.

In this more mainstream usage, imperialism is a previous state of affairs and the debate is whether it is coming back, or alternatively, whether it is a good thing for it to come back.

From the standpoint of the classical anti-imperialist tradition, imperialism never went away. It just mutated from an overtly colonial form to another, variously called neocolonial or dependency. The freedom of the Third World nations is a sham, a purely formal freedom. The Third World state is dependent, severely circumscribed in its freedom of action, and above all, economically shackled to the North. Direct military occupation is therefore just another mode of domination, which makes transparent what was previously obscured from view. 'Imperialism' therefore describes the whole stage of history through which we are now living, in continuity with Lenin's own usage: 'Imperialism, the latest stage of capitalism.' It is implicitly assumed that no subsequent, and still later stage has been reached – we are merely living through various mutations of the stage that started around 1873.

This intellectual tradition has hitherto been marginalised but cannot be omitted from an integrated understanding of the new stage of world history. One of the purposes for this book is to set the framework for a genuine encounter, within the parameters of the movements for global justice and peace, between this intellectual tradition and the newer ideas of the present generation.

A second purpose is to point out, sharply, the need for a more serious academic recognition of the theoretical contribution of the classical anti-imperialist tradition. This tradition has been, in plain words, suppressed. The ideas of the great political leaders of the past age – Hilferding, Lenin, Trotsky, Luxemburg, Kautsky, and many others – is treated not as subject but object. It is engaged in the same terms that historians more justifiably engage the ideas of Hitler, not to shed light on reality but to understand how a political movement came to achieve its objectives.

The movement for global justice can, and should, come to terms with its earlier heritage, absorb it and learn from it. A proper synthesis between its own intellectual contribution and the classical anti-imperialist tradition is long overdue. It would in any case be stupid not to study the period of high empire with careful attention, if only in order to learn what might be coming down the sewers of history now that the blockages have been removed. But it is also important to recognise that the people who last wrote about empire were the people that lived through it, and moreover defeated it, at great and heroic cost and to the benefit of all of us. Their analysis is not just a body of doctrine but a living connection to a body of human experience.

## Basis for a new intellectual synthesis

There are three problems to be dealt with. First, a genuine synthesis requires a genuine dialogue. Two apparently opposed views about the USA's relation to the New World Order each bring our attention to different aspects of that world order precisely because it is a contradictory order. Simple rejections of anything that does not conform to a preformed doctrine are likely to lead to an understanding of the world that actually misses out or ignores vital aspects of it. Second, the world really has moved on in the intervening seventy years. Maybe the devil is only in the detail but if, as Tariq argues, it is back to business 'in a totally different way' then maybe it is not the same business. It is necessary to assess, dispassionately and objectively, and without loading too much on the meanings of words, what new elements have come into the world since the epoch of high imperialism, and what elements really have not changed at all.

Third, and most vexed for the left, is the process whereby theory has been reconstructed as doctrine, freezing it at a point in time and depriving it of all possibility of evolution. Whenever the left defends its theories by appealing to tradition, it emasculates them. The theory is true because, empirically, it has stood the test of time, not because it was the property of a person, a party or even a country.

Worse still, whenever the left reduces theory to dogma, it participates in the suppression of its own heritage: it places itself in the position of standing guard over the tradition, declaring what is and what is not 'true' Leninism or 'true' Marxism and, in the process, placing a barrier between the movement and Lenin, and the movement and Marx. Almost no-one today is advised to read Marx in the original: instead, they must understand him only through the interpretations of the Marxists. The theoretical heritage of this past age is transmitted by '-ists'. The Marxists, Leninists, Trotskyists, in seeking to become guardians, have become jailors. Their interpretations are frequently shallow, flawed and more vulnerable to the valid criticisms of the neoclassicals than the original work. Ironically, it is those who insist on the universality of their own particular reading of the classics who often create the greatest obstacle to their acceptance.

Theory and history alike must be confronted in their original form. The original form of history is the form in which it is experienced, and the original form of theory is the form in which it is written. The new generation should be allowed, therefore, to read, without prejudice, what Marx, Lenin and Trotsky – or for that matter Luxemburg, Kautsky, Bukharin, Hilferding and their peers, and indeed liberals such as Hobson and Mark Twain – wrote in their own words, and apply it to their own experience, equally without prejudice.

History repeats itself: but it always does so with new elements. Whether or not globalisation is 'simply another name for imperialism', the world has moved on and we need to know what is coming next. If we want to make proper use of historical reasoning – for the editors, the linchpin of a valid and integrated social science – we should try to identify the key elements of the past situation which still persist today, even though organised differently. What are the key elements the classical anti-imperialist tradition considered to define its own stage of history? How relevant are they today? What matters is not the vast weight of interpretative dogma that surrounds these basic elements, but their simple, essential message. It is not what the left disputed, but what it agreed on, that matters.

## The classical anti-imperialist consensus

There are, in our view, three decisive elements of agreement within the classical anti-imperialist tradition:

(1)   The world is divided into two entirely different types of country: dominated and dominant. These have acquired two fundamentally different kinds of nation-state, each of which can only be fully understood through its relation to the other.

(2)   The domination of one nation by another is a product of capitalism. It is not an atavistic survival, for example of dynastic ambition, nor is it an alien imposition, for example by Christian fundamentalism.

(3)   Imperialism is a competitive system, and the struggle for territorial domination is simply the highest form of capitalist competition.

How do these propositions sit in relation to formal globalisation theory? At the most abstract level, globalisation theory has a great deal more in common than it recognises with the ideas of the classical Marxists, for whom the world market was the fundamental economic reality, so that class both nationally and internationally was the underlying, essential basis of the nation and the state. In many important senses, the Communist Manifesto with its appeal to the 'Workers of the World' was the planet's first globalist project, as it went on to demonstrate in a very practical and effective form by creating two mass Internationals (the Second and Third) and in shaping the Internationalist ideals of the Russian Revolution.

A confusing polarisation arises if Marxists are cast, or cast themselves, as the standard-bearers of the nation-state and the modern globalisers as its grave-diggers. A sense of history is needed, and is sadly lacking in many globalist accounts. The twentieth century, Hobsbawm has noted, can ultimately be reduced to a world battle between the Russian working class and the American capitalist class. Every battle produces two stories, two interpretations of history, corresponding to the viewpoints of the two protagonists. Twentieth-century international relations theory was dominated by the ideological struggle between two world projects, each arising from the needs of one side in this battle, and each attempting to deal with the fundamental limitations of the state system of the nineteenth century from the standpoint of its own class. The Communist tradition sought a 'transnational polity' based on the common international interest of people without property. The American tradition sought 'liberal democracy' comprised of independent sovereign nations. Each of them theorised, and to some extend mythologised, the real world they found from within their particular perspectives.

### Liberalism, Marxism and the interpenetration of opposites

Materially as well as theoretically, each project ran up against the limitations of real history. The Communists were confined to a territorial state, the USSR – significantly, by no means a nation-state in the old sense, being formally a federation of nations within an integrated state. The dilemma of whether or how to construct 'socialism in one country' divided the Russian Communists from the very beginning, because socialism was by definition a world project. Territorially confined socialism was a contradiction in terms, and even the victorious Stalin camp was quite explicit that the Soviet system was to be extended worldwide, the issues dividing the Communists being on the one hand how this should be done, and on the other what to do in the meantime within the Soviet Union.

At the same time American capital was in the process of deciding that it wasn't quite good enough to liberate the nations held by the old empires; it needed a sphere for its own world operations. When the Philippines were annexed after they were freed from Spain there was a furious and forgotten debate in the USA. The 'anti-imperialist league' of Mark Twain and his many associates was influential enough that the Democrats ran with an anti-imperialist presidential candidate. The USA in general followed a systematic policy of governance through client states, not through direct rule. Yet two world wars later, it was a global power with troops in more countries than any other nation on the planet.

Thus on the one hand history imposed a national form on the world's most committed globalisers, and on the other it handed a global role to the world's most committed nationalists. The entire modern development of the nation took place not in an abstract political space but in a world dominated by the conflict between these two projects. No capitalist nation concluded a successful colonial agenda as long as the USSR existed, but neither did the USSR transcend its territorial form. A technical agreement resulted – as recently as 1943, it should be remembered – from the tripolar equilibrium between the USA, the USSR and 'Old Europe'. The Third World itself set the seal on this diplomats' world map in a postwar revolutionary and anti-colonial upsurge that trebled the extent of the non-capitalist world. The agreement was a formal decolonisation, an acceptance of the independent nation-state as the generally recognised legal form sanctioned in international law and treaties.

## Contradictions of Westphalian mythology

This system is usually described in international relations theory as the 'Westphalian system'. The Peace of Westphalia, in 1648, settled the end of the religious wars launched by the Protestant Reformation. It (and the Treaty of Augsburg, to which IR theory pays less attention) gave birth to the concept of sovereignty by establishing the right of the 'sovereign' to determine the religion of his subjects, and his formal independence both from the Holy Roman Emperor and from the Catholic Church. Rosenberg[21] argues that

> [f]or international theory, however, (and to some extent in the fields of international law and political theory too) ... [the Westphalian system's] iconic significance extends far beyond any historical term in which its detailed and highly complicated legal and territorial provisions much have continued to apply. Looking back from the twentieth-century world of bordered, sovereign states, Westphalia appears instead as a turning point in world history: the point at which sovereignty (however embryonically conceived or unevenly implemented) began to be consolidated as the organisational principle of a European states-system which would later expand across the planet. Viewed in this light, the Peace of Westphalia reappears as the original dispensation of geopolitical modernity itself. And the present-day international system composed as it still legally is of sovereign, independent states, is therefore often referred to as 'the Westphalian system'.

From the standpoint of the classical anti-imperialist tradition this is mythical. Except for Europe and America and possibly Japan, nation-states did not exist in most of the world until the mid-twentieth century, and the dominant world organisational form in the nineteenth century was the empire. The present system of national states has existed only since 1947 and at that only partially, and it resulted from a stalemate between two projects that completely contradicted it: on the one hand the US role as the *de facto* leader of world capital, and on the other hand the status of the USSR as the *de facto* leader of the world working class.

The key intellectual principle of liberal democracy sits in more or less direct contradiction with the view of classical anti-imperialism. Critical attitudes are also to be found among many writers on globalisation, to which we will return. But we want to draw attention to a specific view that classical anti-imperialism developed, 80 years earlier, and which we consider to be one of the key insights to be brought centre-stage in anti-globalisation thinking. This is the great simplifying proposition that has stood the test of time: that the world of nation-states is divided into two fundamentally different types in a definite relation to one another: dominating and dominated.

This is not the same as saying that the world is unjust, or that it is divided into rich and poor, North and South; it says much more. It is a statement about power. It says that the rich nations *rule* the poor nations. Moreover, this is *why* they are rich. The sovereignty of the rich and the sovereignty of the poor are not, therefore, identical. The first is *unconditional and absolute* and the second is *conditional and relative*.

This distinction oozes from every crevice of actual international relations. Weapons of Mass Destruction were the justification, but not at all the core principle underlying the UK and USA's decision to attack Iraq. These nations applied an already operative doctrine of pre-emptive military intervention – the right to intervene to neutralise a threat that does not yet exist. And who judges whether this threat exists? Certainly not the conquered. It is the sole right of the conquerors. One need only imagine the reaction of the Great Powers if, for example, some coalition of Third World powers decided to apply this principle to the USA, to see that it is a principle that can only be operated by one part of the world that reserves to itself the unconditional right to invade the other half.

### Nominal sovereignty

We hope we can summarise the liberal democratic reaction, with the injustice that all simplifications inflict, as being something like this: while, in the past, the great empires occupied and ruled great territories, they have now withdrawn and so the age of empires has ended. Whatever once existed, there is now a world polity of independent and sovereign nations. How can a sovereign country be ruled if is not occupied?

The idea that a nation can be subordinate, though formally free, should not be alien to globalisation theory. It has been saying this for the last twenty years. It has concentrated all its attention, however, on the transnational institutions, which, it claims, are eroding the power of the national state so that although this state appears sovereign, in fact it is not. It needs to be recognised that, however apologetic it may be in many variants, globalisation theory originates in a break with the Westphalian view. A theoretical leap is needed, however. If the power of a nation-state can be eroded by an international institution, as globalisation theory recognises, why can't it be eroded by another national state as classical anti-imperialism maintains?

Against this, as far as we can see, formal globalisation theory has no defence. It has dug its own theoretical grave. *Once it is conceded* that national sovereignty may be eroded from without, it is also conceded that the classical analysis of imperialism has a perfectly valid case. For, if national states can be overridden by supranational institutions, then using every argument in the globalist book, they can also be overridden by other national states. The issue is then empirical. If we concede that many nations have seen many of their essential functions and powers eroded at the expense of external constraints and influences, is it in fact the case that they have been subordinate mainly to the pressures and influences of supranational institutions – or to those from other states, most importantly, the dominant states? And did the Third World nation-state ever actually possess the freedom and the independence of the First World state in any case?

As Rosenberg argues, globalisation theory seems to attempt its break with liberalism by accepting the Westphalian myth as an adequate description of modernity, but then arguing that post-modernity has left it behind.

This does not accord with history. The advanced country nation-state never confined its sphere of influence to its own borders. The European 'great powers' became nation-states only in and through colonisation. The English, French, Dutch, Spanish and Portuguese nations were born in and through a historical process of conquest. They acquired national identity on their own territory only through domination outside it. The later advanced nations, particularly Italy and Germany, but not forgetting Japan, were compelled into such a drive for overseas expansion that their battle with the earlier powers brought about two world wars.

The Third World nations, on the other hand, went through a completely different process of formation; either they were formed in the battle for independence, as in Latin America, Asia and in the exceptional Middle Eastern case of Turkey, or they were butchered into existence by Great Power settlements, drawing arbitrary lines on maps of the world.

## What did decolonisation really achieve?

But did 'formal' decolonisation really bring about genuine political independence and put paid to the global ambitions of the superpowers? It is not, we think, an accident that the Third World contributors to this volume are the most insistent that the globalised world is an imperial one: this fact simply conforms to direct daily experience outside the charmed circles of Western economic fortresses.

Indeed, a great deal of the cynicism and scepticism found towards academic globalisation theory among Third World activists arises because, it seems to them, Western political theory only seems to have discovered that the national state might not be as sovereign as liberalism maintained, when some of the Western states themselves began losing some of their own sovereignty. Third World sovereignty never existed anyway.

This is dramatically illustrated in the dissolution of the apparent similarities between Chile and Britain. In the 1970s many formal analogies used to be made between the two countries. Each, on the surface, had a parliamentary regime and a reforming socialist party in power. In England, however, capital won over the chancellor; in Chile it shot the president.

Moreover the Chilean coup was directly sponsored by a foreign power, a power that regularly conducts its business in the Third World by financing, supporting, and where necessary helping to power, governments that conform to its foreign policy requirements. Direct military occupation, destabilisation, coups and imposed dictatorships are a part of the daily story of most Third World countries. The idea that a parliamentary interlude of a couple of decades constitutes a serious permanent transformation is viewed with justified scepticism by those for whom jail, state- and paramilitary-sponsored murder, torture and foreign-backed dictators were a recent experience.[22]

Why, then, is it so important to the great powers – above all, the USA – to secure governments that comply with their needs? It is here that the second proposition of the classical tradition also stands up well to the test of time. As Savran notes,

> Iraq taught certain sections of the international left what children already knew in predominantly Islamic countries, i.e. that the Bush administration was waging war for oil and hegemony. (Lest it be thought that I am engaging in pure rhetoric here, let me stress for the benefit of readers from non-Islamic countries that I am speaking quite literally: the majority of the population of Turkey, for instance, before and during the war on Afghanistan, was firmly of the opinion that this was a war for oil.)

The purpose of political domination is economic advantage. This is also one of the great facts of history that, in a certain sense, the movement for global justice has rescued in the face of academic disbelief. The movement for global justice arose because the everyday experience of millions of people is that every time the advanced powers got their way, things got worse.

There is a complex and unfinished debate to be had about the exact mechanism through which the North secures its economic advantages from the South, within both the classical anti-imperialist left and the movement for global justice, not to mention within official economics.[23] But without taking that debate here,[24] it is a pretty good working assumption that if the rich countries have got 20 times richer while the poor have got 30 per cent poorer, and if the rich nation-states of the world are in a position to decide who runs the poor ones, then until the milk of human kindness runs up mountains, they will take decisions that ensure they continue to get richer.

## EXIT GLOBALISATION, PURSUED BY AN EAGLE

We now turn to a second insight from globalisation theory that is relevant and which the classical anti-imperialist tradition needs to grapple with, namely the functional necessity of a world order. This, we think, is indeed one of the key new elements of the post-1945 world with which the anti-imperialist left has been trying, not always successfully, to grapple. It is also the aspect of post-1945 stability that is most threatened by the present crisis, and the key to understanding the dramatic nature of the changes we are now seeing.

In early imperial times, the great powers confined themselves to securing dominion over *one part* of the world. The British got the lion's share, with most of the map coloured red, but each of the others had its equivalent: the French in Africa, the Caribbean and Indo-China, the Portuguese in Southern Africa, Poor Little Belgium in the Congo, the Dutch in South-East Asia, and so on.

One of the great insights of American liberalism is that such a system of divided rule was politically unsustainable. It produced two wars, exhausted European capital and gave rise to Communism in nearly a quarter of the globe. The imperial relation does not reduce to simple private robbery. The market itself produces the rising inequality and clearly raises the average income of the rich countries at the expense of the poor. The function of the political order is to keep these largely unconscious mechanisms working; it is to secure the free functioning of the capital market, weighted of course in the interests of the rich countries wherever possible, because that market, on a world scale, is what delivers their wealth.

What is required, if the system of domination is to sustain itself, is not just a set of private dominions but a world political order. The advanced countries need to maintain whatever it is that keeps the inequality rising and, for this, they need not just a special private relation with a particular territory, but a general organisation of the world within which they can take advantage of their specialisations to extract the super-profits that keep them ahead of their subordinates. In short, the ideal form of organisation for the advanced nation-state is indeed 'global apartheid' as Bond notes – a system of strong and sovereign homeland nations given the run of a subdued but unitary world order outside the fortresses.

### The irresolvable contradictions of ultra-imperialism

In consequence of the above, the system of advanced-country nation-states needs a form of organisation that maintains the dominion of capital on a world scale. This could be stable only if it had no contradictions, that is, if the advanced nations could govern by mutual consent, sharing out surplus profit among themselves either by means of a stable political agreement, or in the self-regulating manner that, for example, ordinary profit is shared out by economic competition between capitalists. Such an arrangement was considered by Kautsky under the name of 'ultra-imperialism' and is the closest that the classical anti-imperialist tradition comes to formal globalisation theory.

It is, however, a catastrophic mistake to assume that because a political system is *necessary*, it is also *possible*. It is precisely because this has not been achieved that the imperialist epoch has been such a brutish one.

The US solution was to project itself as the organiser of this dominion on behalf of all the others, as what Ghosh calls the 'Kindleberger leader' of the great powers; a hegemonic leader that could police the world on behalf of all the so-called 'free world' in such a way that the remaining great powers would retain their advantage over the Third World. In classical Marxist terms, it presented itself as the director-general of a super-imperialist world order. This was in turn close to what Kautsky termed 'super-imperialism'. This was a new historical invention. The question of the age is whether this in turn is capable of stable self-reproduction, or whether it too contains within it contradictions that the USA cannot resolve.

The USA departed decisively from the conduct of the European great powers at the Treaty of Versailles, whose reaction to Germany's defeat was to try and crush Germany out of existence, in effect to reduce it to a Third World power. This stupidity, as Keynes insistently pointed out, played no small part in the rise of German Fascism; it meant that many Germans saw the choice facing them not as between fascism and democracy but between fascism and social destruction.

The USA to the contrary reconstructed Japan and Germany after the war and poured capital into Europe and Asia. It did so principally, of course, to stop the spread of Communism. But it could not do this without sustaining these countries themselves as great powers, for which purpose it had to maintain the set of relations *as a whole* between the advanced nations and the Third World. That is, it had to create a world political order.

In doing so it represented, for a while, capital as a whole. It even organised a kind of functional division of labour between the advanced nations. The Second World War victor Britain was allocated the military and financial functions, that is, it was permitted to run a kind of empire but in junior partnership with the USA and according to the principles of US liberal democracy. The defeated powers, Japan and Germany, were constitutionally confined to barracks and utterly shorn of their empires but forced to undertake an 'intensive' capitalist development. Since they had almost no outlet for foreign adventures, their capitals concentrated on securing *technical supremacy* and became the workshops of the capitalist world, with prodigious rates of investment and significantly higher growth rates. Thus each of the advanced powers concentrated on monopolising a particular source of super-profit, a particular means of draining the Third World of its surplus labour, from which all the imperialist nations could draw benefit although the totality was organised by one of them.

It would seem, therefore, that of the three principal tenets of the classical anti-imperialist tradition, though numbers one and two check out, it is number three that has failed the test of time. Where are the great power conflicts? Where is the great power arms race? Where is the competition?

Enter Iraq.

### The contradictions of super-imperialism

We have so far identified only one of the elements leading to the break-up of the 'world globalisation bloc' that has overseen the world order since the early 1980s. This was the erosion of the social base for stable Third World polities capable of delivering compliant social organisation consistent with the domination of the advanced-country bloc. This erosion continued right through the two decades of globalisation. In the second decade, however, a completely new development set in *within* the governing bloc hitherto hegemonised by the USA.

Throughout the first decade of globalisation, the advanced countries as a whole pulled away from the Third World and countries in transition, taking the so-called 'advancing' countries with them. Moreover, through most of this decade, the non-Americans continued to catch up with the Americans and, in particular, regional sub-economies in the German and Japanese zones of influence continued on a trajectory that was launched with the postwar division of labour referred to above. Both their GDP and their GDP per head expanded systematically faster than that of the USA, and their rates of investment – the driver of growth – also exceeded the USA's, in cases such as South Korea reaching double or even treble the US rate. In the 1990s this stopped. Average growth in the USA continued at around 21 per cent over the decade, but South-East Asian growth fell, compared with the previous decade, from 70 per cent to 19 per cent. European growth, in real dollar terms, was actually negative.

The postwar division of labour had provoked a fundamental instability. US hegemony, just like Britain's in the previous imperial epoch, has always depended on its being able to maintain three interlocking functions of world policeman, world banker and world technological leader. Its technological leadership, acquired over 50 years of relatively intensive development on a continental scale, provided it the huge export surpluses through which it funded the Marshall Plan, the fourth Kondratieff golden age and the spectacular expansion of South-East Asia and Western Europe.

## The inevitability of competitive imperialism

The USA has lost its technical leadership, as is clear from its intractable trade deficit. Post-globalisation economic stability therefore rested on, and was in large measure organised to secure, tremendous inflows of capital from the rest of the world to shore up the US deficit. This means that at the most basic level, the interests of the US state, and the interests of US financial capital, no longer coincide with those of advanced-country capital in general. The US is thus less and less able to exercise the role of hegemonic leader because it is less and less able to organise a world political order within which advanced-country capital as a whole can flourish. Policies that benefit one bloc act to the detriment of another; where there are winners, there are losers. Competition, always the most basic law of capitalist development, has once again become a player in world politics.

On the one hand, the USA has experienced a permanent and intractable contradiction between its national interest and its global function of maintaining the world order, as a result of which both its functions as peace-keeper and as world banker are increasingly managed in the private interest of its own economy.

On the other, its partner-rivals are being called on to accept a supporting role for the US economy, in the name of supporting its world leadership, which is ever more damaging to their own economies. US control over the financial institutions became ever more a private weapon not just to strengthen the hands of the Wall Street financial dealers and hedge fund managers, but as an instrument of statecraft specifically directed against countries it increasingly perceived as a threat.

The financial crisis of 1997 laid this process bare. It is worth citing at length Gowan's[25] incisive account of events because it clarifies the extent to which the 'blind' operation of the market was consciously managed by a state whose objectives no longer reduced to simple world leadership:

> those states which had succumbed to the pressures of the US government, the IMF and the Wall Street institutions to open their capital accounts and domestic financial sectors to some extent were allowing their economies and populations to enter a mortally dangerous trap: the inflows of the hot money and short-term loans arrived like manna from heaven, because they seemed to enable these states to evade the effects of currency from the Anglo-America financial centres. But it was not manna; it was bait. When the financial sectors of the region bit into it they were hooked, trapped in the sights of the US hedge funds, sitting ducks for financial warfare. The hedge funds struck, the lines of credit were wrenched back into London and New York, and economy after economy was dragged, writhing like a wounded animal, on to the operating table of the IMF and the US Treasury.
>
> ... those which had refused to bow to American pressure to dismantle their capital account controls escaped the onslaught because the hedge funds could not hit them. The factor that turned a state's failure of macroeconomic adjustment into a catastrophe was the degree to which the Asian development model had been breached by liberalisation of the capital account. Those countries which had largely kept their capital controls were protected from the financial attacks which followed: China, Taiwan, Vietnam and India. Those that had liberalised in the key areas found their macroeconomic management failures exploited by devastating speculative attacks ...
>
> The US Treasury was to view the crisis as an historic opportunity which, if seized, could transform the future of American capitalism, anchoring its dominance in the twenty-first century.

Europeans could only view with alarm a world financial system increasingly functioning as the partisan instrument of a single player. Great emphasis has been placed on the neo-liberal foundations of the Maastricht Treaty with its enormous emphasis on price stability at the expense, essentially, of employment. Nevertheless the enormous stress on financial probity and currency stability had a second objective. On the day the euro was launched, the European press outside Britain was ecstatic – about the arrival of a rival to the dollar. By late 2002, 56 countries had adopted the euro as currency of reference – including most of the Middle Eastern countries.[26] At the same time, the percentage of short-term obligations among capital inflows to the United States had reached 80 per cent.

## ANOTHER WORLD IS INDISPENSABLE

We are by no means predicting a reversion to full-blown colonialism or an immediate run-up to a Third World War. However, two empirical facts must be noted, and incorporated into the whole way that we now think about the world.

First, if the present world order is in fact in continuity with classical imperialism – whose date of origin should probably be located in or around 1873 – and if, furthermore, we are content to accept 1789 as the date of the capitalist mode of production proper – that which Marx designated the 'formal subsumption of the means of production by capital' – then imperialism as such has now lasted longer than its pre-imperialist phase.

Second, we now face the world dominion of capital, to be sure in a relation with many other classes, but having now proved its political independence of all pre-capitalist classes after surviving over a century in its own right. We are no longer living in a system that can be treated as some kind of admixture of capitalism with something else, some kind of incomplete transition. This, folks, is it: this *is* world capitalism, and the way it survived was to become imperialist.[27]

A racist subtext of much development theory, including unilinear Marxist variants, is the idea that dependency is a failure to become properly capitalist.[28] Gunder-Frank's seminal 'Development of Underdevelopment'[29] reconstituted a basic insight of classical anti-imperialism, that the underdevelopment of the dependent countries is a primary means by which capitalism in the dominant countries reproduces itself.

The fundamental question of world politics is whether the survival of capitalism is possible without imperialism.[30] We believe, and the evidence supports us, that it is not. If so, then there are a series of practical implications:

(1)   There is no *capitalist* alternative to imperialism. To put it another way, there is no justice without socialism. No matter how long and how difficult the road to socialism, and indeed no matter whether it is even possible, nothing else will put things right. The division of the world into two completely unequal halves, and

the maintenance of this division by a world political tyranny, is not an option for capital but a condition of its existence.

(2)   Consequently, *peace* under capitalism is an impossibility. War is the unavoidable outcome of the division of the world into rich and poor, both because without it the poor cannot be forced to stay poor, and because the rich can never settle on a stable division of the world as a result of the competition between blocs of dominant capital.

(3)   There is no *partial* road to lasting justice. The entire existence of capitalism is bound up with the imperialist system, and it can afford no permanent accommodation with reforms or national experiments that call into question the division of the world into rich and poor. As Nicaragua and Chile demonstrate, imperialism does not heed calls to justice or appeals to its better nature. It does not *have* a better nature. If anything the more just and democratic the alternatives thrown up by popular resistance, the more determined are the great powers to crush them and the more barbaric the means adopted.

(4)   At the same time there is no *short* road to socialism. Imperialism has emerged relatively triumphant from a century of the most heroic sacrifices. It is clear that it can be defeated only by an opposite and greater force; such a force, however, does not at present exist and has to be constructed.

### Utopianism, fatalism or realism?

The above does not, it has to be said, make life easy. The difficulty of the task facing all movements of resistance, arduous though it may be, is that they bear responsibility both in the day-to-day battle for justice and equality, and in the long-term battle to secure them for posterity. The fatalism these difficulties engender is clear from David Harvey's recent work, which in many ways expresses the potential lines of an emerging 'liberal consensus':

> The danger is that anti-imperialist movements may become purely and wholeheartedly anti-modernist movements rather than seeking an alternative globalization and an alternative modernity that makes full use of the potential that capitalism has spawned.
>
> There are multiple movements around the world in motion searching for some such alternative (as symbolized by the World Social Forum). These are full of interesting ideas and partial

victories have been won. But I do not believe the anti-capitalist and anti-imperialist movement is currently strong enough or even adequately equipped, theoretically or practically, to undertake such a task. This then poses the question of what to do in the immediate present, in the face of a very dangerous political and economic situation.

In my own view, there is only one way in which capitalism can steady itself temporarily and draw back from a series of increasingly violent inter-imperialist confrontations, and that is through the orchestration of some sort of global 'new' New Deal. This would require a considerable realignment of political and economic practices within the leading capitalist powers (the abandonment of neo-liberalism and the reconstruction of some sort of redistributive Keynesianism) as well as a coalition of capitalist powers ready to act in a more redistributive mode on the world stage (a Karl Kautsky kind of ultra-imperialism). For people on the left, the question is whether we would be prepared to support such a move (much as happened in leftist support for social democracy and new deal politics in earlier times) or to go against it as 'mere reformism.' I am inclined to support it (much as I support, albeit with reservations, what Luis Inacio Lula da Silva is doing in Brazil) as a temporary respite and as a breathing space within which to try to construct a more radical alternative.[31]

This reveals two conflicting (and often self-reinforcing) trends within the movement for global justice, which we might term liberal utopianism and sectarian utopianism.

Sectarian utopianism arises from the danger, which Harvey justly points out, of acting as if large-scale social justice, or even an immediate strategic defeat for USA foreign policy, were immediately possible. We cannot but agree that 'the anti-capitalist and anti-imperialist movement is [not] currently strong enough or even adequately equipped, theoretically or practically, to undertake such a task'.

It is precisely because of this that the movement finds it has to take careful and cautious stock, at each given moment, of what can be achieved within the existing relation of forces. In particular, it is disastrous for anyone concerned with justice to *withdraw support* from processes that can end in realisable reforms or advances (not least, for example, any movement to curb IMF interference in the affairs of sovereign Third World states) on the grounds that the processes are not led by socialists or do not result in a social justice. The most obvious example is the war in Iraq itself. Saddam Hussein was a barbaric dictator, but as most people in the world understood, an ouster conducted by the very powers that financed and armed him was an advance for nobody.

More subtly, the domestic policies of Mahathir Mohamad were authoritarian, repressive and corrupt – but this does not alter the fact that the government of Malaysia had every right to respond to the Asian crisis of 1997 by cutting off the flows of speculative capital, flying in the teeth of both IMF orthodoxy and US foreign policy. In such a confrontation, no movement for justice can make its opposition to the IMF conditional on the internal conduct of Mahathir.

An equally catastrophic utopianism is, however, to act on the basis that a *pacification* or *humanisation* of imperialism is a valid option. We therefore profoundly disagree that 'the orchestration of some sort of global "new" New Deal' is a practical option. There is no more a 'benign imperialism' than a vegetarian tiger.

The most devastating indictment of the idea of a benign imperialism is the complete lack of historical evidence that it can ever happen. The phase of classical imperialism, lasting up to and including the Second World War, was – with due and equal account taken of its effects throughout the world – the most barbaric in world history. It brought the merciless devastation of the Third World, wholesale battlefield and civilian slaughter in two successive wars, and, not least, the Holocaust.

The methods of US imperialism under 'Pax Americana' are no more 'civilised' than its European precursors. It launched the nuclear age by deploying nuclear weapons against Japan, engaged in gratuitous and systematic bombing to economically devastate North Korea in the final stages of the war on that peninsula; made repeated military incursions in Latin America, the Middle East and Africa, and killed two million people in Vietnam.

It propped up the great majority of the most odious and repressive regimes in the world (four decades of support for apartheid South Africa, support for Franco, Salazar, successive Guatemalan regimes, Israel, the Shah of Iran, Pinochet, Marcos, Somoza, the Greek colonels, Saudi Arabia and until it became inconvenient, Saddam Hussein and indeed, Osama bin Laden themselves). Via the IMF and the WTO it is responsible for the deaths of millions of people, having reacted with supreme indifference to the crushing of billions by poverty and the deaths of tens of millions from preventable or containable diseases. It tolerates and actively fosters systematic domestic racism and judicial terror against its own black population, it is busily destroying the world environment, and uses aggressive military force against all those who oppose it. It moves daily closer to its stated strategic goal of deploying battlefield and theatre nuclear weapons as an instrument of foreign policy.

A century of barbarity cannot in all conscience be reduced to a lack of moral fibre. It is not the result of a succession of electoral accidents but of the most profound economic imperatives.

## Living with a dying animal

But there is a second respect, perhaps the most important, in which a fatalistic judgement is catastrophically misleading: these actions of imperialism arise not from its strength but its weakness. The USA today is driven to intervene militarily because it can no longer sustain its rule peacefully. In turn, this failure arises from a deep-seated and ineradicable weakness: *economically*, imperialism does not work. It does not regulate itself. It does not sustain social and political formations that are capable of perpetuating themselves indefinitely. No amount of weaponry can correct this; on the contrary, it makes it worse.

If the dominion of the United States, and imperialism in general, were so strong and eternal that left to its own devices, it could last indefinitely, then, terrible as its consequences are, there would be little to be done about it and there would indeed be little alternative but to hold out for a little bit of justice and seek the most minimal reforms.

The problem is that this dominion is not self-perpetuating. It constantly lays the foundations of its own destruction. The issue, therefore, is what comes out of this destructive process. On the one hand, if 'good people do nothing' then all the evidence is that things will continue to get worse, as the Holocaust shows. On the other, it is precisely because imperialism ultimately cannot sustain its own rule that it can and will create the forces capable of replacing it with something better. Whether they do so is not an automatic outcome. We have a choice. Another world is possible, and another world is necessary, but it may not happen. It depends on what we do.

## Alliances in the age of barbarism

It is the self-destructive aspect of imperialism that dictates the need for resistance. The discussion is not, in fact, about whether to pursue 'revolution' instead of reform or 'socialism' instead of redistribution. This counterposition is a vacuous one. A revolutionary is no more nor less than a reformist who does not give up. What distinguishes the world's great revolutionaries is not their immoderate demands ('bread, peace, land') but the fact that they took the measures necessary to secure them in an age when the existing institutions could no longer tolerate them. Conversely, anyone who rejects reform on the basis that it stands in the way of revolution is a simple sectarian.

Of course any move, no matter how minimal, that reduces the prospect of war by however small an amount, restores any measure of human rights to the racially or sexually oppressed, or that raises the living standards of any wage worker anywhere by no matter how small an amount, deserves the full support of all who seek a better life.

The problem is a different one: it is that almost all proposals for the 'structural reform' of imperialism take the form in practice of a negotiation in which what is sacrificed is not the long-term goal of socialism but short-term goals of non-negotiable and often quite minimal reforms that form in fact the bedrock of any unified practical movement.

It is one thing to say that, for example, the relation of forces makes it hard to halt the Bush camp in its tracks. It is another entirely to say that, in order to persuade it to draw back, movements for justice should give up fighting racism, forget women's rights, abandon the trade unions, leave the Palestinians to their lot, drop any opposition to tearing up the Kyoto accords, give up defending the IMF's victims in favour of 'shrunken' or 'fairer' structural adjustment, or tolerate some kind of watered-down US presence in any country it has illegally invaded.

There *is* no 'breathing space' to be had in this manner, and we hope that this kind of compromise is not what Harvey has in mind. This is, however, the real choice. The only points in world history at which movements have gained a breathing space from imperialism are those at which they have defeated it.

'Pax Americana' and the massive curtailment of European imperial ambition after 1945 was itself in no small measure owing to the success of Soviet forces. The victory of the Vietnamese did indeed buy a 20-year 'breathing space' for the world during which the capacity of the United States to intervene with overt massive force was severely circumscribed. Were the peace movement to secure a halt or even a delay in the WMD programme, this would greatly relieve the pressures bearing down on both China and the rest of the Third World where the consequences of a successful capacity for unilateral US nuclear intervention are almost unimaginable. A military withdrawal from Iraq without a colonial postwar settlement would make it immeasurably harder for the US to intervene effectively in other parts of the world.

Argentina's obstinate refusal (at the time of writing) to honour the largest sovereign debt in world history – not to mention the obstinate refusal of its people to accept any government that threatened to do so – did more to modify IMF and World Bank thinking on structural adjustment than two decades of earnest appeals to the good nature of the banking community.

The alliances that can and should be constructed on this premise cannot begin, of course, by sacrificing present reform to future socialism. That is an absurd equation: socialism can succeed only by emerging as the greatest force for reform. The evidence, however, is that alliances will need to be constructed on the fundamental premise that *no* imperialist intervention is progressive. There is no concession to be made to imperialism for the simple reason that nothing it does makes anything better.

### Class, nation and region

This is precisely why the debates in this book, as well as the agreements, have practical implications. Regardless of particular national forms that are not only mutable but mutating, before our eyes, the fundamental political division of the world is between two halves of its peoples: those that live in the so-called 'advanced countries' and the rest.

Does this perspective, inherited from the high point of opposition to the last phase of 'classical imperialism', imply that the division of the world into classes is no longer of any significance, or that geographical struggles have somehow transcended or overcome class struggles? No; it does however mean that, as the classical anti-imperialists insisted, the working class of the dominant and the dependent countries need a very different structure of alliances – because they live in two very different kinds of state.

In the Third World social advance and national sovereignty are indissolubly linked. More or less any movement that strives to change the share of wealth to the benefit of the poor immediately runs up against the opposition of world capital – in particular, with world financial capital, which is why the IMF is the locus of almost all movements of popular opposition. In standing up to this opposition, it is imperative for such movements that their state itself should be a part of the resistance. Of necessity, therefore, they find they must resist any external encroachment on the sovereignty of the nation, in the interests of democracy itself. This is because by and large, the Third World nation 'faces inwards'; its primary function is defensive. Without mitigating the defence of all the poor and oppressed against all their own capitalists, working-class movements of the Third World have to defend the sovereignty of their state.

In the imperialist countries the story is very different. The 'sovereignty' of the US state is synonymous with that state's *external* power – with its oppression of the great majority of the world. Nor should it be supposed that because European and Japanese empires were so savagely reduced in 1945, that their national states, or the European Community, exist purely to regulate the internal affairs of their peoples. The WTO, IMF and World Bank function as multinational instruments of Third World suppression precisely because of, and through, the partnership of the Europeans and Japanese. Through the manipulation of free trade agreements and through such arrangements as the Lomé accords, these states manipulate the world market to their enormous advantage.

The classical position of anti-imperialism holds good without moderation. The working-class and social movements of the imperialist countries have to take a *different* stance towards the sovereignty of their own nation, above all when the exercise of that sovereignty implies the military and economic suppression of the majority of the world's people.

Does the shape of modern world politics call for any modification of this position? In one important respect, yes. The trend of the twentieth century was towards the formation of continental powers; thus the sovereignty of the Third World nation as it now stands is in many respects insufficient for an adequate economic defence against world capital. If anything, the most difficult task facing Third World movements is to bring about a consistent unification, at regional level, of nations that world capital constantly seeks to pit against each other; conversely, the most difficult task facing movements in the imperialist world is to confront insistent attempts at larger and larger blocs of the oppressors extending even to quasi-formal annexations, whether through the endless expansion of fortress Europe, or through such entities as NAFTA and ALCA, and ensure that they do not become the instruments of 'global apartheid'.

Finally, does this vision of an apparently contradictory approach to 'the nation' in the two parts of the world imply the death of a common, 'proletarian' view that stands higher than all nations? We think not; we see it as merely the modern instantiation of an old, but still perfectly valid dictum of Marx: no nation that oppresses another can ever itself be free. Another world is possible – if, and only if, the power of the dominant nations over the planet is ended, once and for all.

## NOTES

1. There is no multilateral agreement even on how to spell globalisation, let alone define it. In this Introduction we try to reflect the usage that the movement has evolved: thus by 'globalisation', unless we say otherwise we mean the events of the last 20–30 years as defined above; by 'globalisers' we mean the committed advocates of all-out financial deregulation, and so on. To discuss academic theories we use phrases like 'formal globalisation theory' or 'globalisation theory as such'. However as will become clear, we take the defining difference of the past period to be not just the existence and growth of a global *economy* but the special role played by global *political institutions*, notably the WTO, IMF and World Bank.

2. Albeit slowly: in its May 2000 *World Economic Outlook* the IMF felt moved to remark that 'the remarkable strength of the US economy and the robust growth now apparent in western Europe have provided key support for faster than expected recoveries in Asia, Latin America, and other emerging market regions. Determined actions by policymakers in the crisis-affected countries to deepen adjustment and reform efforts, together with support from the international community, have also been important. Directors considered that, at least in the near term, risks for global growth may well be on the upside.'

3. Data from R.J. Schiller (2000) *Irrational Exuberance* (Princeton: Princeton University Press), and the *Financial Times*, daily share price indices.

4. This gives rise to the following, rather significant empirical question, which is quite independent of the extent of global markets: why have multinational *institutions* appeared only now? If global politics are a mere product of market forces, and if the world-historical tendency of these forces is a unilateral extension of the world market at the expense of all national boundaries, then why did these institutions not come into being in 1893?

5. See for example D. Held and Anthony McGrew (2000) *The Global Transformations Reader* (Cambridge: Polity) and, for a contrary view, J. Rosenberg (2000) *The Follies of Globalisation Theory* (London and New York: Verso).

6. Held and McGrew, *Global Transformations Reader*, p105.

7. P. Gowan (1999) *The Global Gamble: Washington's Faustian bid for world dominance* (London and New York: Verso), p4.

8. M.P. Todaro (1994) *Economic Development* (London: Longman), p85.

9. See, for an excellent statistical presentation and political analysis, E.M. Basualdo and Matías Kulfas (2000) 'Fuga de capitals y endeudamiento externo en la Argentina', *Realidad Económica* (Buenos Aires: IADE [Instituto Argentina para el Desarollo Economica]), pp76–103.

10. There are historical precedents. Harold James (2003) *The End of Globalization: Lessons from the Great Depression* (Cambridge, MA, and London: Harvard University Press) suggests globalisation in the nineteenth century sowed the seeds of its own destruction, leading to the Great Depression. One conclusion might be that globalisation in the nineteenth century was 'done wrong' or that the retreat from it was misguided, so that under a different policy framework, it would work. Another equally valid conclusion, better supported by the evidence, is that it does not work under any policy framework and this is why people retreat from it.

11. L. Pritchett (1997) 'Divergence, Big Time', *Journal of Economic Perspectives* (Summer).

12. See Freeman's chapter in this book. In 1980 the richest country was the USA ($5,070 per head) and the poorest Bangladesh ($57 per head); in 2000 the richest was Luxembourg ($45,917) and the poorest Guinea-Bissau ($161). In 2000 the ratio between the average US citizen and the average Bangladeshi was 101.

13. For a detailed discussion of Kondratieff's distinction between reversible and irreversible processes, and between cycle and trend, and its seminal role in subsequent business cycle analysis, see C. Freeman and Francisco Louçã (2001) *As Time Goes By: From the Industrial Revolutions to the Information Revolution* (Oxford: OUP), p77.

14. Modelski and Thompson argue that Kondratieff waves are linked both the the rise and decline of globally significant world industries, and to a cycle of rise and decline of world powers and a change in world political arrangements, referring to this as the hegemonic cycle. G. Modelski and William R. Thompson (1996) *Leading Sectors and World Powers: The coevolution of global economics and politics* (Columbia: University of South Carolina Press).

15. The teleology is odd because globalisation theorists are generally so iconoclastic against the alleged 'single overriding dynamic of transformation' offered by classical theories (cf. A. Giddens (1990) *Consequences of Modernity* (Cambridge: CUP), cited in Rosenberg, *Follies of Globalisation Theory*, p96). Shorn of the ifs and buts in which academics habitually shroud predictions, a surprising swathe of accounts of globalisation offer an almost millenarian determinism when it comes to the 'single overriding dynamic' of time–space compression, the information revolution and the rising tidal flow of almost everything.

16. *Wall Street Journal* dollar share indices. On the same date the S&P500 had attained around five times its 1992 level. It never sank below three times this level.

17. *World Economic Outlook*, May 2000.

18.  For their own peoples. They are generally, of course, extremely enthusiastic about self-determination for other nations' peoples, above all those of their rivals.

19.  *The Economist*, 26 July 2003, p29.

20.  Speech at plenary session of the Conference on Critical Global Studies, University of Santa Barbara, May 2003.

21.  Rosenberg, *Follies of Globalisation Theory*, p280.

22.  A. Giddens (2000) in *The Third Way and its Critics* (Cambridge: Polity), defends the Third Way in the UK on the basis that it is being applied worldwide, notably in Chile. Can one seriously imagine that the Chilean experience of 1974 had no impact on the Chilean programme of 2004? This ultimate decontextualisation implies that the two countries operate under the same, universal, worldwide constraints. It is precisely because the postwar left of the advanced countries never suffered the barbarous elimination of its entire capacity for political resistance that it has succeeded in an obstinate economic resistance that has so far secured it a distinctly better deal.

23.  Thus the Samuelson factor-price theorem (Paul A. Samuelson (1948) 'International Trade and the Equalisation of Factor Prices', *Economic Journal*, no. 58, pp163–84) established in the late 1940s that on the basis of very standard economic assumptions, the prices of labour and capital in national economies would converge over time. Most standard textbooks on international economic theory begin by noticing that what really happens in the world is not explained by the theory; what follows is a long series of adaptations and modifications of the same basically false theory, to explain its failure. Any true science would long ago have treated such a basic conflict of fact with prediction as *prima facie* evidence that the entire foundation of the theory should be thrown out.

24.  The underlying issue is to understand how a profit greater than the average – which Marx termed a surplus profit – can be extracted in a systematic way by organising a specific relation between the capital of one country and the capital of another. Traditional 'Marxism' is incapable of theorising the mechanisms by which this occurs because it is confined to an equilibrium interpretation of Marx. From this standpoint permanent surplus profit, which is in reality an outcome of the dynamics of non-equilibrium growth, cannot logically exist. This rendered the last generation of theories of underdevelopment incapable of uncovering, in a logically coherent manner, the real basis for the economic subordination of dependent economies. See, for example, A. Freeman (2003) 'When Things Go Wrong: The political economy of market breakdown' in A. Zuege and Richard Westra, *Value and the World Economy Today: Production, finance and globalization* (London: Palgrave), and papers on www.iwgvt. org.

25.  Gowan, *The Global Gamble*, pp103–5.

26.  V. Giacchè (2001) 'Perché la Guerra Fa Bene all'Economia (I)', *Proteo* (Roma: CEDES), no. 3, pp111–16.

27.  This does not at all mean that the world is now neatly divided between capitalists and workers; on the contrary, the peasantry and petty-bourgeoisie combined probably still constitute a majority of the world's

population, and the Third World possesses vast classes of the dispossessed. What we mean by this statement is that capitalism now *rules* more or less without reliance on any other propertied class. To put it another way, today's Third World landlord is more likely to be Monsanto than Somoza.

28. Marxists can plead guilty to adopting, often uncritically, an enlightenment view of progress that supposes a unilateral movement through pre-capitalist formations whether feudal, 'asiatic' or composite, to capitalist, and then socialist. This was not the view of Marx: 'The chapter on primitive accumulation does not claim to do more than trace the path by which, in Western Europe, the capitalist economic system emerged... He [my critic] insists on transforming my historical sketch of the genesis of capitalism in Western Europe into an historic–philosophical theory of the general path of development prescribed by fate to all nations, whatever the historical circumstances in which they find themselves.' 'Marx to *Otchestvenniye Zapiski*, November 1877' in K. Marx and Friedrich Engels (1955) *Marx–Engels Selected Correspondence* (Moscow: Progress Publishers), p292.

29. A. Gunder-Frank (1996) 'The Development of Underdevelopment', *Monthly Review Press*.

30. There is an interesting formal analogy with absolutist monarchy. Absolutism was the *form in which* feudalism perpetuated itself but also heightened its contradictions to their sharpest degree, preparing the way for revolutionary movements directed against the monarchy but which also finally swept away feudalism.

31. Interview with David Harvey by Nader Vossoughian concerning D. Harvey (2003) *The New Imperialism* (Oxford: OUP). The interview is published in full on Vossoughian's website at http://agglutinations.com/archives/000013.html.

# 2
# The Inequality of Nations

*Alan Freeman*

## ABSOLUTE DIVERGENCE

### The rich and the rest: The two great blocs of the world economy

Figure 2.1 shows how the income of the world was shared between the countries that the IMF classifies as 'advanced' and all the rest for the period 1970–2000.[1] Figure 2.2 shows the proportions of world population living in these two parts of the world. Between 1970 and 2000 the rest of the world's share shrank from just over 30 per cent of the whole world's income to just under 20 per cent. At the same time, the proportion of people living there rose from 80 per cent to 84 per cent.

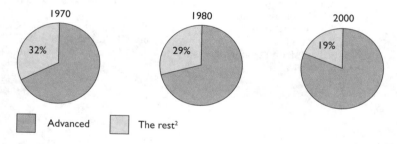

*Figure 2.1* Share of world income

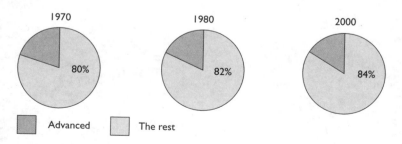

*Figure 2.2* Share of world population

Dating the present stage of globalisation as beginning in 1980, the income of the advanced countries was 11 times larger, in proportion to their population, than the rest of the world. By 2000 this ratio had risen to 23.

Globalisation thus doubled the inequality between the advanced countries and the rest of the world in twenty years. This inequality, measured as the ratio between average income in the two parts of the world, grew at an annual rate of 2.4 per cent in the ten years before globalisation, and an annual rate of 3.9 per cent in the 22 years thereafter.

Globalisation, in a nutshell, equals divergence.

We can express the average incomes in constant 1995 dollars.[3] This is shown in Table 2.1. While output per person in the advanced countries rose from $18,088 in 1980 to $26,201 in 2000, in the rest of the world it fell from $1,690 to $1,160.

*Table 2.1*    GDP per capita in constant 1995 dollars

|  | 1970 | 1980 | 1990 | 2000 | 2002 | Annual growth rate, % 1970–80 | 1980–2002 |
|---|---|---|---|---|---|---|---|
| Advanced countries | 10,473 | 18,088 | 23,989 | 26,201 | 25,672 | 5.6 | 1.8 |
| Rest of the world | 1,248 | 1,690 | 1,356 | 1,160 | 1,100 | 3.1 | −2.1 |
| Ratio of GDP per capita, Advanced/Rest of the world | 8.4 | 10.7 | 17.7 | 22.6 | 23.3 | 2.4 | 3.9 |
| Population of the Advanced countries (millions)[4] | 718 | 778 | 827 | 833 | 845 | 0.4 | 0.8 |
| Population of the Rest of the world (millions) | 2,810 | 3,466 | 4,213 | 4,288 | 4,431 | 1.2 | 2.1 |

Globalisation has thus reasserted, and sharpened to its greatest extent ever, a phenomenon that has dominated world economics and politics for 150 years – the division of the world's nations into two fundamentally unequal blocs.

### The rich fall out: Behind the US miracle

Over the same period there has been a complete reversal in the relation between the USA and the other advanced parts of the world. Table 2.2 compares growth rates over each of the three decades up to 2000, and Figure 2.3 shows the results in detail.

It is well known that the USA led world growth during the 1990s.[5] It is less well known that this was not because it performed any better than at any time in the last half-century, but because everyone else performed considerably worse. A prolonged phase of high growth rates among the USA's principal competitors, lasting from the early 1950s, ended. Their growth rates fell to the level that the USA has suffered since the late 1960s.[6]

*Table 2.2*   Growth rates in the advanced and advancing countries

| Total growth of GDP per capita (% over the decade) | 1970–80 | 1980–90 | 1990–2000 |
|---|---|---|---|
| North America | 24.6 | 24.8 | 20.9 |
| Euro Area | 122.0 | 25.4 | –8.4 |
| South-East Asia | 128.9 | 68.1 | 19.9 |
| Rest of the world | 35.4 | –19.8 | –14.5 |

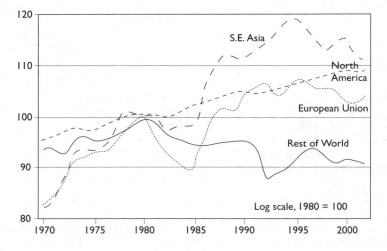

*Figure 2.3*   Real GDP per capita, constant US dollars

This reverses the relation between the US and those wealthy countries that previously functioned as its unquestioning partners. Until 1980 North America was growing slower, in terms of real dollars, than all other parts of the world.[7] Thus, the economic interests of the advanced countries lay in accepting US leadership, not only in the direction of the world economy but in much of world politics as well. German and Japanese strategy was, in essence, to fall in behind the USA politically as a means of outdoing it economically.

Globalisation has undone the material basis for this coalition. The last vestiges of the postwar expansion were crushed out of the USA's rivals in two waves, one in each decade of globalisation.

The second of these two waves was far more decisive. After an initial fall during 1980–85, both Europe and South-East Asia regained ground, and by 1990 Europe had caught up its losses while South-East Asia had resumed its high growth trend, pulling away still further from North America. Thus the opening years of globalisation did much to drive the advanced countries away from the rest, but little to drive the advanced countries apart. The 1990s marked a historical rupture. From around 1995 *all* parts of the world slowed down relative to North America – including the other parts of the 'advanced' world. By 2002 the USA had made good all its previous losses relative to South-East Asia, and, in terms of cumulative GDP per capita growth, had clawed back the historical lead of the European Union.

## ABSOLUTE STAGNATION

In the 1990s, accelerated divergence was joined by a further process: stagnation. This was brought about by the US's own failure to raise its growth rate and by sharp declines in the growth rates of the other major advanced countries. Divergence, combined with stagnation, has produced the present political crisis of world governance.

Stagnation is particularly striking because it has gone almost unnoticed. In a nutshell, as Figure 2.4 shows, world GDP per capita has started going down.

In 1988, the GDP per capita of the world in constant 1995 dollars was $4,885. By 2002, it was $4,778. That is, over the intervening 14 years, in real dollar terms, it fell absolutely. As Table 2.3 shows, prior to the present stage of globalisation world GDP per capita was rising at 3–4 per cent a year. In the first decade of globalisation this

*Table 2.3*   Annual world growth rates, constant 1995 dollars

|  | 1970–80 | 1980–90 | 1990–2000 |
|---|---|---|---|
| World per capita GDP | 4.2% | 0.8% | –0.2% |
| World total GDP | 6.1% | 2.5% | 1.2% |

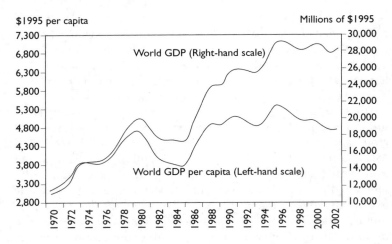

*Figure 2.4*   World per capita GDP and world GDP, constant 1995 dollars

fell to less than 1 per cent, and throughout the 1990s was negative. Globalisation has not increased the rate of world growth: it has diminished it absolutely.

### DIVERGENCE, STAGNATION AND THE END OF GLOBALISATION

Conventional economic wisdom holds that globalisation was an economic success but a political failure. In fact, it has been a political triumph and an economic catastrophe.

Its success lay in creating a governing bloc that regulated the way in which almost all nations participated in the world market, so that despite exceptions – most notably China – a more or less uniform economic order, with a single integrated economic policy, was implemented worldwide. This bloc was dominated by the rich nations and hegemonised by the USA. Its social base included the bulk of the population of the wealthy countries, a majority in their more successful clients, and a minority but governing class in the poorest countries.

European and Japanese support was secure, as was that of the NIACs, as long as the advanced or advancing countries grew at the expense of the rest. Elsewhere, pro-globalisation governments formed wherever substantial elites could reap private benefits, enjoying living standards rising above the general level in their countries – particularly where they were integrated into circuits of world financial capital. In those many countries where the beneficiaries of globalisation were thin on the ground, the bloc governed quite simply through fear: the twin threats posed by debt and capital flight.

Because of this basic consensus, much of the economic regulation of the world could safely be delegated to transnational bodies such as the IMF, the World Bank and the WTO. Enforcement was not a substantive problem because, in each individual state, a politically functional government could be formed that was committed to implementing the global world economic consensus.

But this political pyramid rested on an unsustainable economic base. Political cohesion is incompatible with economic divergence. Generally speaking, the deeper the economic differences between people, the deeper their political antagonisms. Thus the only form of globalisation that can ultimately succeed politically is one based on the reduction of economic difference, not on its increase.

Such political antagonisms can be suspended or offset in a situation where world output is generally increasing, because in that case divergence is only relative. If most of those that are falling behind nevertheless enjoy a rising standard of living, and if growth in the richer parts of the world generates a politically accessible surplus sufficient to head off political conflict, then open national and political conflict can be contained or avoided.

This was the case in the golden age of the 1950s and 1960s when there was a general and prolonged Kondratieff upswing. Although nations continued to move apart from one another, this meant only that some were growing faster than others, so that the number of absolutely poor people was falling. Divergence now, however, combines with stagnation. Conflict ceases to be one of many possible recourses: for more and more people, it becomes the only recourse. This, in effect, removes the entire basis for liberal democracy, since if people have no option but to fight each other in order to survive, no amount of wise regulation is going to stop them.

Through stagnation combined with divergence, globalisation itself is dissolving the pro-globalisation bloc, literally tearing it apart. Large tracts of the world have been rendered ungovernable. At best it is increasingly difficult to form stable governments that can survive politically while carrying out IMF policies, as the case of Argentina dramatically demonstrates. At worst, in cases such as Afghanistan, the Middle East, and increasingly in Africa, political instability dominates an entire region.

The political institutions that have made globalisation possible have thus eroded the economic circumstances that made their own existence possible. This has exposed the absolute limits within which they functioned as world institutions. The basic weakness of the IMF is that it has no means of enforcement. This is particularly important for the market in capital – which is what really distinguishes the period of 'globalisation' from the general expansion of the world market. Without enforcement, a debtor can simply renege, unless legally sanctioned force compels her or him to conform. Hence when the governments of Russia or Argentina simply refused to honour their internationally contracted debts, there was actually nothing the IMF could do except complain.

A nation-state can use internal force, within its boundaries, to distrain any individual or corporate body that fails to comply with its laws. No such sanction exists on the international level. The IMF does not have an army or a police force. Therefore no matter how draconian, its policies, imposed through 'structural adjustment' plans, have always required the consent of the government concerned, in turn coerced by the threat of debt, and it is the national government that has been allocated the awkward job of suppressing domestic opposition. As countries gradually realise that there is indeed a fate worth than debt, it becomes harder and harder to secure this governmental consent; governments that do so consent have simply become politically unsustainable.

This leaves only one recourse if an advanced country wishes to impose policies on countries that cannot sustain governments that consent to them – conquest. If a country's governing institutions refuse to implement measures that are likely to lead to it losing office, there is no alternative but to set up alternative institutions by external intervention. There is no other means of compelling a country to adopt policies, or pay debts, that its government refuses to accept.

The problem with force, and conquest, is that it is basically impossible to secure multilateral consent; *conquering force is therefore the ultimate prerogative of the national state*. On this terrain, there has been no erosion of sovereign national powers whatsoever. Conquest is therefore organised by national states.

This fact ultimately renders a multinational capitalist government impossible. There is a solid material reason; the conquerors are themselves not bound by the laws of contract. They can simply impose economic terms – as is the case, for example, with the disposition of

Iraqi oil. To the conquerors belong the spoils. Conquest and war are, therefore, the ultimate and logical form of economic competition.

This, and not terrorism, is what led the US to revert to a unilateralist agenda and bypass the international institutions. It substituted direct military and political intervention for the old 'hands-off' policy of leaving the IMF to get on with the job on behalf of Wall Street, because the IMF could no longer do the job.

John Williamson,[8] who coined the term 'Washington Consensus', explains this process clearly:

[T]here is no longer any agreement on the main lines of economic policy between the current U.S. administration and the international financial institutions ... there is now a critical difference in attitudes toward capital account liberalization in the emerging market countries, with the IMF having beaten a well-advised retreat since the Asian crisis ... while the Bush administration is still using bilateral free trade agreements to bully countries like Chile and Singapore into emasculating even the most enlightened capital controls. And even on trade, the international financial institutions have expressed strong criticism of U.S. policy on agriculture and steel. So, in this sense, any Washington Consensus has simply ceased to exist – a reflection of the chasm that the Bush administration has opened up between the United States and the rest of the world.[9]

A second process accompanied this, and sealed the fate of the international institutions. At the same time that it lost its capacity to create stable governing blocs in the Third World, the US has lost its political hegemony over its erstwhile partners. Multilateral conquest is bringing no multilateral benefits. A unilateral US agenda means not only that the US administration has abandoned the multilateral institutions, but that it has also made the conscious decision to advance its own interests over those of its erstwhile partners. The Iraq War made this finally clear to everyone. France and Germany opposed US policy in Iraq, not for humanitarian motives,[10] but because their economic needs were too brutally counterposed to those of the USA.

Finally, and not least – since it is probably the reason that this book exists – as the multilateral benefits from globalisation erode away, the fragile support of the working class *within* the advanced countries, above all Europe, has fallen away. This is what really lies behind the startling growth of the 'Northern' component of the anti-globalisation movement and the peace movement alike.

Globalisation, as it has existed for the past 23 years, is self-destructing. It has given birth to a new age: of protectionism, rivalry and war.

## THE NEW AGE OF COMPETITIVE REGIONALISM

What shape might politics take in this emerging brave new world? I will try to answer this question in more detail by looking at its economic underpinnings, examining the possible shape of twenty-first-century politics by looking at the structure of divergence within and between the world's major regions. First, however, some basic methodological questions have to be answered, the first of which is the relation between economics and politics. Most basic of these is: why is the state necessary at all?

A straightforward consequence of standard economic theory[11] is that the 'natural' tendency of markets is convergence. Divergence, according to almost all orthodox theory and quite a lot of heterodoxy, is not produced by markets but happens in spite of them – it is either the result of misguided government, malign forces such as trade unions, terrorists and anti-globalists, or is just a residual effect of a backward past before markets came to the rescue. In technical language, convergence is *endogenous* to the market and divergence is *exogenous*.

This is difficult to square with the evidence, given that the world has been diverging more or less since the world market began by almost any measure that one cares to adopt, and has done so faster when obstacles to it have been weakest.[12] Indeed, it is now harder than ever, since, perhaps for the first time in history, the whole world is basically capitalist. In a certain sense, the past period of globalisation has finally settled the case against all theories of development that seek to explain the world economy as an interaction between capitalism and 'pre-capitalist' obstacles – not least, that of Rosa Luxemburg. No serious pre-capitalist obstacles to the market remain. The jury is no longer out: *capitalism* is responsible for the course of capitalist development.

A number of more or less sophisticated economic theories – the new trade theory, endogenous growth theory, and so on – seek to explain divergence through the interaction of the market with non-market phenomena. But with the exception of Marx's work, no body of economic theory contains within it the natural conclusion that markets create divergence simply because they are markets. If divergence is explained at all, it is explained as an exception. More usually, it is claimed, with an almost religious blindness to basic facts, that divergence does not happen.

What consequence does this have for the future of the state? It is my view that globalisation theory, to a great extent a creation of non-economists, has uncritically and unquestioningly absorbed the outlook of the economists, of whom it should have been far more critical. From the economists, it has become imbued with the idea that the state is an economic anachronism. But what is the theoretical origin of this idea? Basically, from an ideological premise: from the view that, left to its own devices, the market homogenises.

If this were true, it would surely remove one of the basic reasons that sets people against each other. One of the most basic functions of the state – to regulate and contain *conflict* – would, if economic orthodoxy were true, be economically dissolved.

But if divergence is the natural tendency of the market, precisely the opposite conclusion follows. All social conflicts are sharpened by divergence, the ultimate outcome being war. Politics has an indispensable function: to contain – or, indeed, simply cope with – the natural processes of divergence that the market produces. The stronger the divergence, therefore, the greater the demands on the state. One of the important insights of Marx's political economy is an understanding that the nation-state regulates *class* conflict, which in turn is a natural outcome of one of the market's key social products, namely a separation of civil society into classes defined by the source of their income and its relation to property.

Marx's economic theory as such, however, does not dictate that the state should have a *national* form or, indeed, even a territorially bounded form.[13] On the contrary, Marx was in many senses the first globalisation theorist, a fact often forgotten by both the opponents and supporters of globalisation. It was Marx who first recognised that the market forms classes on a worldwide basis, independent of nation-states, and that moreover the basic solidarity of property owners against wage-earners extends over national boundaries and transcends them. The capitalist class, for Marx, was an international class formed by the market. That is why he dedicated himself to constructing international institutions of the working class, to confront it also at international level.

So why can't a world state, or a system of state-like world institutions, play the same role as the nation-state? To succeed in this, the world institutions that arose under globalisation would have had to act, as do national states, to contain divergence and regulate conflict. But the evidence is that they have done exactly the opposite: they have accentuated divergence, and spawned conflict.

Superimposed on the division of the world into classes is a division of the world's territories, arising from a second great imperative of the capitalist market – the geographical concentration of capital, splitting these territories into competing blocs. The analysis of this phenomenon was a theoretical achievement of twentieth-century Marxists; the empirical evidence is that their basic analytical categories are still valid today.

It is true that the most basic economic and social division in the world is that between classes. However, the most fundamental political division is between the 'advanced' countries as a whole and all the others, and this establishes the institutional framework within which class conflict is necessarily played out. This gives rise to a completely different type of state in the two parts of the world – dominant states and dominated states. The typical function of the advanced country state is the extraction of a special advantage from the rest of the world, by monopolising sources of world surplus-profit – an exceptional profit over and above the world average that arises from the functioning of the world market. The typical function of the Third World, or dominated state, is to protect its capitalists against this predation. It does so by facing both ways. On the one hand, it must minimise the surplus profit that they lose through the operation of the world market. On the other, it must suppress the implicit conflict between its own working people and the unholy alliance between the predatory capitalists outside the country, and the subordinated capitalists inside.

'Globalisation' was a particular form in which the predatory states delegated the economic aspect of their domination to the international financial institutions and suppressed the implicit competition between them. It is this delegation that has fallen foul of the destructive consequences of divergence. Increasingly, the dominated states have to organise their own, special, relationship with the rest of the world, just as they did at the end of the nineteenth century in the age of classical imperialism.

But the problem is that the system of dominating states is inadequate for this purpose because it consists of a single continental state – the USA – and a collection of national states, none of which is adequate on its own to confront the power of the USA, and each of which is being crushed by the fatal combination of political power and economic weight that the US state puts at the disposition of its capitalists. It is for precisely this reason that the politics of the twenty-first century reduces to the political economy of *regional state-building* projects, regional alliances and rival regional trading projects – the EEC, ALCA, Mercosur, APEC, and so on.[14]

First, the Europeans have to try and construct a continental power adequate to confront the USA economically, politically and ultimately militarily. Second, the Third World countries are driven, on pain of dissolution and extinction, to construct regional blocs and proto-states adequate to defend them both against the emergent superpowers. And third, the policies of both the USA and Europe are directed constantly towards the political division of the Third World, as they were in the epoch of classical imperialism.

The most decisive political objective is to ensure that no continental Third World state can emerge. This made destruction of the Soviet Union the prime objective of the pro-globalisation bloc. It is what requires it to demonise Islam, with its pan-national aspirations; it makes the dissolution of India a constant subtext; and it makes China, already in effect a continental economy, the principal obstacle to the world order that the advanced countries require. 'Terrorism', in effect, is a codeword for the ever-present threat of continental Third World alliances – for the danger of a pan-national Third World coalition of sufficient weight, and with sufficient separation from the market in capital, to chart an independent path of development.

It is thus perfectly true that the present system of states is absolutely inadequate to regulate the economic consequences of globalisation. And it is equally perfectly untrue that a world system of governance can replace it. In consequence we have entered a period of generalised crisis of world governance. This process is leading not to the abolition of the state, but to a completely new structure of states and territories, driven by two phenomena: an increasingly political struggle of the dominant bloc against the rest of the world on the one hand, and the polarisation of the dominant bloc on the other.

The real issue, therefore, is to study the structure of economic divergence region by region, to discard all utopian illusions, and ask where it is driving the corresponding structures of political domination. In order to do this, however, we need the soundest possible instruments of analysis. The next section is therefore addressed to questions of methodology, and the last section will apply them concretely to analysing the new structure of the world's economic geography.

## THE LIMITS OF STATISTICS

How much reliance can be placed on numbers derived by adding up world GDP statistics, and how much can we trust the conclusions? I will single out three questions, which I think are central to obtaining an accurate and complete picture of the economic geography of the twenty-first century.

First, GDP statistics are available for whole countries only, and there is obviously differentiation within each country as well as between countries. Do national boundaries obscure the true geography of poverty? To put it more starkly, does poverty have no geography?

Second, I have studied the figures by converting them into world money. I have studied inequality in strictly monetary terms, that is, in terms of *ability to pay* – to be precise, I have expressed them in US dollars at current market exchange rates. There are other measures of both income and output – for example, purchasing power parity (PPP) dollars. They often give rise to different conclusions, which is why the international institutions, which were until the early 1990s quite suspicious of them, have now enthusiastically adopted them. So is inequality nothing more than a statistical construct?

The third issue is the particular significance of China, which does have a continental economy, which still maintains its independence from the market in capital, and which has seen unprecedented and sustained growth over the recent period of globalisation. China's actual policies are very remote from the ideals the IMF sold to the rest of the world from 1982 onwards, maintaining strict capital controls and rejecting the 'shock therapy' that devastated the Economies in Transition (among which, we should note, the IMF does not include China). Is China proof of the success of globalisation – or is it proof of the opposite? And how should it be treated in the statistics to give an accurate picture of what is really going on?

## THE USE AND MISUSE OF AVERAGES

Statistical agencies are geared up to collect data on a national basis. Access to data on world income distribution that cross country boundaries is virtually impossible to come by, and awareness of this fact is only now beginning to reallocate some fairly small resources to this question.

However, some simple arithmetic shows there are basic limits within which actual income in a country can range above or below national averages. This becomes clear once we start to think about the most basic issue socially, namely, how many rich people, and how many poor people, can logically exist within a certain territory, given its average income?

### Advanced Third World countries?

First, as regards the general scale of inequality – that is, the relation between the number of poor people in the world and the number of rich people in the world – it is statistically impossible that differences between averages, on the scale we see in the world today, can co-exist with declining, or even low, levels of inequality. The views expressed below in *The Economist* on 26 June 2003 represent, frankly, wishful thinking:

> Far from rising, global inequality has actually been falling substantially. Not when measured as the gap between the very richest and the very poorest. Nor when measured, as has until recently been the rather odd norm, as the difference between the average incomes of each country, regardless of population (thus counting Chad and China as if they were of equal size). But if it is measured in the way which is normal within countries, as the distribution of individual incomes, it has narrowed considerably.

I agree that inequality, properly presented, does not reduce to comparing average income in one country with average income in another. But this is not the same as saying that geography counts for nothing. At the beginning of this chapter I did not compare one country with another. I compared the whole of one part of the world with the whole of the other part.

All I did was to divide the world in two, using the IMF's own classification. If world income is a cake, then before this phase of globalisation began, 82 per cent of the people in the world got 29 per cent of this cake to share between themselves. When it had finished, 84 per cent of them had to share 19 per cent of it between themselves. To present this as anything other than an increase in inequality is an act of statistical deception.

To fix ideas, I will define 'poor' simply to mean living at or about an income equal to the average of the 'rest of the world' – that is, \$3 per day in 1995 dollars.[15] It is then arithmetically impossible for the number of poor people to decrease as long as average inequality is rising. This is such a basic statistical fact that faced with its persistent denial we can only conclude that the faculty of reason is being replaced by something else.

Let us first suppose for the sake of argument that individual incomes within countries are in fact growing closer today – a questionable result in the light of figures cited by Robinson in Chapter 6 of this book. In that case, if average incomes in the two parts of the world are growing apart, the divergence between incomes of people living in them must also be diverging. Thus, consider the extreme case where everyone in each part of the world earns the same income. In that case, country averages would be a perfect guide to personal inequality. Every individual in each country would be earning exactly the same. Every one of the 4,288 million people in the 'rest of the world' would be earning 23 times less than every one of the 833 million people in the 'advanced countries' – just over twice the differential that existed at the beginning of globalisation.

Thus if, as *The Economist* suggests, incomes within each part of the world are becoming more equal, then this can only mean, since the average income in the two parts of the world has diverged, that individual incomes in these two parts of the world have also diverged. Nothing else is statistically possible.

Let us look at an alternative possibility. Suppose instead that inequality within countries is large, or getting larger, compared with the differences in average income. But this too, given the averages reported above, would have to mean that the great majority of the world's population is at least relatively poor, and growing poorer. Suppose, for example, that the entire average GDP of \$1,160 in the 'rest of the world' in the year 2000 was appropriated by a rich class securing the same income as the average in the advanced countries – quite a modest idea, really. Their income would then be 23 times greater than the average in the Third World. But this entire class has to fit inside the share of the cake, which, in 2000, took up 19 per cent of the whole world's income. This places an absolute limit on the size of this class: it cannot possibly make up more than one-twenty-third of the population. For it to do so, the average for the whole of the 'rest of the world' would have to rise above \$1,160 or, to put it in its most direct form, the share of the cake would have to get bigger.

Moreover, even in that extreme case, the remaining population would have to earn nothing at all. Either, therefore, this rich class must be poorer than even the average for the advanced countries, or it must be very small. There is a simple trade-off from which *The Economist*'s anonymous writer must choose. *Either* this class is not really very rich, or it is not really very big. A class that is both rich and big simply cannot exist, statistically, in a section of the world that contains four-fifths of its people and appropriates a fifth of its income.

It is technically possible – in a different world – to have a large number of people with high incomes, even though average incomes are very far apart. The arithmetical condition for this is that the number of people living in impoverished countries would have to be small compared with the world's population. In that case, we could see a small and desperately poor underclass, largely confined to marginal parts of the globe, against a background of generally increasing wealth.

Since the existence of poor people is hard to deny, this is the way that their numbers are usually presented. This is, in essence, the analytical framework of the 'Third Way'. This is articulated as if the political problems of globalisation were confined to relatively small and manageable layers of socially excluded and marginalised individuals. Globalisation is treated as if the number of people living in a each slice of the cake was proportional to the size of the slice. The problem of liberal democracy is then to ensure that this small number of marginalised individuals is included in a general process of progress.

However, the great majority of the world live in the small slice, and moreover the proportion is getting bigger. The 80/20 vision of the Third Way breaks down statistically once we reckon with the fact that this 'marginalised' layer consists of most people in the world. Actually, in terms of population, the world's 'marginal' people are those living in the advanced countries. The sheer number of people living in poor countries dictates, statistically, that the overwhelming majority of the world's people must also be poor, and any attempt to avoid this basic arithmetic fact is either wishful sophistry or wilful ignorance. In a world whose majority is poor, the marginals are the rich. This is why they have no option but to sustain their wealth by directly political domination. The political 'integration' of a majority by a minority is not a caring liberal democracy: it is a dictatorship with a conscience.

### Third World advanced countries?

Only one other statistical possibility works in the opposite direction. This has been suggested by Paul Krugman. It corresponds politically to the outlook of Negri and Hardt,[16] who seek to demonstrate, in essence, an unmediated identity of political interest between the poor of the First World and the mass of the Third World. It could be that the high average incomes of the advanced countries are caused by the distillation of a super-rich class in the advanced countries, which raises the average although the majority in these countries live in Third World conditions. It is beyond the scope of this chapter to investigate this empirically.

However, we must note, first, that it could provide no comfort to pro-globalisers, since in this case political instability would be all the worse: the number of relatively poor people in the world would be understated by the averages rather than overstated. Second, however, it suggests that no significant section of the working classes of the advanced countries should have much interest in supporting their own imperialism's activities. It is difficult to reconcile this with the level of support that, in the past, the working-class organisations of the advanced countries have given to the wars of conquest of their own nations. And, finally, it is only possible arithmetically if inequality within the advanced countries were substantially greater than between the advanced countries and the rest of the world. This is empirically a hard thesis to sustain.

### WHAT DOES MONEY BUY?
### PURCHASING POWER, PAYING POWER, AND GROWTH

The figures used in this chapter were calculated, as has been said, by converting national GDPs into dollars at current exchange rates. Anyone with access to the Internet, incidentally, can verify them, since the IMF distributes them free of charge.

This method, widely used by the IMF until the early 1990s, presents a different picture from that generally now produced when institutions attempt to assess the results of globalisation. In short, the globalisers have shifted the goalposts. Output is now usually presented for the purpose of comparing country outputs in purchasing power parity (PPP) dollars.

A PPP dollar is a fictitious currency unit, which is supposed to represent the same quantity of goods in every place, at every time. No-one in the world actually consumes what a PPP dollar buys. It is constructed by calculating an 'ideal' basket of goods representing the average consumption of an imaginary world citizen.

Such a citizen does not exist, because patterns of consumption are widely different in different parts of the world. Indeed, as we shall see, under globalisation consumption patterns have themselves diverged. Moreover, PPP dollars do not exist, in a very fundamental sense: they cannot be used to pay bills or settle debts. A PPP dollar is not means of payment. It is not even a unit of account that can be used in international settlements like the European 'green pound'. In particular, debtor countries cannot use them to pay their creditors, and if they could, the world's debt would be reduced by three-quarters.

There is no single consistent PPP measure, and it is generally acknowledged that such a measure is theoretically impossible. In particular, a PPP measure that is good for making comparisons between country price levels is bad at estimating aggregate output, and vice versa.[17] Worse still, a single measure of output that is valid both for comparisons in time and in space is not possible, and one can therefore either compare countries' absolute levels using one PPP measure, or their growth rates using another – but not both, with the same measure. In short, it is theoretically impossible for a single PPP measure to serve as an indicator of both divergence and stagnation. For this reason the OECD took a decision as early as 1990 to disseminate two different sets of PPP measures:

> In 1989 UNSTAT, the OECD and Eurostat jointly convened an expert meeting to discuss the aggregation methods used in the calculation of PPPs and real expenditures. The experts recognised that the results of such calculations are used for many different purposes and that *there is no one method of aggregation which can be considered satisfactory for all these purposes*. They recommended the calculation and dissemination of two sets of results: one set to be aggregated using the EKS method, the other to be aggregated using the GK method [emphasis in original].[18]

This does not prevent most agencies, particularly in publications aimed at the general public, writing as if there were only one such measure or, worse, choosing the particular measure that proves the point they wish to make and then speaking authoritatively as if it were the only one available. This extends even to statistical authorities, as the OECD acerbically comments:

Both Eurostat and the OECD have accepted the experts' recommendations in principle, but there is a practical difficulty of particular importance to Eurostat. The results for Community countries are used for administrative purposes as well as for economic analysis. For this reason, Eurostat requires that only one set of results be recognised as the official results for the Community.

That is, although it is theoretically ridiculous, politically the Europeans will do it anyway. So much for the enlightenment.

### Globalisation and the movement of world prices

Let us for the sake of argument set aside for now all the above difficulties, and simply compare the results of measuring output in current dollars and in PPPs. Table 2.4 shows, for the bottom and top group of countries, the ratio of PPP output to dollar output in 1999 after adjusting world totals to be the same.

It can be seen that the output of the advanced countries is estimated as systematically lower, and the output of the Third World systematically higher, in PPPs than in dollars. The effect is huge: for example, when Sri Lanka at the bottom of the table is compared with Japan at the top, it will be treated as seven times less unequal in PPPs than in current exchange dollars. To put it another way, when Sri Lanka is paying its debts it will be allowed seven times less purchasing power per dollar than when it puts its case against structural adjustment.

To some degree (though, because of theoretical imperfections in the PPP method, not entirely), a country whose PPP output is high compared with its dollar output will have lower prices. Hence if a country's domestic products are cheap in comparison with their price in the USA, the international agencies will record it as producing more than it can actually raise by selling its produce in the world market; in some cases a great deal more. For example, as can be seen from the Table, in the IMF or World Bank's estimates of the performance of China and India, they will multiply China's actual money output by 4.38 and India's by 4.23.

But the IMF only does this when it wishes to prove that India is doing well as a result of globalisation, not when it enquires whether it can pay its bills. That is, the IMF uses ordinary dollars to assess whether a country has complied with its policies, and PPPs to assess whether they worked.

Table 2.4    Ratio of PPP and dollar GDP, highest and lowest in 1999[*]

| Country | Ratio of PPP GDP to dollar GDP at market exchange rates | Country | Ratio of PPP GDP to dollar GDP at market exchange rates |
|---------|-------------------------------------------------------|---------|-------------------------------------------------------|
| Japan | 0.62 | Bangladesh | 2.39 |
| Switzerland | 0.63 | Jordan | 2.44 |
| Denmark | 0.69 | Colombia | 2.48 |
| Norway | 0.73 | Philippines | 2.50 |
| Sweden | 0.75 | Iran | 2.91 |
| Germany | 0.78 | Kenya | 3.09 |
| Austria | 0.79 | Thailand | 3.22 |
| Finland | 0.80 | Ghana | 3.23 |
| Ireland | 0.81 | Bulgaria | 3.26 |
| United Kingdom | 0.83 | Ethiopia | 3.97 |
| Belgium | 0.85 | Nigeria | 4.15 |
| France | 0.86 | India | 4.23 |
| Netherlands | 0.86 | China | 4.38 |
| United States | 0.87 | Pakistan | 4.70 |
| Italy | 0.93 | Indonesia | 4.81 |
| Israel | 0.95 | Syria | 7.11 |
| Slovenia | 1.01 | Sri Lanka | 7.13 |

* After adjustment so that totals are the same

## PPP and the contribution of India

The cases that illustrate the problem most clearly are those of India and China, above all India, which, unlike China, is yet to undergo a prolonged period of sustained growth, as Jayati Ghosh makes clear in Chapter 4 in this book. There is no doubt that China has undergone a real and sustained growth, which I assess in the next section. But China does not rightfully belong in the category of 'globalised' countries. The statistical effect of PPP measurements is to make it appear as though China and India were engaged in an identical process, and to use this falsely inflated growth as 'proof' of globalisation's success.

The GDP of India measured in 1996 PPPs was $1,783 billion but in 1990 current-exchange-rate dollars it was $441.7 billion, because in India a dollar buys over four times as much as in the USA, as already shown in Table 2.4. Thus whereas the combined national output of India and China in 1999 was worth $1,428 billion at current exchange rates, the IMF reports it as $5,932 billion, nearly as much as the output of Europe, which in PPP terms was $7,203 billion.

China and India have a specific statistical impact because, since globalisation began, their output measured in PPP terms has increased exceptionally rapidly. Figure 2.5 shows the ratio of GDP, for China and India, measured in PPPs and constant US dollars at current market exchange rates. It can be seen that the GDP of these two countries, measured in PPPs, has effectively been multiplied by 250 per cent since the present phase of globalisation began.

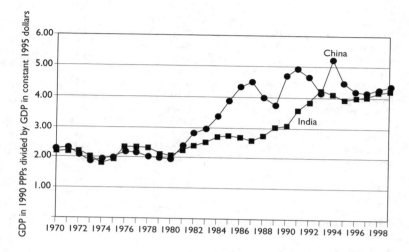

*Figure 2.5*  Ratio of real dollar and PPP dollar measures of GDP, for China and India

This rise in the PPP dollar is clearly itself a specific effect of globalisation. The capacity of these nations to appropriate wealth in the world market has fallen precipitately, because local prices have fallen much faster than US prices. It is moreover unique to the developing countries, not least India and China.

This has two profound implications. First, it means that globalisation has worsened the terms of trade. An Asian producer must work on average over four times longer to acquire US goods than a US producer, and seven times more than a Japanese producer to acquire Japanese goods. Developing countries, particularly Asian countries, are far less equipped to acquire on the market the produce of the advanced countries – which is precisely what they need in order to invest competitively, and which moreover are precisely the goods the IMF structural adjustment plans oblige them to buy. A central feature of these plans is that the developing countries are supposed to concentrate on exporting labour-intensive, primary produce. The substantial extra supply of these goods created has played a major role in producing a catastrophic fall in commodity prices, vitiating the whole strategy.

Although the divergence of PPP and current-exchange measures is universal throughout the non-advanced countries, its statistical effect on aggregates is heavily concentrated on China and India because of their size. If these two large Asian countries are removed from the calculation, the divergence evident in real dollar terms reappears even in PPP terms. As Table 2.5 shows, divergence, measured in PPP terms, appears over the period of globalisation to have fallen from 7.4 to 6.9. But if Asia is removed from the calculation, this ratio has risen from 3.5 to 5.1 during the period of globalisation, having remained virtually constant in the preceding four decades.

*Table 2.5* Growth of GDP per capita with and without Asia, in PPP dollars

| GDP per capita in 1990 PPP dollars | 1950 | 1960 | 1970 | 1980 | 1990 | 1999 |
| --- | --- | --- | --- | --- | --- | --- |
| Rest of the world | $845 | $1,147 | $1,464 | $1,936 | $2,341 | $3,124 |
| Rest of world without Asia | $1,712 | $2,244 | $3,060 | $4,059 | $3,875 | $4,239 |
| Advanced or advancing countries | $5,480 | $7,569 | $11,190 | $14,402 | $18,190 | $21,539 |
| Divergence ratio with Asia included | 6.5 | 6.6 | 7.6 | 7.4 | 7.8 | 6.9 |
| Divergence ratio with Asia excluded | 3.2 | 3.4 | 3.7 | 3.5 | 4.7 | 5.1 |

**The law of two prices**

Actually, the very fact that GDP measured in real dollars is diverging from GDP measured in PPPs signifies that something new is going on. Thirty years ago world output was rising unambiguously, and now it is not. The most definite post-modern statement that can be made, by anyone who wishes to argue that globalisation works, is that this view is supported only if one measures output in one particular way.

The divergence of PPP measures of income from a simple monetary measure shows something else: it shows that globalisation has produced a divergence not just in incomes but in *prices*. Paradoxically globalisation, which was supposed to act to bring about a harmonised world market, is creating a dual system of world prices. In particular we can summarise its overall effect quite simply: it has driven apart the cost of *wages* and *capital*. We have, in effect, a global cost of capital and a local cost of labour.

It is precisely because of this bipolar price system that a single PPP measure cannot convey what is really going on. Moreover, it is in any case nonsensical to argue that the key process in the world is the formation of an integrated world market, and then study it by concentrating on local differences.

What we must really study is the *combined* effect of price differentiation and output differentiation, and understand that they are not two separate phenomena but completely interdependent. To be absolutely precise, price differentiation is a *consequence* of income differentiation and is part of the proof that it is happening. If incomes really were converging, then why on earth should prices be diverging? It makes no sense at all. The actual outcome, statistically, of measuring output in PPPs is that the reality – income divergence in money terms – produces an effect – price differentiation – that is then used to hide the original cause, namely, the income differentiation.

It is really not hard to see why the two measures of output are diverging: it is because low incomes are possible only on the basis of low wages. Low wages exist both because people consume less, and because the products that make up the wage-basket (so-called 'non-traded goods') are themselves cheaper. What the PPP measure actually does, reduced to its essence, is to treat all wage-baskets as if they were equal, even though they cost different amounts.

This might be valid were it not for the fact that there *is* a world market and world prices for the produce of the advanced countries – that is, high-tech investment goods. The divergence of world prices is, primarily, a divergence of country wages from global capital goods. The growing gap between PPP and monetary measures of output is merely a reflection of this price divergence: a country whose wages are low is artificially accounted as having a high output, by multiplying these wages by the price differential for wage products in the two parts of the world.

There are numerous reasons to suppose that this obscures the real process. Most importantly, it mixes up the direction of causality. In a commodified world people do not make money because they live well; they live well because they make money. The first thing we must understand, if we want to know whether a country can or cannot extract itself from poverty, is *how much money it has at its disposal with which to do it.*

This is particularly important since a country's income is not just used to live on, but to invest and grow. It is a fund from which all expenditures must be met, and the crucial factor is the cost, not of wage-goods, but of investment goods – which are, generally, world goods produced in the advanced countries and which cost advanced-country prices.

How can a poor country escape poverty? It must grow faster than an advanced country. To do this it must invest. It then has two choices: it may produce investment goods itself, or it may buy them on world markets. But investment goods are precisely that part of the 'world basket' that is expensive to produce locally, because they involve technology, and technology is what costs money. If, therefore, a country produces investment goods locally, it will not be able to use the advantages of cheap local wage-goods or even cheap local labour to anything like the extent it can with consumer goods, because technologically sophisticated processes command high salaries.[19] If, on the other hand, it purchases investment goods on world markets – the fate allotted it in any case by the IMF policies – then it will pay, not local but global prices. It will pay, in fact, the *same* amount of money as must be paid by its competitors in the advanced countries.

The difference between PPP and current-exchange measures of income boils down to this: the world is divided, and there is no single, theoretically consistent measure of output volume that is valid for both parts of the world. We must choose whether to measure economic performance on the basis of the price structure of the advanced and dominant part of the world or that of the dominated, dependent part of the world.

We wish to compare the growth prospects of the two parts of the world – advanced and non-advanced. The advanced countries are characterised above all by their near-total monopoly of technology – that is, of the means to make investment goods. The remainder can close the gap only by acquiring this technology, embedded in investment goods, which it is the special privilege of the advanced countries to sell into the world market. If we want to find out whether a poor country can cease being poor, we must find out whether it can buy the advanced capital goods it needs in order to raise its rate of productivity growth above that of the global North. These goods are generally made in the advanced countries, and moreover form a proportionally larger part of their annual expenditure. It is therefore the price structure of the *advanced countries themselves* that must be used as the basis of comparison, and that is why we have chosen to study world output and inequality in terms of the most dominant and largest advanced country – the USA.[20]

In the latter case the determining factor that decides whether much a country may catch up with or even hold its own against the technologically advanced nations, is its ability to purchase this technology on the world market; that is, the rate at which its own produce exchanges for the products of the advanced countries. GDP in real dollars measures this capacity: the ability to acquire the means to compete globally, in global markets. The figures above show that, above all, globalisation is destroying the poorer nations' capacity to grow. It is steadily reducing, or at best holding constant, their capacity to purchase what they need to stop being poor. It is inevitable, unless countervailing forces are brought into play, that this will work its way through into declining relative incomes and, as long as general stagnation persists, declining absolute incomes and declining standards of living.

## THE STATISTICAL SIGNIFICANCE OF CHINA

Bodies with an interest in beating the drum for globalisation tend to conceal China's specific role by including it in aggregate figures but omitting it as an individual entity. The IMF, for example, simply includes it statistically in the region of 'Asia' – yet it places the central Asian republics in 'Transcaucasus and Central Asia'. Notably also, it does not classify China as 'transitional'.

In some cases the presentation of China's data is downright tendentious. Our anonymous *Economist* writer says:

> countries in Asia have actually been narrowing the gap substantially: there, excluding already-developed Japan, in 1950–2001 income per head increased fivefold. In the early decades, Asian growth could be dismissed as exceptional, given that it was limited mainly to the city states of Hong Kong and Singapore, and two politically anomalous countries, Taiwan and South Korea. But since 1980, not only has growth spread to South-East Asia but it has also accelerated in the world's most populous countries, China and India. Given that Asia as a whole is home to well over half of the world's people, such progress can no longer be dismissed.

It is true that Asia should not be dismissed. But if we leave out China, then even in PPPs, the measure applied by *The Economist*'s author, income per head in Asia rose by 205 per cent, a considerably slower rate than 'fivefold' and, in fact, equivalent to a rather pedestrian annual growth rate of 2.25 per cent, somewhat less than the world average over the same period.

The effect of China on the 'rest of the world' category is equally salutary. Table 2.6 shows the annual growth rates of GDP per capita of the advanced regions, and of the rest of the world with and without China.[21]

Table 2.6  Growth of GDP per capita with and without China

| Ten-year total growth of GDP per capita in constant 1995 dollars | 1970–80 | 1980–90 | 1990–2000 |
|---|---|---|---|
| Rest of world | 35.4% | −19.8% | −14.5% |
| Rest of world without China | 32.6% | −20.2% | −25.1% |

Without China, the 'rest of the world' was declining almost twice as fast. The statistical impact of this fast growth of China is most marked in the 1990s. This highlights the problem with another tendency in the literature, which is to link China and India together as if they were part of a common 'Asian miracle'. But as Table 2.7 shows, from 1990 onwards China's growth began to outstrip that of India, in real dollar terms, beyond all recognition. Moreover, the change in the performance of the economy of China is of an entirely different order of magnitude. When an economy doubles in size in a decade, and above all when it contains between a quarter and a fifth of the world's people, it does not merely make it a 'bigger' economy but transforms world politics.

Table 2.7  Growth of GDP per capita of China and India

| Ten-year total growth of GDP per capita in constant 1995 dollars | 1970–80 | 1980–90 | 1990–2000 |
|---|---|---|---|
| China | 55.0% | −26.7% | 103.4% |
| India | 13.0% | −4.1% | 1.1% |

By 2010, if current growth trends were sustained, China would produce an output worth more in dollars than Japan's, and by 2023 it would produce more than Europe. In PPP terms it is widely reported that its GDP will equal America's by 2015, and it already has the second largest output in the world. An implication not lost on strategic planners is that China has the capability in our lifetimes to become a military rival of the USA, which completely changes the world relation of forces. It would, for example, make nonsense of the idea that the present century will be an American one.

This process has already transformed China's relation to the developing world, and thereby the developing world itself, as Figure 2.6 shows. This plots the GDP per head of China and India, relative to the average of all the other developing countries excluding China and

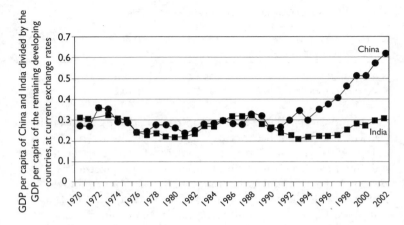

*Figure 2.6* GDP per head of China and India, measured at current exchange rates

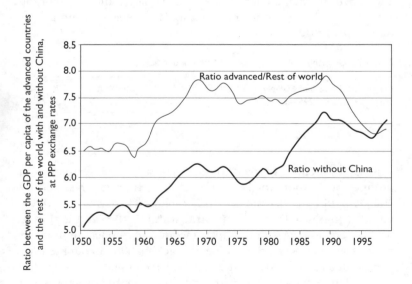

*Figure 2.7* Inequality with and without China, measured at PPP exchange rates

India. In 1990, both China and India were well below the average. But by 2000, China's GDP per head placed it within striking distance of the average.

The effect of this transformation on the growth of inequality between the developing and advanced countries is so striking that it clearly shows up even in PPP dollars. If China is included in the numerator and denominator, inequality measured in this way (in PPP dollars) has hardly risen at all since 1950. But if China is excluded, there is a clear rising trend, which moreover accelerated sharply in 1975 and after a brief fall, resumed its upward trend in 1995.

Figure 2.7 shows the inequality ratio between the advanced countries and the rest of the world, with and without China, measured in PPPs.

### Is China really growing?

Faced with the above facts, a considerable discussion has been going on about what the GDP of China actually is. In and of itself, this reflects the very fact that China's economy is far from simply capitalist; for example, there is no reliable expenditure measure of production in China because so much of it is not for money. On an extreme view, China's statistics therefore distort its output so much that most of its recorded growth is a fake.

Very well, consider the extreme opposite view, that in reality, China's income growth rate is little more than 2 per cent per year. But the IMF accepts China's statistics more or less at face value, and the conclusions the IMF draws about world output depend on this assumption. If the value recorded by Chinese statisticians for China's output is false, then most of the figures recorded by the IMF for the world are themselves false, and with them most of the claims of the globalisers in which, implicitly or explicitly, China's success is included in the success of globalisation.

For this reason, in the last part of this chapter, we will study the dependent world as it should be studied, independent of China.

## THE NEW REGIONALISM AND THE POLITICAL GEOGRAPHY OF DIVERGENCE

Divergence is not uniform. The advanced countries have moved away from the developing countries, the advanced countries have divided among themselves and, not least, the countries in transition have undergone a particularly sharp divergence, which dates very precisely from the moment of the dissolution of the USSR. However, within regions the process is more variable. Is divergence nothing more than a geographical process, in which some regions have done well and others have not? This is certainly one aspect of divergence. Thus, for example, South-East Asia has grown substantially faster than Sub-Saharan Africa.

Nonetheless, the evidence is clear that the separation of the developing from the advanced countries impacts on every region and overrides regional differentiation. There is thus no evidence that any regional group of developing countries is 'pulling away from the pack', with the specific exception of the group of 'Newly Industrialised Asian Countries' (NIACs) – whose population, it should not be forgotten, is in total smaller than most major European countries.

So what processes of divergence and differentiation are actually at work? In order to go any deeper, some means of investigation is needed. When the IMF or World Bank divides the world into the 'advanced countries' and the rest, they employ a clear prior concept of what the advanced countries are, using a classification that does not itself presuppose wealth or poverty. The starting point is a form of economic organisation; a manner in which these countries arrange to extract surplus from the world's resources. The question of whether they are rich or poor is an outcome, an object of enquiry, not an initial part of the definition.

If we have no prior classification in mind, we are obliged to begin from what the data itself provides. We have to study the distribution of wealthy and poor as such and ask whether the evidence suggests that the wealthy are becoming more wealthy, relative to the poor. There are then two difficulties.

The first problem, dealt with earlier, is that data is almost all available on the basis of countries, rather than peoples. We do not know the income distribution within each country and so it is difficult to study income distribution completely independent of geography. Indeed, it may not be right to do so, if it turns out that nations and national states, despite globalisation, remain a fundamental determinant of the path of economic development a country and its people can follow. Nevertheless, since this is one of the things we are trying to ascertain, we cannot begin by supposing it.

Studies have slowly begun to emerge that attempt to correct for this. The problem is that their starting point is the study of *poverty* as such, and so the measure they concern themselves with is personal income. But, as we have already pointed out, personal income is only one part of the total money wealth a given country acquires on the world market. It is a caused factor rather than a causal factor, and does not allow us to get to the bottom of the real process of divergence. In point of fact the real figure we are after is the productivity of labour; it is the wealth generated by the activity of the country.

As most economists recognise, GDP per capita is actually a proxy for this magnitude. What should be measured, if the figures were available, is the distribution of wealth-creating capacity or, to be precise, value-creating capacity. This would yield a very different distribution than personal income since badly paid people in a poor country are often very productive of wealth, as is clear from the large profits of multinationals that employ this labour.

The second problem is how to measure divergence in any case. What should be compared with what? When we had made a prior separation of the world into developed and advancing countries we could simply compare the income of one group with the income of another group. But now there are no 'natural' groupings to compare. Here we combine three procedures.

First, we can try to ascertain the *geographical* distribution of income. Relatively well-defined regions of the world exist such as Latin America, Africa, and so on. Are they diverging from each other, and are incomes diverging within them?

Second, since we already know that the advanced countries and the developing countries follow a very different path, we will confuse what we wish to study if we mix them up. We should therefore study geographical relations in, and between, the non-advanced countries.

Third, in order to see what is going on independent of geography, the simplest procedure is to divide the population into groups of equal size, and rank them. The commonest summary measure is quintiles, groups of 20 per cent of the population, and this is what we will study.

In the absence of figures on this quantity we have to adopt the most neutral assumption, which is that on average, everyone in a country generates the same wealth. All quintiles in this section have been calculated on this basis.[22] The figures are very striking.

Table 2.8 shows the ratio of each quintile to the average; Table 2.9 shows the per capita income of each quintile in real 1995 dollars. It must be stressed, as throughout this chapter, that measures of divergence, which is a ratio of incomes, do not depend on any particular method of price deflation or indeed on using any particular currency. They depend only on measuring incomes in terms of their purchasing power on the world market, at current exchange rates.

Table 2.8   Quintiles of GDP per capita of the non-advanced countries (without China) as a proportion of average GDP per capita

|  | 1970 | 1975 | 1980 | 1985 | 1990 | 1995 | 2000 | 2001 | 2002 |
|---|---|---|---|---|---|---|---|---|---|
| Bottom 20% | 0.27 | 0.01 | 0.23 | 0.30 | 0.25 | 0.19 | 0.20 | 0.21 | 0.22 |
| Second 20% | 0.38 | 0.01 | 0.26 | 0.37 | 0.36 | 0.30 | 0.34 | 0.36 | 0.39 |
| Third 20% | 0.42 | 0.01 | 0.46 | 0.45 | 0.40 | 0.34 | 0.36 | 0.39 | 0.42 |
| Fourth 20% | 0.84 | 0.03 | 0.87 | 0.94 | 0.98 | 0.93 | 0.83 | 0.86 | 0.93 |
| Top 20% | 3.10 | 0.08 | 3.17 | 2.94 | 3.02 | 3.25 | 3.28 | 3.19 | 3.05 |

Table 2.9   Quintiles of GDP per capita of the non-advanced countries (without China) in real dollars at current exchange rates

|  | 1970 | 1975 | 1980 | 1985 | 1990 | 1995 | 2000 | 2001 | 2002 |
|---|---|---|---|---|---|---|---|---|---|
|  |  |  |  |  | $ |  |  |  |  |
| Bottom 20% | 277 | 396 | 384 | 323 | 284 | 239 | 239 | 234 | 234 |
| Second 20% | 390 | 451 | 441 | 392 | 421 | 376 | 408 | 402 | 413 |
| Third 20% | 437 | 597 | 771 | 476 | 460 | 423 | 431 | 431 | 436 |
| Fourth 20% | 868 | 1,104 | 1,451 | 999 | 1,135 | 1,167 | 986 | 956 | 976 |
| Top 20% | 3,213 | 3,471 | 5,280 | 3,127 | 3,495 | 4,074 | 3,913 | 3,567 | 3,200 |
| Average | 1,036 | 1,203 | 1,665 | 1,063 | 1,157 | 1,254 | 1,194 | 1,117 | 1,050 |

If there was substantive divergence going on within the developing countries – either because an especially rich or an especially poor layer were distilling out – we should expect to see the lower ratios falling and the upper ratios rising. In fact over 30 years there has been almost no change at all, either in the relative position of any the developing country quintiles, or in their absolute level. In the ten years before the current phase of globalisation the top three quintiles, most notably the first, rose by around 60 per cent – and then fell back. The fourth quintile has grown by little under 80 per cent.

Apart from that the picture is almost completely static. The ratio between the top quintile and the bottom – the most usual measure of divergence – was 11.6 in 1970, and 13.7 in 2002. The ratio between the fourth and bottom quintile rose from 3.1 to 4.2. These ratios should be contrasted with the relation between the average GDP of the advanced countries and the average GDP of the developed countries, already mentioned above, which rose from 8.4 to 23.3. The net effect of globalisation is to drive a gigantic wedge between the advanced countries as a whole and the developing countries as a whole, while at the same time producing almost zero net growth and almost no divergence between the developing countries.

Indeed, the stability of developing country GDP per capita is so remarkable that it is an accurate first approximation to say that developing country GDP is effectively constant, which implies that the advanced countries have become organised, through globalisation, to extract from the developing countries all the gains of productivity; that is, all excess profit above the bare minimum required simply to maintain the peoples of these countries, on average, at a fixed rate of value-appropriating capacity.

This enables us to create what is, in effect, an absolute standard of divergence; we may measure the GDP per capita of any country, group of countries, or group of people, as a proportion of average developing country GDP. This standard is a useful one to chart, therefore, two things: first, the divergence between the principal geographical regions of the world and, second, within these geographical regions.

*Table 2.10*   Regional per capita incomes relative to the average per capita income of the rest of the world, without China

|  | 1970 | 1975 | 1980 | 1985 | 1990 | 1995 | 2000 | 2001 | 2002 |
|---|---|---|---|---|---|---|---|---|---|
| Asia without China | 0.4 | 0.5 | 0.4 | 0.4 | 0.4 | 0.5 | 0.4 | 0.4 | 0.5 |
| Africa | 0.7 | 0.9 | 0.9 | 0.7 | 0.7 | 0.5 | 0.5 | 0.5 | 0.5 |
| Transition | 4.2 | 3.8 | 3.0 | 5.0 | 4.7 | 1.5 | 1.4 | 1.7 | 2.0 |
| LA | 2.2 | 2.3 | 1.9 | 2.4 | 2.6 | 3.0 | 3.1 | 3.1 | 2.8 |
| Mideast | 1.7 | 2.9 | 3.1 | 2.9 | 2.7 | 2.3 | 2.6 | 2.5 | 2.6 |
| Advanced SE Asia | 5.2 | 7.4 | 7.4 | 10.8 | 18.2 | 24.4 | 21.2 | 19.6 | 20.1 |
| Euro | 7.4 | 10.3 | 10.3 | 10.2 | 18.6 | 19.2 | 16.7 | 17.5 | 20.0 |
| USA | 16.4 | 15.6 | 12.8 | 22.1 | 22.7 | 22.0 | 26.5 | 28.1 | 30.2 |

On the basis of this standard, we can take an overview of the principal regions of the world and including the advanced countries as a comparison. This is shown in Table 2.10, and displayed graphically in Figure 2.8.

The pattern is a very clear one and completely confirms the division of the world into two quite distinct blocs. The developing regions have, if anything, converged. The countries in transition were plunged into the ranks of the developing countries, which in turn have converged into two groups: Latin America, the Middle East and the countries in transition, with average incomes about three times those of the developing countries as a whole; and Asia

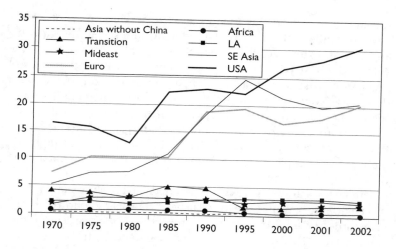

*Figure 2.8* GDP per capita of the world's regions, as a proportion of GDP per capita of the developing countries, without China

and Africa, whose incomes have also converged and are about half that of the developing countries as a whole. The wealthiest and least wealthy group of developing countries (the Middle East and Asia) are separated by a factor of just over six.

In contrast the advanced countries pulled away sharply, in the course of the only real departure from an extremely static geopolitical division, namely, the very rapid growth of the small group of NIACs, included here in the category of advanced South-East Asia, along with Japan, New Zealand and Australia. Thus, in sum, only four countries have broken away from the group of developing countries, with a total population amounting to 82 million in 2002.

Among the advanced countries, however, a new development set in during the late 1990s, namely the rapid relative growth of advanced South-East Asia came to an abrupt halt and began to reverse, as did that of Europe. The USA pulled away from everyone. This polarisation of the advanced countries themselves highlights the onset of a intensified phase of rivalry *between* the principal geographical groups.

Do the regional aggregates conceal a differentiation within regions? Only here is the picture more mixed. To study it (Tables 2.11 to 2.15), we present the more usual measure, discussed above, of the ratio of each quintile's average income to the average of the first quintile.

*Tables 2.11–2.15*   Ratio of quintile GDP to GDP of bottom quintile

*Table 2.11*   Latin America

|    | 1970 | 1975 | 1980 | 1985 | 1990 | 1995 | 2000 | 2001 | 2002 |
|----|------|------|------|------|------|------|------|------|------|
| Q2 | 1.26 | 1.44 | 1.28 | 1.79 | 2.38 | 1.77 | 2.01 | 1.73 | 1.65 |
| Q3 | 1.42 | 1.54 | 1.32 | 1.93 | 3.15 | 2.23 | 2.29 | 1.87 | 1.72 |
| Q4 | 2.60 | 2.77 | 2.94 | 2.49 | 3.17 | 2.61 | 3.43 | 3.35 | 2.36 |
| Q5 | 5.24 | 3.84 | 3.95 | 3.39 | 3.72 | 3.45 | 4.33 | 4.20 | 4.22 |

*Table 2.12*   Middle East

|    | 1970 | 1975 | 1980 | 1985 | 1990 | 1995 | 2000 | 2001 | 2002 |
|----|------|------|------|------|------|------|------|------|------|
| Q2 | 1.24 | 1.87 | 2.28 | 1.28 | 1.19 | 1.25 | 1.06 | 1.14 | 1.15 |
| Q3 | 1.61 | 2.66 | 2.95 | 1.53 | 1.30 | 1.58 | 1.19 | 1.31 | 1.43 |
| Q4 | 2.24 | 3.48 | 4.37 | 1.81 | 2.10 | 2.93 | 2.27 | 1.64 | 2.25 |
| Q5 | 5.20 | 8.71 | 17.82 | 6.37 | 5.02 | 7.78 | 6.79 | 6.48 | 6.94 |

*Table 2.13*   Countries in transition

|    | 1970 | 1975 | 1980 | 1985 | 1990 | 1995 | 2000 | 2001 | 2002 |
|----|------|------|------|------|------|------|------|------|------|
| Q2 | 1.70 | 1.48 | 1.57 | 1.51 | 1.75 | 2.27 | 2.02 | 2.16 | 2.39 |
| Q3 | 2.19 | 2.29 | 2.47 | 2.81 | 3.78 | 4.87 | 3.37 | 3.75 | 4.23 |
| Q4 | 2.31 | 2.58 | 2.81 | 3.20 | 4.29 | 5.27 | 3.42 | 3.89 | 4.37 |
| Q5 | 2.36 | 2.61 | 2.84 | 3.23 | 4.33 | 8.46 | 8.01 | 8.40 | 9.38 |

*Table 2.14*   Asia without China

|    | 1970 | 1975 | 1980 | 1985 | 1990 | 1995 | 2000 | 2001 | 2002 |
|----|------|------|------|------|------|------|------|------|------|
| Q2 | 1.46 | 1.06 | 1.16 | 1.18 | 1.42 | 1.15 | 1.23 | 1.27 | 1.25 |
| Q3 | 1.47 | 1.06 | 1.16 | 1.18 | 1.42 | 1.15 | 1.23 | 1.29 | 1.26 |
| Q4 | 1.54 | 1.23 | 1.73 | 1.37 | 1.53 | 1.52 | 1.31 | 1.34 | 1.35 |
| Q5 | 2.74 | 2.16 | 3.13 | 2.39 | 3.16 | 4.16 | 2.65 | 2.50 | 2.67 |

*Table 2.15*   Africa

|    | 1970 | 1975 | 1980 | 1985 | 1990 | 1995 | 2000 | 2001 | 2002 |
|----|------|------|------|------|------|------|------|------|------|
| Q2 | 1.85 | 2.24 | 1.94 | 1.47 | 1.50 | 1.79 | 2.24 | 2.16 | 2.30 |
| Q3 | 2.15 | 3.35 | 3.12 | 2.02 | 1.82 | 2.24 | 3.15 | 3.07 | 3.12 |
| Q4 | 3.53 | 4.13 | 4.67 | 2.76 | 3.94 | 3.80 | 4.08 | 3.99 | 4.22 |
| Q5 | 9.48 | 9.89 | 10.23 | 8.85 | 10.61 | 18.24 | 18.61 | 17.04 | 17.63 |

In only two cases is there significant divergence within the region: Africa, where the top 20 per cent has reached a GDP equal to 17.6 times that of the poorest; and the countries in transition (in fact, the former Soviet Union and former Eastern Europe).

### Nation-building and nation-destruction

In the case of the countries in transition a point has to be made: a decisive impact of the globalisation process was a dramatic growth in divergence precisely in that situation where it was accompanied politically by the dissolution of a territorial state. Moreover, the most rapid phase of divergence came after, not before, the territorial state was dissolved. The territorial state, whatever its other economic weaknesses, clearly constituted a substantial barrier to divergence.

Contrary to the assertion of the globalisation thesis, the real process was not that first the economic processes took shape, and then the state dissolved or lost its power but precisely the opposite: first the state was dissolved, then the economic processes took over.

It is in this light that we turn to the last and most interesting regional process, namely the situation in the euro zone, shown in Table 2.16. It is here, and only here, that we note a strong process of convergence: by 2002 a factor of no more than 1.77 separated the richest 20 per cent from the poorest 20 per cent. This is where a territorial state is in the process of formation.

*Table 2.16*   Euro zone ratio of quintile GDP to GDP of bottom quintile

|    | 1970 | 1975 | 1980 | 1985 | 1990 | 1995 | 2000 | 2001 | 2002 |
|----|------|------|------|------|------|------|------|------|------|
| Q2 | 1.57 | 1.31 | 1.49 | 1.65 | 1.48 | 1.31 | 1.43 | 1.40 | 1.37 |
| Q3 | 1.76 | 1.64 | 1.75 | 1.74 | 1.59 | 1.65 | 1.58 | 1.52 | 1.47 |
| Q4 | 1.89 | 1.95 | 1.96 | 1.86 | 1.63 | 1.93 | 1.63 | 1.58 | 1.54 |
| Q5 | 2.26 | 2.33 | 2.28 | 2.28 | 1.91 | 2.17 | 1.87 | 1.80 | 1.77 |

This also directly contradicts the principal thesis of globalisation, which is that the state is powerless in the face of economic forces. In the case of Europe, the national states were of *insufficient size* to counter the enormous economic and political weight of the USA. Actually, what we see in Europe is not the dissolution of the power of the territorial state but a drive to constitute a new, continental, territorial state. This process is driven by an economic imperative, namely, to constitute itself as a more effective appropriator of the value created in the Third World than the USA itself.

In summary, the post-globalisation world is neither the outcome of a teleological and unstoppable process of nation dissolution, nor is it the result of a conscious and organised plot hatched in the USA. It is an outcome of a contradiction driven by the market's inexorable tendency to geographical polarisation. The capitalist world order has shown itself unable to escape the requirement of a system of territorial states. But, on the other hand, the existing system of territorial states is clearly absolutely inadequate for its requirements. The capitalists of the USA and of Europe are intervening in this process with a strategic vision, which is to reconstitute themselves as dominant continental powers capable of intervening on a world scale with political and military might to secure what the economic legacy of globalisation has failed to deliver.

At the same time within the non-advanced countries, economic convergence with each other, in contradiction to their divergence from the advanced countries, poses them a possibility and a sharp choice. What is possible is mutual self-defence. The relation of forces, to be sure, is not adequate for reconstituting such bodies as the non-aligned movement. But the G21, and Mercosur, have both shown that they have an unused capability. What prevents them using this capability is the capacity of the dominant powers to buy off and divide the elites of these countries, who have so far risen with the tide of globalisation and have no interest in confronting the dominant powers. It falls, therefore, to their popular classes themselves to intervene politically on the world stage, recognising the fundamental identities of interest that are created by the polarisation of the world.

## NOTES

1. The economic data used in this chapter were extracted from GDP data published by the IMF in its World Economic Outlook database, with data before 1992 on the countries in transition from the Groningen Growth and Development Centre, and population data from the US Bureau of the Census.

2. Shares of world income measured in dollars at current exchange rates. The IMF defines the advanced countries to be the 'Major Industrial Countries' (France, Germany, Italy, United Kingdom, Japan, the United States, and Canada) together with the remaining countries of the European Union, the 'Newly Industrialised Asian Countries' or NIACs (Taiwan, Hong Kong, Singapore and South Korea), and a group of six 'other countries' (Australia, Iceland, Israel, New Zealand, Norway, Switzerland). The 'rest of the world' comprises the IMF group of 'Developing' countries and the IMF

group of 'Countries in Transition'. A group of around 30 countries that are classified by the Bureau of the Census, with a population estimated at 1.7 million, are not classified by the IMF. I have omitted from the comparisons the following countries for which a continuous data series from 1970, compiled on a comparable basis, could not be obtained: Bosnia, Bulgaria, Cambodia, Croatia, Czech Republic, Eritrea, Macedonia, Slovakia, Slovenia, Yemen.

3. Although the ratios are, of course, independent of currency units.
4. Total population is less than the total population of the world because of countries omitted for lack of usable data: see note 2 above.
5. With the exception of China, which I deal with later.
6. I have modified the IMF classification to reflect the regional character of these differences. 'South-East Asia' comprises Japan and the NIACs. Europe is the European Union. North America is the United States plus Canada.
7. Although, since Europe and South-East Asia were growing much faster than both the USA and the developing countries, the rest of the world was still falling behind the advanced countries as a whole.
8. J. Williamson (2003) 'From Reform Agenda to Damaged Brand Name: A short history of the Washington Consensus and suggestions for what to do next', *Finance and Development* (IMF), September.
9. Ibid.
10. France's objections to military intervention evaporated when it saw the opportunities arising from participating in the ouster of Haiti's Aristide.
11. By the term 'standard theory' I mean any approach ontologically constructed around the principle of general equilibrium. See A. Freeman (1999) 'The Limits of Ricardian Value: Law, contingency and motion in economics', Annual Conference of the Eastern Economic Association (EEA), March, available on www.iwgvt.org.
12. For an authoritative account of world divergence, see L. Pritchett (1997) 'Divergence, Big Time', *Journal of Economic Perspectives*, Summer; available on http://econ.worldbank.org/files/375_wps1522.pdf.
13. A territorial state is by no means necessarily the same as a nation-state. The Austro-Hungarian and Ottoman empires (not to mention the pre-capitalist empires) were territorial state forms, but they were not nation-states. The nation-state is a contradictory combination of territorial extent with ethnic descent, which accounts for the peculialy barbaric forms it has taken in the last two centuries.
14. It should be noted that the articles of the WTO quite specifically assign an exceptional role to free trade zones that effectively exempts them from its rules, a point that has eluded much academic globalisation theory. Article XXIV of the GATT proposes stringent conditions that a Free Trade Area must satisfy, but these are never applied. As of 1990, only four working parties (of a total of over 50) could agree that any regional agreement satisfied Article XXIV, three of these before 1957. 'The GATT's experience in testing FTAs (Free Trade Areas) and customs unions against Article has not been very encouraging ... It is not much of an exaggeration to say that GATT rules [on regional agreements] were largely a dead letter'

(B. Hoekman and Michel Kostecki (1995) *The Political Economy of the World Trading System: From GATT to WTO* (Oxford: OUP), p219). See A. Freeman (1998) 'Gatt and the World Trade Organisation', *Labour Focus* no. 59, pp74–93.

15. It might be thought that this definition begs the complex question of what 'poverty' means. Actually it sets the ceiling rather low: $3 per day is hardly higher than the UNCTAD definition of poverty ($2 per day). There is not an advanced country in the world that would not treat one of its own citizens, earning such an income, as near to destitution.

16. A. Negri and M. Hardt (2001) *Empire* (Cambridge, MA: Harvard University Press).

17. Generally speaking two measures are in use: the Etelto-Köves-Schultz (EKS) method and the Geary-Khamis (GK) method. Neither is judged satisfactory, but EKS PPPs are considered better for comparing countries, and GK PPPs better for measuring aggregate output for a group of countries. Effectively, the GK method treats a group of countries as if they were a single country with a single pattern of expenditure while the EKS method affords more recognition to the difference in expenditure patterns in different countries.

18. OECD (1990) *Purchasing Power Parities and Real Expenditures*, Vol. 2 (Paris: OECD Statistics Directorate), p4.

19. Not least, a country that fails to pay global rates for skilled technology will find its skilled workforce systematically evaporating to the places in the world that are content to pay for it, and whose objections to immigration mysteriously evaporate confronted with a skilled workforce whose education they never had to pay for.

20. This is thus the opposite of the neoclassical view, which, instead of asking whether the poor countries can buy the produce of the rich countries, asks how easy it is for the rich countries to buy the produce of the poor. This is not a measure of economic capacity but of availability for plunder.

21. In 1995 constant dollars, the measure used in this chapter wherever an absolute estimate of 'real incomes' is given, unless explicitly stated to the contrary.

22. A spreadsheet that carries out the calculation, and which also carries the underlying data, can be obtained on www.iwgt.org/quintiles.

# 3
# The Crisis of the Globalist Project and the New Economics of George W. Bush

*Walden Bello and Marylou Malig[1]*

In 1995, the World Trade Organisation was born. The offspring of eight years of negotiations, the WTO was hailed in the establishment press as the gem of global economic governance in the era of globalisation. The nearly 20 trade agreements that underpinned the WTO were presented as comprising a set of multilateral rules that would eliminate power and coercion from trade relations by subjecting both the powerful and the weak to a common set of rules backed by an effective enforcement apparatus. The WTO was a landmark, declared George Soros, because it was the only supranational body to which the world's most powerful economy, the United States, would submit itself.[2] In the WTO, it was claimed, the powerful USA and lowly Rwanda had exactly the same number of votes: one.

Triumphalism was the note sounded during the first ministerial of the WTO in Singapore in November 1996, with the WTO, IMF and the World Bank issuing their famous declaration saying that the task of the future was the challenge to make their policies of global trade, finance, and development 'coherent' so as to lay the basis for global prosperity.

## THE CRISIS OF THE GLOBALIST PROJECT

By the beginning of 2003, the triumphalism was gone. It has not come back. As the fifth ministerial of the WTO approached, it became clear that the organisation was in gridlock. A new agreement on agriculture is nowhere in sight as the US and the European Union stoutly defend their multibillion dollar subsidies. Brussels is on the verge of imposing sanctions on Washington for maintaining tax breaks for exporters that have been found to be in violation of WTO rules, while Washington has threatened to file a case with the WTO against the EU's *de facto* moratorium against genetically modified foods. Developing countries, some once hopeful that the WTO would in fact bring more equity to global trade, unanimously agree that most of what they have reaped from WTO membership are costs, not benefits. They are dead set against opening their markets any further, except under coercion and intimidation. Instead of heralding a new round of global trade liberalisation, the Cancun ministerial is likely to announce a stalemate.

The context for understanding this stalemate at the WTO is the crisis of the globalist project – the main achievement of which was the establishment of the WTO – and the emergence of unilateralism as the main feature of US foreign policy.

But first, some notes on globalisation and the globalist project. Globalisation is the accelerated integration of capital, production and markets globally, a process driven by the logic of corporate profitability.

Globalisation has actually had two phases, the first lasting from the early nineteenth century till the outbreak of the First World War in 1914; the second from the early 1980s until today. The intervening period was marked by the dominance of national capitalist economies characterised by a significant degree of state intervention and an international economy with strong constraints on trade and capital flows. These domestic and international constraints on the market, which were produced by the dynamics of class conflict internally and inter-capitalist competition internationally, were portrayed by the neoliberals as having caused distortions that collectively accounted for the stagnation of the capitalist economies and the global economy in the late 1970s and early 1980s.

As in the first phase of globalisation, the second phase was marked by the coming to hegemony of the ideology of neoliberalism, which focused on 'liberating the market' via accelerated privatisation, deregulation and trade liberalisation. There were, broadly, two versions of neoliberal ideology – a 'hard' Thatcher–Reagan version and a 'soft' Blair–Soros version (globalisation with 'safety nets'). But underlying both approaches was an unleashing of market forces and removing or eroding constraints imposed on transnational firms by labour, the state and society.

## THREE MOMENTS OF THE CRISIS OF GLOBALISATION

There have been three moments in the deepening crisis of the globalist project.

The first was the Asian financial crisis of 1997. This event, which laid low the proud 'tigers' of East Asia, revealed that one of the key tenets of globalisation – the liberalisation of the capital account to promote freer flows of capital, especially finance or speculative capital – could be profoundly destabilising. The Asian financial crisis was, in fact, shown to be merely the latest of at least eight major financial crises since the liberalisation of global financial flows began in the late 1970s.[3] How profoundly destabilising capital market liberalisation could be was shown when, within a few weeks, 1 million people in Thailand and 21 million in Indonesia were pushed below the poverty line.[4]

The Asian financial crisis was the 'Stalingrad' of the IMF, the prime global agent of liberalised capital flows. Its record in the ambitious enterprise of subjecting some 100 developing and transitional economies to 'structural adjustment' was revisited, and facts that had been pointed out by such agencies as the United Nations Development Programme (UNDP) and United Nations Conference on Trade and Development (UNCTAD) as early as the late 1980s now assumed the status of realities. Structural adjustment programmes designed to accelerate deregulation, trade liberalisation, and privatisation had almost everywhere institutionalised stagnation, worsened poverty and increased inequality.

A paradigm is really in crisis when its best practitioners desert it, as Thomas Kuhn pointed out in his classic study *The Structure of Scientific Revolutions*.[5] Something akin to what happened during the crisis of the Copernican paradigm in physics occurred in neoclassical economics shortly after the Asian financial crisis, with key intellectuals leaving the fold – among them Jeffrey Sachs, noted earlier for his advocacy of 'free market' shock treatment in Eastern Europe in the early 1990s; Joseph Stiglitz, former chief economist of the World Bank; Columbia Professor Jagdish Bhagwati, who called for global controls on capital flows; and financier George Soros, who condemned the lack of controls in the global financial system that had enriched him.

The second moment of the crisis of the globalist project was the collapse of the third ministerial of the WTO in Seattle in December 1999. Seattle was the fatal intersection of three streams of discontent and conflict that had been building for some time:

- Developing countries resented the inequities of the Uruguay Round agreements that they felt compelled to sign in 1995.

- Massive popular opposition to the WTO emerged globally from myriad sectors of global civil society, including farmers, fishermen, trade unionists and environmentalists. By posing a threat to the well-being of each sector in many of its agreements, the WTO managed to unite global civil society against it.
- There were unresolved trade conflicts between the EU and the US, especially in agriculture, which had been simply been papered over by the Uruguay Round agreement.

These three volatile elements combined to create the explosion in Seattle, with the developing countries rebelling against Northern diktat at the Seattle Convention Center, 50,000 people massing militantly in the streets, and differences preventing the EU and US from acting in concert to salvage the ministerial. In a moment of lucidity right after the Seattle debacle, British Secretary of State Stephen Byers captured the essence of the crisis: '[T]he WTO will not be able to continue in its present form. There has to be fundamental and radical change in order for it to meet the needs and aspirations of all 134 of its members.'[6]

The third moment of the crisis was the collapse of the stock market and the end of the Clinton boom. This was not just the bursting of the bubble but a rude reassertion of the classical capitalist crisis of overproduction, the main manifestation of which was massive overcapacity. Prior to the crash, corporate profits in the US had not grown since 1997. This was related to overcapacity in the industrial sector, the most glaring example being seen in the troubled telecommunications sector, where only 2.5 per cent of installed capacity globally was being utilised. The stagnation of the real economy led to capital being shifted to the financial sector, resulting in the dizzying rise in share values. But since profitability in the financial sector cannot deviate too far from the profitability of the real economy, a collapse of stock values was inevitable, and this occurred in March 2001, leading to the prolonged stagnation and the onset of deflation.

There is probably a broader structural reason for the length of the current stagnation or deflation and its constant teetering at the edge of recession. This may be, as a number of economists have stated, that we are at the tail end of the famous 'Kondratieff cycle'. Advanced by the Russian economist Nikolai Kondratieff, this theory suggests that the progress of global capitalism is marked not only by short-term business cycles but also by long-term 'supercycles'. Kondratieff cycles are roughly 50–60-year-long waves. The upward curve of the Kondratieff cycle is marked by the intensive exploitation of new technologies, followed by a crest as technological exploitation matures, then a downward curve as the old technologies produce diminishing returns while new technologies are still in an experimental stage in terms of profitable exploitation, and finally a trough or prolonged deflationary period.

The trough of the last wave was in the 1930s and 1940s, a period marked by the Great Depression and the Second World War. The ascent of the current wave began in the 1950s and the crest was reached in the 1980s and 1990s. The profitable exploitation of the postwar advances in the key energy, automobile, petrochemical and manufacturing industries ended while that of information technology was still at a relatively early stage. From this perspective, the 'New Economy' of the late 1990s was not a transcendence of the business cycle, as many economists believed it to be, but the last glorious phase of the current supercycle before the descent into prolonged deflation. In other words, the uniqueness of the current conjuncture lies in the fact that the downward curve of the current short-term cycle coincides with the move into descent of the Kondratieff supercycle. To use the words of another famous economist, Joseph Schumpeter, the global economy appears to be headed for a prolonged period of 'creative destruction'.

## THE NEW ECONOMICS OF GEORGE W. BUSH

The intersecting crises of globalisation, neoliberalism, overproduction and capitalist legitimacy provide the context for understanding the economic policies of the Bush administration, notably its unilateralist thrust. The globalist corporate project expressed the common interest of the global capitalist elites in expanding the world economy and their fundamental dependence on one another. However, globalisation did not eliminate competition among the national elites. In fact, the ruling elites of US and Europe had factions that were more nationalist in character as well as more tied for their survival and prosperity to the state, such as the military-industrial complex in the US. Indeed, since the 1980s there has been a sharp struggle between the more globalist fraction of ruling elite, stressing the common interest of the global capitalist class in a growing world economy, and the more nationalist, hegemonist faction that wanted to ensure the supremacy of US corporate interests.

As Robert Brenner has pointed out,[7] the policies of Bill Clinton and his Treasury Secretary Robert Rubin put prime emphasis on the expansion of the world economy as the basis of the prosperity of the global capitalist class. For instance, in the mid-1990s, they pushed a strong dollar policy meant to stimulate the recovery of the Japanese and German economies, so they could serve as markets for US goods and services. The earlier, more nationalist Reagan administration, on the other hand, had employed a weak dollar policy to regain competitiveness for the US economy at the expense of the Japanese and German economies. With the George W. Bush administration, we are back to economic policies, including a weak dollar policy, that are meant to revive the US economy at the expense of the other centre economies and push primarily the interests of the US corporate elite instead of that of global capitalist class under conditions of a global downturn.

Several features of this approach are worth stressing:

- Bush's political economy is very wary of a process of globalisation that is not managed by a US state that ensures that the process does not diffuse the economic power of the US. Allowing the market solely to drive globalisation could result in key US corporations becoming the victims of globalisation and thus compromising US economic interests. Thus, despite the free market rhetoric, we have a group that is highly protectionist when it comes to trade, investment and the management of government contracts. It seems that the motto of the Bushites is protectionism for the US and free trade for the rest of us.
- The Bush approach includes a strong scepticism about multilateralism as a way of global economic governance since, while multilateralism may promote the interests of the global capitalist class in general, it may, in many instances, contradict particular US corporate interests. The Bush coterie's growing ambivalence towards the WTO stems from the fact that the US has lost a number of rulings there, rulings that may hurt US capital but serve the interests of global capitalism as a whole.
- For the Bush people, strategic power is the ultimate modality of power. Economic power is a means to achieve strategic power. This is related to the fact that under Bush, the dominant faction of the ruling elite is the military-industrial establishment that won the Cold War. The conflict between globalists and unilateralists or nationalists along this axis is shown in the

approach toward China. The globalist approach put the emphasis on engagement with China, seeing its importance primarily as an investment area and market for US capital. The nationalists, on the other hand, see China mainly as a strategic enemy, and they would rather contain it than assist its growth.

- Needless to say, the Bush paradigm has no room for environmental management, seeing this to be a problem that others have to worry about, not the USA. There is, in fact, a strong corporate lobby that believes that environmental concerns such as that surrounding GMOs is a European conspiracy to deprive the US of its high-tech edge in global competition.

If these are seen as the premises for action, then the following prominent elements of recent US economic policy make sense:

- *Achieving control over Middle East oil.* While it did not exhaust the war aims of the administration in invading Iraq, it was certainly high on the list. With competition with Europe becoming the prime aspect of the transatlantic relationship, this was clearly aimed partly at Europe. But perhaps the more strategic goal was to pre-empt the region's resources in order to control access to them by energy poor China, which is seen as the US's strategic enemy.[8]

- *Aggressive protectionism in trade and investment matters.* The US has piled up one protectionist act after another, one of the most brazen being to hold up any movement at the WTO negotiations by defying the Doha Declaration's upholding of public health issues over intellectual property claims by limiting the loosening of patent rights to just three diseases in response to its powerful pharmaceutical lobby. While it seems perfectly willing to see the WTO negotiations unravel, Washington has directed most of its efforts to signing up countries into bilateral or multilateral trade deals such as the Free Trade of the Americas (FTAA) before the EU gets them into similar deals. Indeed the term 'free trade agreements' is a misnomer since these are actually preferential trade deals.

- *Incorporating strategic considerations into trade agreements.* In a recent speech, US Trade Representative Robert Zoellick stated explicitly that 'countries that seek free-trade agreements with the United States must pass muster on more than trade and economic criteria in order to be eligible. At a minimum, these countries must cooperate with the United States on its foreign policy and national security goals, as part of 13 criteria that will guide the US selection of potential FTA partners.' New Zealand, perhaps one of the governments most doctrinally committed to free trade, has nevertheless not been offered a free trade deal because it has a policy that prevents nuclear ship visits, which the US feels is directed against it.[9]

- *Manipulation of the dollar's value to stick the costs of economic crisis on rivals among the centre economies and regain competitiveness for the US economy.* A slow depreciation of the dollar vis-à-vis the euro can be interpreted as market-based adjustments, but the 25 per cent fall in value cannot but be seen as, at the least, a policy of benign neglect. While the Bush administration has issued denials that this is a beggar-thy-neighbour policy, the US business press has seen it for what it is: an effort to revive the US economy at the expense of the EU and other centre economies.

- *Aggressive manipulation of multilateral agencies to push the interests of US capital.* While this might not be too easy to achieve in the WTO owing to the weight of the EU, it can be more readily done at the World Bank and the IMF, where US dominance is more effectively institutionalised. For instance, despite support for the proposal from many European governments, the US Treasury recently torpedoed the IMF management's proposal for a Sovereign Debt Restructuring Mechanism (SDRM) to enable developing countries to restructure their debt while giving them a measure of protection from creditors. Already a very weak mechanism, the SDRM was vetoed by US Treasury in the interest of US banks.[10]

- *Finally, and especially relevant to our coming discussions, making the other centre economies as well as developing countries bear the burden of adjusting to the environmental crisis.* While some of the Bush people do not believe there is an environmental crisis, others know that the current rate of global greenhouse emissions is unsustainable. However, they want others to bear the brunt of adjustment since that would mean not only exempting environmentally inefficient US industry from the costs of adjustment, but hobbling other economies with even greater costs than if the US participated in an equitable adjustment process, thus giving the US economy a strong edge in global competition. Raw economic realpolitik, not fundamentalist blindness, lies at the root of the Washington's decision not to sign the Kyoto Protocol on Climate Change.

## THE ECONOMICS AND POLITICS OF OVEREXTENSION

Being harnessed very closely to strategic ends, any discussion of the likely outcomes of the Bush administration's economic policies must take into account both the state of the US economy, the global economy and the broader strategic picture. A key base for successful imperial management is expanding national and global economies – something precluded by the extended period of deflation and stagnation ahead, which is more likely to spur inter-capitalist rivalries.

Moreover, resources include not only economic and political resources but political and ideological ones too. For without legitimacy – without what Gramsci called 'the consensus' of the dominated that a system of rule is just – imperial management cannot be stable.

Faced with a similar problem of securing the long-term stability of their rule, the ancient Romans came up with the solution that created what was till then the most far-reaching case of collective mass loyalty ever achieved and prolonged the empire for 700 years. The Roman solution was not just or even principally military in character. The Romans realised that an important component of successful imperial domination was consensus among the dominated of the 'rightness' of the Roman order. As sociologist Michael Mann notes in his classic *Sources of Social Power*, the 'decisive edge' was not so much military as political. 'The Romans,' he writes, 'gradually stumbled on the invention of extensive territorial citizenship.'[11] The extension of Roman citizenship to ruling groups and non-slave peoples throughout the empire was the political breakthrough that produced 'probably the widest extent of collective commitment yet mobilized'. Political citizenship combined with the vision of the empire providing peace and prosperity for all to create that intangible but essential moral element called legitimacy.

Needless to say, extension of citizenship plays no role in the US imperial order. In fact, US citizenship is jealously reserved for a very tiny minority of the world's population, entry into whose territory is tightly controlled. Subordinate populations are not to be integrated but kept in check either by force or the threat of the use of force or by a system of global or regional rules and institutions – the WTO, the Bretton Woods system, NATO – that are increasingly blatantly manipulated to serve the interests of the imperial centre.

Though extension of universal citizenship was never a tool in the American imperial arsenal, during its struggle with Communism in the post-1945 period Washington did come up with a political formula to legitimise its global reach. The two elements of this formula were multilateralism as a system of global governance and liberal democracy.

In the immediate aftermath of the Cold War, there were, in fact, widespread expectations of a modern-day version of Pax Romana. There was hope in liberal circles that the US would use its sole superpower status to undergird a multilateral order that would institutionalise its hegemony but assure an Augustinian peace globally. That was the path of economic globalisation and multilateral governance. That was the path eliminated by George W. Bush's unilateralism.

As Frances Fitzgerald observed in *Fire in the Lake*, the promise of extending liberal democracy was a very powerful ideal that accompanied American arms during the Cold War.[12] Today, however, Washington or Westminster-type liberal democracy is in trouble throughout the developing world, where it has been reduced to providing a façade for oligarchic rule, as in the Philippines, pre-Musharraf Pakistan and throughout Latin America. In fact, liberal democracy in America has become both less democratic and less liberal. Certainly, few in the developing world see as a model a system fuelled and corrupted by corporate money.

Recovery of the moral vision needed to create consensus for US hegemony will be extremely difficult. Indeed, the thinking in Washington these days is that the most effective consensus builder is the threat of the use of force. Moreover, despite their talk about imposing democracy in the Arab world, the main aim of influential neo-conservative writers like Robert Kagan and Charles Krauthammer is transparent: the manipulation of liberal democratic mechanisms to create pluralistic competition that would destroy Arab unity. Bringing democracy to the Arabs is not even an afterthought as a slogan that is uttered tongue in cheek.

The Bush people are not interested in creating a new Pax Romana. What they want is a Pax Americana where most of the subordinate populations like the Arabs are kept in check by a healthy respect for lethal American power, while the loyalty of other groups such as the Philippine government is purchased with the promise of cash. With no moral vision to bind the global majority to the imperial center, this mode of imperial management can only inspire one thing: resistance.

The great problem for unilateralism is overextension, or a mismatch between the goals of the US and the resources needed to accomplish these goals. Overextension is relative, that is, it is to a great degree a function of resistance. An overextended power may, in fact, be in a worse condition even with a significant increase in its military power if resistance to its power increases by an even greater degree. Among the key indicators of overextension are the following:

- Washington's continuing inability to create a new political order in Iraq that would serve as a secure foundation for colonial rule;
- its failure to consolidate a pro-US regime in Afghanistan outside Kabul;
- the inability of a key ally, Israel, to quell, even with Washington's unrestricted support, the Palestinian people's uprising;
- the inflaming of Arab and Muslim sentiment in the Middle East, South Asia, and South East Asia, resulting in massive ideological gains for Islamic fundamentalists – which is what Osama bin Laden had been hoping for in the first place;
- the collapse of the Cold War Atlantic Alliance and the emergence of a new countervailing alliance, with Germany and France at the centre of it;
- the forging of a powerful global civil society movement against US unilateralism, militarism and economic hegemony, the most recent significant expression of which is the global anti-war movement;
- the coming to power of anti-neoliberal, anti-US movements in Washington's own backyard – Brazil, Venezuela and Ecuador – as the Bush administration is preoccupied with the Middle East;
- an increasingly negative impact of militarism on the US economy, as military spending becomes dependent on deficit spending, and deficit spending become more and more dependent on financing from foreign sources, creating more stresses and strains within an economy that is already in the throes of stagnation.

In conclusion, the globalist project is in crisis. Whether it can make a comeback via a Democratic or Liberal Republican presidency should not be ruled out, especially since there are influential globalist voices in the US business community – among them George Soros – that are voicing opposition to the unilateralist thrust of the Bush administration.[13] In our view, however, this is unlikely, and unilateralism will reign for some time to come.

We have, in short, entered a historical maelstrom marked by prolonged economic crisis, the spread of global resistance, the reappearance of the balance of power among centre states and the re-emergence of acute inter-imperialist contradictions. We must have a healthy respect for US power, but neither must we overestimate it. The signs are there that the US is seriously overextended and what appear to be manifestations of strength might in fact signal weakness strategically.

**NOTES**

1. This chapter appears in another form in the Fall 2004 issue of *New Labor Forum*.
2. George Soros (2002) *On Globalization* (New York: Public Affairs), p35.
3. See United Nations Conference on Trade and Development, *Trade and Development Report 1998*; and B. Eichengreen and Donald Mathieson (1998) *Hedge Fund and Financial Markets*, Occasional Paper 166 (Washington, DC: International Monetary Fund).
4. Chomthongdi Jacques-chai (2000) 'The IMF's Asian Legacy', in *Prague 2000: Why We Need to Decommission the IMF and the World Bank* (Bangkok: Focus on the Global South), pp18, 22.
5. T.S. Kuhn (1962) *The Structure of Scientific Revolutions* (Chicago and London: University of Chicago Press).
6. Quoted in 'Deadline Set for WTO Reforms', *Guardian News Service*, 10 January 2000.
7. See R. Brenner (2002) *The Boom and the Bubble* (New York: Verso), pp128–33.
8. David Harvey, Speech at Conference on Trends in Globalization, University of California at Santa Barbara, 1–4 May 2003.
9. 'Zoellick Says FTA Candidates Must Support US Foreign Policy', *Inside US Trade*, 16 May 2003. This article summarises a speech by Zoellick made on 8 May 2003.
10. For the sharpening conflicts between the US Treasury Department and IMF officials, see Nicola Bullard (2002) 'The Puppet Master Shows his Hand', *Focus on Trade*, April; http://focusweb.prg/popups/articleswindow.php?id=41.
11. Michael Mann (1986) *The Sources of Social Power*, Vol. 1 (Cambridge: CUP, 1986), p254.
12. Frances Fitzgerald (1973) *Fire in the Lake* (New York: Random House), p116. 'The idea that the mission of the United States was to build democracy around the world had become a convention of American

politics in the 1950s. Among certain circles, it was more or less assumed that democracy, that is electoral democracy combined with private ownership and civil liberties, was what the United States had to offer the Third World. Democracy [provided not only the basis for American opposition to Communism but the practical method to make sure that opposition worked.'

13. See George Soros, 'America's Role in the World', Speech at the Paul H. Nitze School of Advanced International Studies, Washington, DC, 7 March 2003. Noting that he was for intervention in the Balkans, including a 'NATO intervention without UN authorization', Soros denounced the war with Iraq on the grounds that it stems from a fundamentalism that is unsound and wreaking havoc with the US's relations with the rest of the world. The arguments he musters are those heard not only in liberal democratic circles in Washington but also in 'pragmatic' Republican Party circles and Wall Street.

# 4

# Imperialist Globalisation and the Political Economy of South Asia

*Jayati Ghosh*

## IMPERIALISM AND THE GLOBAL ECONOMY AT THE START OF THE TWENTY-FIRST CENTURY

Two features of the capitalist world economy in the early years of the new century must be noted at the outset. The first is the continuing, indeed overwhelming, significance of imperialism as the defining feature of global economic relations, with imperialism broadly defined as the struggle by large capital over control of economic territory of various types. The second is that this current imperialism is different in several crucial ways from that described by Lenin nearly a century ago as the monopoly stage of capitalism. To some extent the differences are simply the result of history, the evolution of both the institutions and processes of capitalism. But they are also the result of the effects of the recent processes of deregulation of trade and capital markets as well as other forms of economic liberalisation (constituting the essence of what is typically called 'globalisation'), which have given the new imperialism its cutting edge.

In terms of the current world economy, therefore, a number of important differences from the imperialist globalisation of the late nineteenth century can be identified. These include:

- the implications of accentuated internationalisation and concentration of both production and finance;
- the greater domination and changed nature of finance capital;
- the effects on inter-imperialist rivalry (or the lack of it);
- the use of multilateral institutions and rule-based regimes to further the aims that in earlier periods of history were resolved through more direct militaristic or political means;
- the changed nature of the systemic instability of global capitalism;

- the new forms of economic territory that are currently being contested;
- technological changes that have furthered the process of global corporate dominance as well as allowed for the possibility of confronting it at an international level; and the implications of the global spread, privatisation and concentration of media industries.

It is obvious that the processes of concentration and centralisation of capital, as well as the internationalisation of production, have gone much further, with some important implications. The recent phase of globalisation has been marked by some of the strongest and most sweeping waves of concentration of economic activity that we have known historically. In terms of multinational firms' activities, the possibility of vertical disintegration of production, which has allowed parts of the production process to be relocated and geographically separated, has been associated with greater vertical integration of the control (and ownership) of production internationally. In addition, the past decade in particular has witnessed a wave of cross-border mergers and acquisitions across not only major manufacturing industries but even in the services sector and in utility provision. The increased concentration of economic activity in general could reflect the recession and slump in recent years: concentration is always more marked in the downswing phase of economic cycles. But the process is also evident in some of the more 'dynamic' sectors, such as telecoms, the media and entertainment industries, and even during the expansionary phases of such sectors. This process should not however be misinterpreted to imply that the links between multinational conglomerates and their home governments have disappeared: they may appear to be more tenuous, but nevertheless still exist and continue to influence geopolitical and economic strategies of the major capitalist powers.

Internationalisation is, of course, most marked for finance. The domination of financial flows in cross-border transactions, as well as the greater role played by speculative elements and the separation (and to some extent supremacy) of finance capital and productive capital, are too well known to require further discussion. However, some of the more significant implications of these processes may be noted. They include:

- the enhanced differentials in speeds of adjustment between capital markets and the markets for goods and services, implying both more rapid changes in terms of financial variables and more accentuated effects on real economies;
- the destabilising role played by speculative capital flows, leading to more volatility of relative prices in general and periodic crises of varying intensity in particular economies;
- the constraints on, and deflationary impetus imparted to, national economic policy-making, especially fiscal and monetary policies in almost all countries, and the heightened inability of states (independent of political persuasion) to ensure basic needs and minimum socio-economic rights to all citizens;
- the necessity on the part of finance for constantly (if temporarily) discovering new avenues (or emerging markets) for investment, which ensures that deflation is not a uniform process across the world economy, but is always accompanied by a few pockets of capital-inflow-led boom.

The domination of finance capital has had effects on the nature of inter-imperialist rivalry as well. The point is essentially as follows: when finance capital, independent of national origin, seeks to ensure the stability of its investments, then it will be especially concerned about the some degree of stability at the capitalist core, notably in US government and private securities. This means that (notwithstanding the recent decline of US stock markets, the revulsion away from US financial assets and the associated decline of the US dollar in world currency markets) there will be attempts to maintain some degree of stability in terms of the most important financial assets available, and therefore to reinforce the geopolitical arrangements that underlie such stability. This requirement creates a different source of pressure from that determined solely by US military domination. It means that in crucial political and economic areas, the important capitalist powers have tended to act together or at least implicitly endorse the positions taken by the US, whether in the WTO negotiations, or in the use of the IMF to determine country policies to directly or indirectly benefit US-based capital, or in the 'war on terror' and treatment of so-called 'rogue states', and so on. It also means that US unilateralism in economic and political matters has tended to be accepted (if not condoned), whether in terms of allowing the continued use of unilateral protectionist measures such as Super 301 etc., or the US Farm Bill, or in terms of pushing for greater enforcement of multilateral liberalisation in precisely those sectors in which the US economy is perceived to have competitive advantage, or in terms of military engagements with what it chooses to define as 'rogue states'.

It is worth noting that the new imperialism, in addition to utilising new institutions and international rules and protocols to its own end, is also about the struggle to control newer forms of economic territory. This is not to deny the continuing significance of economic territory as traditionally conceived, that is, natural resources, markets and labour. Indeed, control over natural resources – particularly energy and oil resources – remains central to imperialist preoccupation. This is demonstrated by a number of recent and current events: the significance of the proposed (and soon to be constructed) oil pipeline in Afghanistan to the US military intervention and ongoing geopolitics of the region; the (failed) attempt to instigate and support a military coup in Venezuela against a president elected by a huge popular margin; the US administration's continuing obsession with forcibly instituting regime change in Iraq using whatever means possible. While these are in fact the most blatant political expressions of imperialism today, it is in the area of developing new markets that the economic implications are most pronounced.

These new markets are sought to be developed and made accessible in two ways. The first is the opening up of existing markets in developing and formerly socialist countries through the processes of trade and investment liberalisation, using the agencies of conditional lending by the IMF and World Bank and, more recently, the rules and dispute settlement procedures of the WTO. Such opening up, especially if it involves the relative deindustrialisation of the newly liberalised economies, contributes new markets for manufactured goods and services for the core capitalist countries. It is surely not an accident that, despite fears of manufacturing jobs being 'exported' from North to South, in fact the manufacturing trade balance of the South with the North remains negative, and indeed the deficit has been growing. Associated with this is the lowering of world prices of Southern exports, which stems from the fallacy of composition problem, as more and more developing countries are forced to increase export volumes either to repay debt or pay for more imports, or simply because they have been told that it is good for them to do so. This is turn provides the related advantage of cheaper imports to the core countries, not only of raw materials and tropical agricultural commodities, but also of the manufactured goods that developing countries have been encouraged to specialise in and which are now characterised by massive overcapacity internationally.

The more innovative form of finding new markets in the recent past has been that of creating markets where none previously existed, that is, by encouraging and furthering the commercialisation of activities that were earlier not perceived as commercial, or were defined in the public domain, or were only enabled by social intervention. The push towards commercialisation and then privatisation of a range of public services – such as power, telecommunications, and now water and sanitation – is the most obvious expression of this. The proliferation of new forms of commerce has never been so rampant. Knowledge and what is defined as intellectual property, rights to energy use, pollution control certificates, all are now subject to trading; and even the media for trade have expanded to include e-commerce and the like. The forced commercialisation of a wide range of services therefore provides the newest and most promising hinterland for capitalist expansion.

One aspect of this is also that information and entertainment have themselves become not just commercialised but have emerged as major industries; indeed, they are now the fastest-growing segments of the global economy. They are also among the most concentrated and centralised of all sectors. The multimedia boom has spawned large multimedia companies that can now be counted among the largest multinational corporations. This is really a phenomenon of the last decade, or at most the last 15 or so years, as giant media firms have sought 'synergy' not just through vertical integration but by effectively 'acquiring control of every step in the mass media process, from creation of content to its delivery in the home'.[1] The 1990s witnessed an unprecedented wave of mergers and acquisitions among global media giants.[2] Many of these firms have explicitly rejected national identities and posited themselves as global or internationally based corporations. Nevertheless, and despite the attempts to programme according to local sensibilities, the bulk of the content, the forms of expression as well as the structures of ownership and management, reflect the domination of the core capitalist countries, especially the US.

In sheer quantitative terms, the most important new markets are of course the financial ones, and the explosion of financial activity reflects the ability of capitalism to create and enlarge the spheres of economic activity even where material production is flagging. In addition, financial services such as banking and insurance – an area in which companies based in the core capitalist countries clearly have competitive advantage – have been among the fastest-growing areas of world trade. The huge cross-border and intra-border flow of financial resources often reflects trade in commodities that are purely notional, such as derivatives trading. That huge profits can be made from this pyramiding of financial assets reflects the ingenuity of capitalism, but it also marks speculative bubbles, which do have to burst eventually.

In addition, the new imperialism seeks to make use of particularly the skilled labour to be found in some developing countries. This has meant greatly enhanced labour mobility of a small section of highly skilled and professional workers, even as other labour finds it much more difficult to move, and aggregate rates of labour migration are lower than they have been in the history of capitalism. This in turn has contributed in no small measure to the enthusiasm for the process of global integration among such groups of skilled workers in developing countries. In fact, it can be argued that one important reason for the success of imperialist globalisation has been its ability to draw local elites and middle classes across the world into its own ranks, to offer part inclusion into a privileged international space within which the travails of the local working poor can be forgotten, even while their crucial role in generating productive surplus is sustained.

Despite the appearance of complete domination by a single and determined superpower, which has been a requirement for a period of stable world capitalism in the past, the current world economy is an unstable one, which is prone to systemic instability and constant possibility of crisis. This emerges from the following factors:

First, the US is not currently fulfilling its role (in the Kindleberger sense[3]) of leader in the world economy to maintain stability. Such a role requires the fulfilment of three functions at a minimum: discounting in crisis; countercyclical lending to countries affected by private investors' decisions; and providing a market for net exports of the rest of the world, especially those countries requiring it to repay debt. The absence of discounting in crisis is not universal; there are countries that have received large bailouts orchestrated by the US Treasury and the IMF. But the spectacular collapse of Argentina, the bleeding of Sub-Saharan Africa despite impending large-scale famine, and the indifference to implosions in Eastern Europe and elsewhere, bear witness to the fact that the US administration does not see its responsibility to discount in crisis in terms of salvaging the larger system. Similarly, countercyclical lending has been discouraged, as private finance (including portfolio capital) has been associated with creating sharp boom-and-bust cycles rather than mitigating them, and US policy has been geared towards protecting such behaviour rather than repressing it. Finally, while the US did play a crucial role as engine of world trade by running very large external trade deficits in the 1990s, that role has been much diminished after 2000. Indeed, even before then, the import surplus in the US reflected private investment-savings deficits, as the government's budgetary role became more contractionary.

Second, partly because of this inadequately accepted role of the leader, and partly because of the deflationary impulse provided by the greater mobility of finance capital, aggregate growth in the world capitalist system has been far below expectations in the recent phase of globalisation. It is now clear that the period has been associated with a deceleration of economic activity in much of the developed world, a continuing implosion in vast areas of the developing world including the continent of Africa, and a dramatic downslide in what had hitherto been the most dynamic segment of the world economy – East and South-East Asia.[4] These processes are reflected in rates of growth of world trade (in value terms), which have decelerated despite the enforced liberalisation of trade in most countries, as well as in declining rates of greenfield investment across the world.

Third, the recent process of imperialist globalisation has been marked by greatly increased disparities, both within countries and between countries.[5] While there is – inevitably – a debate over this, most careful studies find increased inequality within and across regions[6] as well as a stubborn persistence of poverty, and a marked absence of the 'convergence' predicted by apologists of the system. In addition, the bulk of the people across the world find themselves in more fragile and vulnerable economic circumstances, in which many of the earlier welfare state provisions have been reduced or removed, public services have been privatised or made more expensive and therefore less accessible, and employment conditions have become much more insecure and volatile.

Fourth, these features in themselves have led to a major crisis of legitimisation for the system. Not only are the basic tenets of the neoliberal argument (which forms the theoretical support for the current pattern of imperialist globalisation) under question, but increasingly the institutions that serve to uphold it (the IMF, the WTO and so on) lack popular support and legitimacy. The anti-globalisation umbrella movement is one expression of such growing dissent in local and national contexts. One important – and new – feature is that the process of integrating elites from developing countries, and rewarding them materially for their active co-operation in furthering corporate globalisation, has slowed down. As argued above, the complicity and participation of local elites has been a potent force in ensuring the success of global capitalist integration – but as the world recession bites and rewards become more scarce, such complicity can no longer be taken for granted. Since the political economy of resistance movements everywhere requires the involvement of at least some middle-class and professional elements and often some local elites as well, this may prove to be a critical development.

Fifth, imperialism has an increasingly ambiguous relationship with various backward-looking, revanchist and reactionary tendencies in different parts of the world. At different times and places, such tendencies have been encouraged and allowed to spread, but increasingly many of them are now seen as threats to the system, to be rooted out and destroyed. All of those currently seen as enemies of the US and therefore as the objects of attrition in the current 'war against terror' – Osama bin Laden, Al Qaeda and the Taliban, Saddam Hussein – have been at one time or the other overt or covert darlings of the US administration, used against other perceived enemies or simply to destabilise regions. Even now, in clientelist regimes such as that in Saudi Arabia, reactionary forces have been allowed to grow. Elsewhere, US imperialism has turned a blind eye or even implicitly encouraged the growth of semi-fascist movements (such as the Hindutva tendencies in India) as well as separatist forces, which encourage the disintegration of large nations. However, many of these movements now threaten to spin out of control and to destabilise the system itself, even if only partially. The terrorist attacks of September 2001 mark a watershed only insofar as they forced a realisation of this tendency towards destabilisation; they do not mark any major changes in basic organisation of the system itself, which is still run as cynically as before.

Finally, one important contradiction looks likely to become more significant in the near future. This is the requirement of deflation, which predatory finance capital imposes on the system as a whole even while it encourages differential rates of deflation in different areas so as to maximise its own profits. A sustainable prey–predator relation requires the continued existence of the prey, but widespread deflation makes this less likely. The current downslide in the major equity markets, and especially in the US, suggests that while finance can be separated from real economic trends for extended periods, and can even profit by such separation, it cannot do so indefinitely.

All this means that, while the world capitalist system may not yet be in full-fledged crisis (even though parts of it clearly are) there are systemic instabilities, which suggest that the current pattern cannot continue without some changes or even substantial overhaul in the medium term.

## SOUTH ASIA IN THE ERA OF GLOBALISATION

As background, it is worth noting the significance of the South Asian region (broadly interpreted to include an area from Afghanistan to Myanmar) for the imperialist core, and in particular the United States. While the economic significance may appear to be less than for other regions, in terms of both markets and resources, this is not completely the case. The Indian economy was viewed as a major market for a range of consumer goods, and even the limits of that market given the prevailing income distribution have not completely diminished expectations. In addition, there are large possibilities in terms of introducing commercialisation and the possibility of private profit generation into activities that have not previously been treated as commercial in India, either because of lack of development or because of the role played by the public sector. There are other sources of interest. Geopolitically, the region is viewed both in terms of its capacity (especially that of India) to assist in the containment of the potential power of China, and as a means of providing access to the oil and mineral resources of Central Asia and the Bay of Bengal area. The region is also the location for struggle for control over other, newer forms of economic territory, such as certain types of skilled labour.

The economies of South Asia – and especially India – are often portrayed in comparative discussion as among the 'success stories' of the developing world in the period since the early 1990s. The sense that the Indian economy performed relatively well during this period may simply reflect the much more depressing or chaotic experiences in the rest of the developing world, with the spectacular financial crises in several of the most important and hitherto dynamic late industrialisers in East Asia and Latin America, and the continuing stagnation or even decline in much of the rest of the South. Compared to this, the Indian economy, and indeed those of most of the smaller economies in the region, was largely stable and has been spared the type of extreme crisis that became almost a typical feature of emerging markets elsewhere. But the picture of improved performance is a misleading one at many levels, since in fact both India and the entire South Asian region as a whole experienced economic growth that was less impressive than the preceding decade. Further, across the region this growth pattern was marked by low employment generation, greater income inequality and the persistence of poverty. In other words, despite some very apparent successes in certain sectors or pockets, on the whole the process of global economic integration did little to cause a dramatic improvement in the material conditions of most of the population, and added to the greater vulnerability and insecurity of the economies in the region.

In India, the rate of growth of aggregate GDP in constant prices was between 5.5 per cent and 5.8 per cent in each five-year period since 1980, and the process of accelerated liberalisation of trade and capital markets did not lead to any change from this overall pattern.[7] Further, while investment ratios increased (as share of GDP) this reflected the long-term secular trend, and in fact the rate of increase decelerated compared to earlier periods. More significantly, the period since 1990 has been marked by very low rates of employment generation. Rural employment in the period 1993–94 to 1999–2000 grew at the very low annual rate of less than 0.6 per cent per annum, lower than any previous period in post-Independence history, and well below (only one-third) the rate of growth of rural population. Urban employment growth, at 2.3 per cent per annum, was also well below that of earlier periods, and employment in the formal sector stagnated.[8] Other indicators point to disturbing changes in patterns of consumption. Thus, per capita foodgrain consumption declined from 476 grams per day in 1990 to only 418 grams per day in 2001.[9] The National Sample Survey data also suggest that even aggregate calorific consumption per capita declined from just over 2,200 calories per day in 1987–88 to around 2,150 in 1999–2000. Given aggregate growth rates and the evidence of improved lifestyles among a minority, this points to substantially worsening income distribution, which is also confirmed by survey data. While the evidence on poverty has been muddied by changes in the procedure of data collection, which have made recent survey data non-comparable with earlier estimates, overall indicators suggest that while the incidence of head-count poverty had been declining from the mid-1970s to 1990, subsequently that decline has been slowed or halted.[10] Meanwhile, declining capital expenditure by the government has been associated with more infrastructural bottlenecks and worsening provision of basic public services.

The major positive feature that is frequently cited, that of the overall stability of the growth process compared to the boom-and-bust cycles in other emerging markets, reflects the relatively limited extent of capital account liberalisation over much of the period, and the fact that the Indian economy was never really chosen as a favourite of international financial markets during this time. In other words, because it did not receive large inflows of speculative capital, it did not suffer from large outflows either. Meanwhile, stability to the balance of payments was imparted by the substantial inflows of workers' remittances from temporary migrant workers in the Gulf and other regions.

In other countries of the region, the economic growth experience subsequent to liberalisation has been even less impressive in most cases. In Pakistan, average annual growth rates plummeted in the 1990s compared to the earlier decade, by about one-third. Industrial growth rates almost halved from 8.2 per cent to 4.8 per cent per annum. The earlier success at reducing poverty was reversed in the 1990s, as the proportion of households living in absolute poverty increased from 21.4 per cent in 1990–91 to 32.6 per cent in 1998–99. Unemployment rose, real wages fell and income distribution worsened. All this occurred within much greater macroeconomic instability than in the past.

In Bangladesh, while aggregate growth rates over the 1990s were marginally higher than in the earlier decade, the overall incidence of poverty (at around 45 per cent of the population) has been stubbornly resistant to change. Indeed, the rate of poverty reduction slowed down after 1994–95, because of both lower growth of production and lower employment generation. Industrial growth was positively affected by the expansion of the export-oriented textile sector (taking advantage of previously unutilised MFA quotas) but other than textiles and garments, most manufacturing sectors have stagnated or declined. All the productive sectors have been adversely affected by trade liberalisation in India, given the porous border, which allows for the possibility of substantial smuggling. Thus import penetration has adversely affected production and employment in both agriculture and most manufacturing, and even sectors of rural economic diversification such as livestock and poultry rearing. Income distribution worsened over the 1990s.

The economy of Nepal has been similarly affected by Indian trade liberalisation because of its open border with India. Growth in the productive sectors has been weak, especially in agriculture where the removal of subsidies was not accompanied by public investment in rural infrastructure.

In Sri Lanka, relatively low growth in the 1990s (especially in the agricultural sector) was associated with high macroeconomic imbalances, high trade deficits and reduced employment generation. Domestic political strife and the state of war in the north were only partly responsible for this; an important role was played by the decline in value of agricultural exports, the mainstay of Sri Lanka's economy.

Throughout the region, therefore, the process of increased integration with the global economy was not associated with higher GDP growth or more productive employment generation, or improved performance in terms of poverty reduction. Rather, employment possibilities became more fragile and there were clear income distributional shifts towards increased inequality. In all countries, attempts to impose 'fiscal discipline' by cutting public expenditure resulted in adverse consequences for producers as well as reduced quality and quantity (in per capita terms) of physical infrastructure and basic public services. The loss of revenues from import tariffs, the associated necessary declines in domestic duties, and the need to provide incentives to capital through tax concessions, all led to declines in tax–GDP ratios across the region, further reducing the spending capacity of the states.

If such have been the consequences of the process of global integration, adversely affecting the material circumstances of the large bulk of citizenry in the region, the question may be asked as to what has influenced government policy in all these countries to make the neoliberal economic strategy so inevitable nonetheless? In other words, what was the domestic political and social support for the process of liberalisation that made it fit so neatly into the requirements imposed by international imperialism? Obviously, the political economy processes involved are complex and vary from country to country. But some idea may be had from a more detailed consideration of the Indian experience in particular.

One of the interesting features of the political economy of the Indian strategy of liberalising economic reform has been the first conditional and subsequently more unqualified support extended to it by various elements of the large capitalist class and other social groups that have substantial political voice, such as middle-class and professional groups. To some extent this can be explained by the proliferation and diversification of the Indian capitalist class that took place during the years of import-substituting growth and later. There were three factors that led to this.[11] The first was related to the process of introduction of new products and markets. In India over time there were a number of areas outside the traditional bases of existing monopolistic groups, such as trade, services of various kinds and operations abroad by Non-Resident Indian groups, which served as sites for primary accumulation of capital. A typical example is trade, which saw the growth and proliferation of relatively independent capitalist groups, some of which on occasion made relatively successful forays into industrial production.[12] Another example was finance. While the ability of domestic capital to use the financial sector as a site for accumulation was earlier contained by the presence of a large public sector in banking, matters changed substantially from the 1980s, especially when the stock market came into its own. The subsequent periods of speculative boom in the stock market allowed some insiders within the erstwhile financial community to accumulate substantial sums of capital, most often at the expense of the small middle-class investor.

Over time, groups that had accumulated capital in this fashion sought to diversify into manufacturing, not only by entering new niche markets, but also by investing in large capacities in industries characterised by economies of scale. This created a direct challenge for several of the traditional business groups. These traditional monopolies had in the past been protected by the barriers to entry created by the government's industrial and trade policies, which involved not just import substitution but also substantial regulation of capacity creation and production. They had therefore been able to hedge against risk by investing small sums embodied in uneconomic plants in each individual industry, given the narrow domestic market base for most manufactured goods. This meant that they were unable to compete successfully with the new entrants, who because of newer technology were also less averse to import competition.

Established big capital, insofar as it could not enter into certain spaces and was not able to take full advantage of the entry of new products, found its relative position worsening in the economy over time. To reverse this decline, it looked for new avenues, including expansion abroad. It is necessary to distinguish here between two different types of expansion abroad. One is simply expanding activities abroad, which requires little export of capital from the domestic economy since it is largely locally financed. The other involves the export of capital through the non-repatriation of exchange earnings which, at the very least, involves the acquisition of rentier status, but may help the expansion of activities as well. The non-repatriation of exchange earnings, for a given level of domestic activity being maintained, has to be financed for the economy as a whole through larger international borrowing.

The second avenue open to established big business was to move into the space occupied by the public sector or smaller capitalists; and hence they also demanded an opening up of space through industrial deregulation. This was achieved by the elimination of anti-monopoly legislation, the lifting of licensing requirements, the removal of legislation 'reserving' certain sectors for small capitalists, a regime of high interest rates that squeezed small capitalists, the privatisation of a number of profitable public sector units, and the delinking of the public sector from budgetary support of any kind. In short, even the established big businesses that were, to start with, the beneficiary of state controls of various kinds, began to chafe against these controls at a certain stage. Hence large capital extended at least qualified support to the neoliberal 'liberalisation' programme, no matter how uneasy it may have felt about some other aspects of the programme, such as import liberalisation.

Among certain other sections such as agricultural capitalists the regime change met with qualified approval, though parts of it were objected to. Agricultural capitalists, while being hostile to the withdrawal of subsidised inputs and directed credit, favourably anticipated the prospect of exporting at favourable prices in the international market. In the event, a substantial section of domestic capital was willing to make compromises with metropolitan capital on the terms that the latter demanded. It was therefore all for allowing metropolitan capital to capture a share of the Indian market even at the expense of the entrenched capitalists, not to mention the public sector, in the hope of being able to better its own prospects as a junior partner, both in the domestic as well as in the international market. It was thus in favour of import liberalisation, a full retreat from state interventionism, and accepting the kind of regime that metropolitan capital generally, and the World Bank and the International Monetary Fund as its chief spokesmen, had been demanding.[13]

Support for liberalisation was growing not just among a section of industrial and agricultural capital. A whole new category of an altogether different kind of businessman was coming up, containing those who were more in the nature of upstarts, international racketeers, fixers, middlemen, often of 'non-resident Indian' origin or having NRI links, often linked to smuggling and the arms trade. Such private agents in any case did not have much of a production base, and their parasitic intermediary status as well as the international value of their operations naturally inclined them towards an 'open economy'. And finally, one should not exclude a section of the top bureaucracy itself, which had close links with the IMF and the World Bank, either as ex-employees who might return any time to Washington DC, or through being engaged in dollar projects of various kinds, or as hopeful aspirants for a lucrative berth in Washington DC; the weight of this section in the top bureaucracy had been growing rapidly, and its inclination naturally was in the direction of the Washington Consensus-style policy regime. Thus, quite apart from the growing leverage exercised by the international agencies in their capacity as 'donors', the internal contradictions of the earlier economic policy regime generated increasing support within the powerful and affluent sections of society for changing this regime in the manner desired by these agencies.

Besides this support from large corporate capital, the large and politically powerful urban middle classes, along with more prosperous rural farming groups, whose real incomes increased in the consumption-led boom of the 1980s, actively began to desire access to international goods and gave potency to the demands for trade liberalisation. And of course the technological and media revolutions, especially the growing importance of satellite television, imparted a significant impetus to the international demonstration effect, which further fuelled liberalising and consumerist demands.

One important social change, which was arguably influential in creating pressures for the shift in macroeconomic strategy, was the accelerated globalisation of a section of Indian society. Apart from the media, one major instrument of this was the postwar Indian diaspora. The 'NRI phenomenon', by means of which a qualitatively significant number of people from the Indian elites and middle classes actually became resident abroad, contributed in no small measure to consumerist demands for opening up the economy. Non-Resident Indians were important not only because they were viewed as potentially important sources of capital inflow, but also because of their close links with (which in many cases made them almost indistinguishable from) dominant groups within the domestically resident society. It should be remembered that while the liberalising reforms failed in the aggregative sense and also in terms of delivering better conditions for most of the Indian population, there was anticipated and achieved a definite improvement in material conditions for a substantial section of the upper and middle classes. Since these groups had a political voice that was far greater than their share of population, they were able to influence economic strategy to their own material advantage. It is in this sense that local elites and middle classes were not only complicit in the process of integration with the global economy, but active proponents of the process.

While the neoliberal economic reform programme entailed a changed relationship of government interaction with economy and polity, it was not a 'withdrawal of the state' so much as a change in the character of the association. Thus, while the state effectively reneged on many of its basic obligations in terms of providing its citizens access to minimum food, housing, health and education, state actions remained crucial to the way in which markets functioned and the ability of capital to pursue its different goals. Government and bureaucracy were central to economic functioning at the end of the decade of reforms; in fact the overall context was one of greater centralisation of economic and financial power. Many had believed that a 'retreat of the state' and the exposure of the economy to the discipline of the market would cut out arbitrariness of decision-making and the corruption that is inevitably associated with it. It would streamline the functioning of the economy by making it a 'rule-governed system', though admittedly the rules of the market. What happened instead in the Indian economy during this period of neoliberal structural adjustment was an increase in the level of corruption, cronyism and arbitrariness to unprecedented levels. The privatisation exercise became another vehicle or primitive accumulation by private capital as it acquired public assets cheaply. Precious natural resources, hitherto kept inside the public sector, were handed over for a pittance (and alleged 'kickbacks') to private firms with dubious objectives. With the wider corruption that increasingly pervaded the system, the 'discipline of the market' proved to be a chimera.

Across the South Asian region, indeed, and not confined only to India, the period has witnessed an increase not only in levels of open corruption but also in a decline in substantive democracy and acceptance of basic socio-economic rights of citizens. While the formal denial of democracy has been more limited (as in Pakistan) across the region, the states have in effect become more centralising and more authoritarian in certain ways, even as their ability to control events and processes becomes more tenuous.

It could be argued that the centralised, centralising and increasingly authoritarian state is in fact a necessary requirement for this type of liberalisation, which is based more on external legitimisation (from foreign financiers and the perceived discipline of international markets) than on internal legitimacy derived from the support of the majority of its citizens. Such a change in the nature of the state may therefore be a fallout of the substantially increased income inequalities associated with liberalisation and the social and political processes that they unleash. These inequalities have accentuated certain longer-term structural features of South Asian societies, whereby more privileged groups have sought to perpetuate and increase their control over limited resources and channels of income generation in the economy. This in turn has involved the effective economic disenfranchisement of large numbers of people, including those who occupied particular physical spaces in rural areas, or were urban slum dwellers who constituted both the reserve army of labour for industrialisation and the most fertile source of labour supply for extra-legal activities. The basic disregard for 'rule of law' which has characterised economic functioning in most parts of South Asia over several decades, became even more pronounced in this period, with both economic and other lawlessness becoming accepted features pervading all aspect of civil society, and allowed everything – even the rights of citizens – to become marketable and negotiable. Meanwhile ordinary citizens tended to experience reduced civil liberties and security along with worsening socio-economic rights, which may even have been necessary to allow the more centralised state to direct particular forms of lawlessness to the benefit of powerful agents and groups

These concomitant trends of greater economic and financial centralisation and increased income inequality in turn operated to aggravate the various regional, fissiparous and community-based tensions that have become such a defining feature of South Asian societies and polities. One of the features of the region as a whole has been an increase in the degree of instability and the growing absence of security. It has been reflected not only in greater cross-border tension, as between India and Pakistan, but also in civil and communally inspired clashes within national boundaries. These conflicts both emerge from the prevailing material contradictions and contribute to them. They also serve the very important political economy function (for the states concerned) of distracting people from the real and pressing issues resulting from the governments' denial of basic economic responsibility, and serve to direct anger in other less potentially threatening directions.

Obviously, not all such tension has had a direct and monocausal material underpinning. Nevertheless, it is true that the combination of greater material insecurity in terms of both lower real incomes and more precarious employment opportunities for a very large section of the population, with the explosion of conspicuous consumption on the part of a relatively small but highly visible minority, can have very adverse social and political consequences. The frustration that may arise because of the gap between aspiration and reality for growing numbers of people in the system can be only too easily directed towards any apparent or potential competitor in such a system, or even to those who are not in competition but simply represent a group that can be attacked with relative ease. The streak of venom that has been periodically directed towards various minority groups across the region can be seen as one expression of this trend. The inability to confront those who are responsible for the system, or actually benefiting from it, or even the lack of desire to confront these much more powerful elements, given that they still have the power to distribute some amount of material largesse, has meant that they could not become the direct objects of any aggressive vent for frustration. Rather, the outlet was increasingly found in terms of growing antagonism, increasingly finding violent expression, towards other categories of people who are nearer home, closer in terms of lifestyle and more susceptible to such attack. It is worth noting that often these groups are already the most disadvantaged and materially weak sections of society.

There is a broader international context to this, which is particularly reflective of this phase of imperialist globalisation. Across the world, in both developed and developing countries, there is a greater tendency on the part of the rulers, and those who are privileged in society, to ignore the interests of the majority and to blatantly push for those policies that will only benefit a small minority. The rise of finance capital and the hugely powerful role played by speculative capital in determining the fortunes of even large industrial countries has made this even sharper. Increasingly, governments point to the threat of capital flight as the reason why they cannot undertake basic measures for the welfare of most of the citizens, since anything that involves more expenditure for the people is inherently viewed with disfavour by international capital. Of course, this international tendency then has its counterpart in each national economy, as particular groups that actually benefit from the process seek to establish that 'there is no alternative'. Which is why we have the spectacle of local elites and governments not just advocating, but also able to continue to push through, policies that are likely to be to the detriment of most of the people. The situation is neither inevitable nor permanent, however, and the contradictions in the global system that were outlined earlier in this chapter mean that even in particular regions, forces that will instigate change are likely to surface.

## NOTES

1. B. Bagdikian (1997) *The Media Monopoly* (Boston, MA: Beacon Press).
2. As a result, the top six multinational conglomerates – News Corporation, AOL TimeWarner, Disney, Bertelsmann, Viacom and TCI – now effectively own and control huge swathes of the media, publishing and commercial entertainment activities across the world.
3. C. Kindleberger (1970) *Power and Money: The politics of international economics and the economics of international politics* (New York: Basic Books).
4. Global output growth, which averaged 3 per cent in the period 1990–97, was less than half that rate in 1998–2000, and even worse subsequently. Nearly 40 developing countries have experienced declines in per capita income since 1990. (Data from UN DESA, 2002, Office of the Under-Secretary General for Economic Affairs.)
5. The gap in per capita income between industrial and developing worlds has more than tripled between 1960 and 1990. Between 1960 and 1991, the income share of the richest 20 per cent of the world's population rose from 70 per cent to 85 per cent, while the income share of the poorest 20 per cent of population fell from 2.3 per cent to 1.4 per cent. In fact, the income shares of more than 85 per cent of the world's population actually fell over this period. The ratio of shares of the richest to the poorest groups doubled from 30:1 to 60:1. Subsequent data indicate a marked worsening of such disparities. (Data from UNDP *Human Development Report 2001*.)
6. See Giovanni Andrea Cornia and Sampsa Kiiski (2001) 'Trends in Income Distribution in the Post-World War II Period: Evidence and Interpretation', WIDER Discussion Paper no. 89 (Helsinki: United Nations University World Institute for Development Economics Research); Branko Milanovic (2001) 'World Income Inequality in the Second Half of the 20th Century', World Bank Research Paper, March.
7. Figures in this section are from CSO: National Income Accounts of India, various issues; detailed tables based on author's calculations available in C.P. Chandrasekhar and Jayati Ghosh (2002) *The Market that Failed:*

*A decade of neoliberal economic reforms in India*, (New Delhi: Leftword Press); National Sample Survey Organisation: Estimates of Consumer Expenditure, various rounds up to 55th Round for 1999–2000, New Delhi.

8. The only positive feature in employment patterns was the decline in educated unemployment, largely related to the expansion of IT-enabled services in metropolitan and other urban areas. However, while this feature, along with that of software development, has received much international attention, it is still too insignificant in the aggregate economy to make much of a dent.

9. Of course, it has been argued that this can represent a positive diversification of consumption away from foodgrain that is associated with higher living standards. But it is usually the case that aggregate foodgrain consumption does not decline because of indirect consumption of grain (for example, through meat and poultry products that require feed). In any case, the overall decline in calorific consumption (covering all food products) suggests that the optimistic conclusion may not be valid.

10. See Abhijit Sen (2002) 'Agriculture, employment and poverty: Recent trends in rural India', in V.K. Ramachandran and Madhura Swaminathan (eds) *Agrarian Studies* (New Delhi: Tulika Books).

11. This argument is elaborated in Chandrasekhar and Ghosh, *The Market that Failed*.

12. This has been particularly true of groups operating in areas (like steel, tyres and cement), which for one reason or another have been through periods of shortage, a burgeoning black market and extremely high margins from trade.

13. It is true that the more powerful and the more entrenched monopoly houses were more circumspect. They would not have minded import liberalisation in areas other than their own, including in areas dominated by the public sector; they would not mind collaborating with foreign capital to add to their empires and hence a degree of relaxation of controls to further facilitate such collaboration; but they would not like encroachments by metropolitan capital upon their own empires. Their attitude towards neoliberal economic liberalisation therefore was more ambiguous.

# 5

# Globalisation and the New World Order: The New Dynamics of Imperialism and War

*Sungur Savran*

After the international movement against neoliberal globalisation, the powerful protests against the war on Iraq all over the world have once again reminded everyone that historical development is not simply the product of the schemes devised by the dominant forces of society, but the outcome of a struggle of contending forces, among which working people and the oppressed masses are a power to be reckoned with. The weekend of 15–16 February 2003 promises to go down in history as a landmark. It is perhaps the first time ever in history that between 10 and 15 million people in scores of cities on five continents came out together to put forward the same demand. Even the *New York Times*, the voice of the establishment *par excellence* was so impressed as to imaginatively dub the movement the 'second superpower'.

For all of us who are proud to be part of this movement, it is now time to ask ourselves the question whether this 'superpower' has the clarity of vision to be able to counter effectively the twin scourges of neoliberal globalisation and war and militarism. Quite often in history, when there is a surge in the mass movement after a period of sustained inaction, consciousness cannot keep apace with the readiness to act. Close to a quarter of a century of defeats, demoralisation and inaction have made the masses of working people and left-wing movements vulnerable to ideologies that, at best, declare that only partial and piecemeal change is feasible and, at worst, reproduce the pervasive feeling of helplessness that has beset many a thinker and activist. In the spheres of theory and analysis, this has given rise to a superficial diagnosis of the world situation economically and politically. Just to cite the most recent instance, the dominant analysis of the post-September 11 world situation suffers from an extreme shallowness. Taken aback by the shock of the tragedy of the Twin Towers, major sections of the left, at least in the West, felt that the US intervention in Afghanistan was really about the struggle against terrorism. The political discourse of the US administration was taken seriously and the war treated as if it were an act of 'retribution'. Those who insisted that the war on Afghanistan was part and parcel of an American policy long in preparation aiming for the domination of Eurasia remained a small minority.

The real test came, however, with the Iraq war. There could of course be no wavering here, since the reasons adduced by the US–UK alliance for military intervention in Iraq were transparently false. Iraq taught certain sections of the international left what children already knew in predominantly Islamic countries, that is, that the Bush administration was waging war for oil and hegemony. (Lest it be thought that I am engaging in pure rhetoric here, let me stress for the benefit of readers from non-Islamic countries that I am speaking quite literally: the majority of the population of Turkey, for instance, before and during the war on Afghanistan, was firmly of the opinion that this was a war for oil.) Adamant in eschewing systemic analysis, superficiality then assumed a different form. The cruel and disastrous policy followed by the US was presented as the work of a small clique of neo-conservatives, popularly dubbed the 'neo-cons', headed by Vice-President Dick Cheney. The corollary for the politics of the movement is that if this clique is removed from power, the cause of peace and justice will prevail.

It is, of course, useful, even necessary, to expose the reactionary ideas of those in power in the US. The problem lies not in the exposition of the machinations of the neo-cons, but in the fact that the systemic tendencies of world capitalism and of the US state as the hegemonic power are left unexplored. Once the clique in power in the US is made to bear the whole responsibility for what is happening, the political recipe for the movement becomes a search for an alliance with alternative forces within the ruling classes. Differences within the establishment are exaggerated. We end up with France and Germany as an axis of peace as opposed to the US–UK alliance. The United Nations is declared to be the international forum that the mass movement should rest its hopes on.

In order to create an alternative to this perspective, what is needed is a serious analysis of the underlying forces for the strategy of the New World Order, announced with great fanfare in 1990, on the eve of the first Gulf War, by George Bush senior. This concept has too often been dismissed on the left on the pretext that it is hardly anything more than a New World Disorder. This appellation may be useful for purposes of propaganda, but it is hardly sufficient in coming to grips with the real content of the concept, which overlaps with the overall political and military strategy of the US at the present stage of world development. To state that what is presented as a 'new order' is in fact a new kind of disorder hides from view the fact that the disorder in question is not a matter of a failure on the part of the proponents of the strategy in question, but resides in the very nature of the NWO. This is conceived by US imperialism as the ultimate destination to be reached through a series of cataclysms in the existing world order. Hence the disorder that is time and again denounced is in fact the path that the world has to travel in order to reach that ultimate destination. It is, in other words, *order through disorder* by its very nature. Thus the NWO is, in fact, a dialectical unity in the true sense of the term: the old order has to be negated violently so that the new order may be established as a synthesis of order and disorder. Pure denunciation also makes it more difficult to analyse the methods and modalities through which the new order aspired to is being built. To state that US imperialism is seeking world hegemony will not do. We have to come to grips with the mechanisms and modalities through which it is doing so.

In its turn, the NWO cannot be understood in isolation but only as the political superstructure of the economic strategy of 'globalisation'. Hence the structure of the present chapter. The first section will deal with the myth and the reality of 'globalisation' and seek to understand the major driving forces behind this new phase in the contradictory history of the internationalisation of capital. The next section will build on this to identify the specific characteristics of the strategy of the NWO as imperialist politics. This will then allow us to situate the developments in Eurasia and the Middle East in the overall context of imperialist strategy at the dawn of the twenty-first century. The concluding section will try to bring out the contradictions inherent in the world imperialist system under the combined strategies of globalism and the NWO, provide a prognosis for the foreseeable future and draw lessons for the struggles against imperialist capitalism.

## 'GLOBALISATION': THE UNFETTERED CIRCULATION OF CAPITAL

The use of the term 'globalisation' to characterise advances in the integration of the world economy immediately confronts theory with the task of defining what is new in capitalism and which structural characteristics of the older capitalism still hold sway. For 'globalisation' is but one element in that series of theoretical concepts such as post-Fordism, post-modernism, the information society etc. that form the basis of the overall claim that the nature of society and the economy have undergone such complete transformation that all conceptual frameworks hitherto utilised to understand the world have now become wholly inadequate for the task. The end of everything from history and work all the way to capitalism itself has been loudly and proudly proclaimed. There is no doubt that certain traits of capitalism as a world system have indeed changed. But the indispensable task of any theoretical effort to understand the present world is to separate the reality of *change within continuity* from the myth of *total transformation*. We will then start out with a critique of the myths of 'globalisation' theory.

### 'Globalisation' as technological fatality

The advances in the internationalisation of capital and the integration of the world economy in the recent period have been codified within the framework of the bourgeois liberal theory of 'globalisation', whose assumptions and conclusions were later adopted unquestioningly by many on the left (most notably by Michael Hardt and Antonio Negri in their much acclaimed *Empire*).[1] 'Globalisation' theory has become so influential that it is now common sense, so to speak, for the thinkers of and spokespeople for the establishment, its major ideas being circulated in the popular media in the form of incontrovertible dogma. The core of this theory can be summed up in four major propositions: (1) 'globalisation' is the direct product of the recent wave of technological progress, that is of the new information and communication technologies; (2) 'globalisation' is an inevitable and irreversible process; (3) the new integration of the world economy has rendered the nation-state obsolete as a historical category or, in more restrained versions of the theory, paved the ground for this; (4) it has opened up a new stage in the historical development of capitalism distinct from the imperialist stage. None of these propositions can withstand the test of a confrontation with the facts of present-day world capitalism.

It is certainly true that the widespread application of new information-processing and communications technologies and new materials to the spheres of production and circulation have opened up fresh horizons for the mobility of capital. But this in no way warrants a jump to the conclusion that it is this development in productive forces exclusively and in unmediated fashion that has set in motion the whole new process of economic integration on a world scale. Behind this integration lies a host of factors, which are of a socio-economic and political nature. Some of these factors will be taken up later on. Suffice it to say, at this stage, that were it not for the successful attempt of the international bourgeoisie to establish neoliberalism as the hegemonic strategy of economic policy and to progressively provide for the unfettered circulation of money, commodities and productive capital since the era of Thatcher and Reagan starting in the late 1970s and early 1980s, no amount of technological change would have brought about the present level of economic exchange in the international arena. Thus the thesis that 'globalisation' flows directly from technological change, without the mediation of socio-political factors, reveals itself as a crass kind of technological determinism. It is indeed ironic to see bourgeois liberal theory committing the very sin it has constantly accused Marxism of in the past.

The thesis of inevitability and irreversibility in fact flows directly, if somewhat implicitly, from this technological determinism and therefore stands or collapses with it. It is enough to ask why the IMF goes to such pains to impose liberal policies consonant with the 'realities of globalisation' on each country it has dealings with or why the WTO has to have recourse to round after round of negotiations in order to liberalise world trade to see the absurdity of the claim of inevitability and irreversibility. At a more general level, the irreversibility argument evacuates human agency from the unfolding of history, treating the latter as a process 'without a subject' bound by iron laws. The masses have refuted such a view of history, voting with their feet against 'globalisation' from Seattle to Genoa, from the streets of Paris in 1995 to the Parque Centenario in Buenos Aires in 2001–02.

The third claim with respect to the growing obsolescence of the so-called nation-state is a much more complex question. It is based, among other arguments, most importantly, first, on the irrelevance of national borders in the face of global forces and flows of economic exchange, and, secondly, on the supposed 'multinational' or even 'transnational' character of capital itself. The idea that, with the tremendous increase in international flows of money, commodities and productive capital, national borders have lost their meaning and that the world economy has become a uniform and homogeneous entity is both theoretically fallacious and inconsistent with facts (and, in fact, with the economic recipes that flow from 'globalisation' theory itself).

Certain traits that derive from the very essence of statehood such as a national currency, the existence of a public finance system, a specific labour relations regime and an overall economic structure distinguish the economic territory of each nation-state from the others. (Note that we are not simply referring to uneven development in general: these are factors that distinguish between *states*, as opposed to other factors that are the consequences of pure uneven development and distinguish economic *regions* from each other, including within the borders of a single state.) The first three of these factors contribute specific effects that go into determining three key economic variables (namely the rate of exchange, the rate of interest and the wage rate), which typically (along with other specificities) set out a differential path for each national economy within the overall context of the current forces of the world economy. The latter is thus by no means a uniform and homogeneous whole.

Quite the contrary: the capitalist world economy presents itself as an integrated whole with tendentially ever-increasing cross-border flows, separated, however, into national domains with specific characteristics of their own. It is not a 'smooth' space (Hardt and Negri), but a closely knit patchwork of national economies. That this is so is confirmed by the irreducible fact that diversities between the different national economies are one of the fundamental determinants of the investment decisions of the so-called 'multinational' companies. Investment is but the mediated form of the accumulation of capital, itself the central process of the capitalist mode of production. Hence the laws that determine the spatial development of this key process are indissociably linked with the continuing existence of the so-called nation-state. As much is admitted by the advocates of 'globalisation' theory itself when they advise governments to harmonise their economic policies with the requirements of the 'global economy' in order to be able to attract foreign capital, which is but a roundabout way of admitting the specificity of national economies and the difference national economic policy can make.

This brings us to the second major proposition behind the claim regarding the obsolescence of the category nation-state. According to this second argument, capital no longer has 'national allegiances': so-called 'multinational companies' (MNCs) or 'transnational companies' (TNCs) are said to have no interest in any single country, since capital seeks nothing but profit and these companies do this at the world level. The terms 'multinational' and, *a fortiori*, 'transnational' are clearly misnomers for this type of company. There are very few among these whose capital is jointly controlled by capitalists of different nations (some prominent examples being ABB, Unilever or Royal Dutch-Shell – even the case of Daimler-Chrysler is deceptive notwithstanding the name, for this company is clearly controlled by the German partner). The overwhelming majority are companies effectively controlled by capitalists of single nations, or, in the case of Europe, where cross-border centralisation is occurring at an increasing pace, of the new European proto-state. In principle, each nation-state in question protects and supports the companies that originate in it as against foreign companies, according to a 'well-defined strategy that is based on a 'survival of the fittest' pattern, so that some companies are sacrificed at the altar of the general interests of national capital. A wealth of empirical material can be adduced to show that this is the case. The sight of so many governments scrambling for a piece of the cake for their national companies in the so-called reconstruction of Iraq should have reminded the theorists of globalisation that nation-states still represent the interests of their own capitals. The role assumed by US and EU authorities in the competition between their respective national (or supranational in the case of the EU) capitals is another clear example. The French newspaper *Le Monde* carried the following headline in its issue of 19 June 2001 (p20): 'The European Commission wishes to act as "legal shield" to Airbus'. The subtitle read: 'In an interview given to *Le Monde*, Pascal Lamy, European Commissioner for Trade, explains that the European constructor needs Europe in the face of the American menace. He denounces the political deviation of the General Electric–Honeywell merger.' In place of the misnomers 'multinational companies' or 'transnational companies' then, one can propose a more adequate terminology, 'companies with international activity', with the fitting abbreviation of CIAs.

All this goes to show that at the present stage of the development of the capitalist world economy, so-called nation-states still have considerable weight within the world economy and define distinct sub-units within this integrated whole. But irrespective of the validity of all these arguments, nation-states are of paramount importance for capitalism for another entirely different reason: each nation-state is still the locus of class power. Whatever the degree of influence international organisations (say the IMF or the World Bank) have on the policies followed by different states, this influence still has to be relayed into the domestic policies of each country by the state in question. The ruling class of each nation has to consolidate its rule at the national level. Conversely, the conquest of power by the working class and the oppressed masses still has to make its debut on the national arena. It is true that such conquest, wherever and whenever that may be, will meet with sanctions and aggression by the imperialist powers (by the other imperialist powers if the country in question happens to be one that is at present an imperialist country itself), but that does not negate the fact that this intervention will have to fight *a new state* that has at its disposal the means of an army to defend itself. In any case, outside intervention against the conquest of power by the working masses has been a constant of the history of capitalism from the Paris Commune through the October Revolution to Cuba and Nicaragua, and cannot be considered a *differentia specifica* of the present period.

The final claim that the imperialist stage has been transcended thanks to 'globalisation' is perhaps the most insulting of all to the collective intelligence of the masses when considered in the light of the crystal-clear fact that inequality between nations has, if anything, greatly increased within the last several decades thanks to the functioning of the system of 'globalisation'. Neither does this claim hold water at the theoretical level. All the characteristics of imperialism depicted by the classical Marxist theory of imperialism, developed by Hilferding, Bukharin and Lenin, with significant contributions by Luxemburg and Trotsky, are truer today than when formulated at the beginning of last century. Gigantic units of capital (called *monopolies* at that early stage) organised as large groups bring together the power of financial and industrial capital and diversify into all spheres of the valorisation of capital (named *finance capital* by the pioneers of the theory of imperialism). They thrive more than ever on the *export of capital*, which has not only become the characteristic feature of world capitalism but has even gone on to subsume the export of commodities under its logic (witness intra-firm exchange of goods and services as a constantly rising proportion of international trade). Giant banks and companies compete to carve out profitable shares in the four corners of the world, and imperialist states are in a constant but temporarily muted struggle for control over bigger portions of the planet. For various reasons, it can even be claimed that the Leninist theory of imperialism is now more relevant than it was when first propounded. To cite a single example: at the beginning of the twentieth century, competition between the capitals of the imperialist countries took, in principle, the roundabout form of investments in the subordinate countries, whether colonies, semi-colonies or independent nations. Today, on the contrary, the overwhelming part of both foreign direct investment and portfolio investment flows between the imperialist countries themselves, with the corollary that the struggle is now played out not only in the regions outside the imperialist heartlands (although that also rages on as never before), but in the respective homes of the capitals in question.

At the stage we have reached, we feel entitled to state clearly that the specific theses of bourgeois liberal 'globalisation' theory are mere fancies and that the imperialist nature of capitalism has hardly changed at all. It is now time to turn to the new reality, of which 'globalisation' theory is but a symptom and a refracted image.

## Globalism as capitalist assault

Despite the continuity in the inner nature of the world system of imperialism, it is hardly deniable that, since the late 1970s and early 1980s, there is much that is new in the concrete forms of functioning of the world capitalist system that deserves attentive study. The dismantling of barriers in the way of cross-border flows of money, commodities and productive capital, accompanied by extensive privatisation of state enterprises, and even of infrastructural establishments, the abrupt or gradual erosion, depending on the case, of social services, through cuts, commodification or outright privatisation, the penetration of the private sector into governmental functions, especially at the municipal level (conceptualised under the high-sounding label 'governance'), the flexibilisation of the labour market and the rapid spread of lean production techniques, have all added to create an entirely new set-up with tremendous consequences for the balance of forces between the classes at the international and national levels. In order to come to grips with this new situation and explain the dynamics behind the panoply of new instruments deployed by the international bourgeoisie, we have to take into consideration three developments of a world-historical nature that have stamped the recent period with their indelible mark.

Foremost among these is the rise of what I propose to call, for lack of a better alternative, *mega-capital* as the dominant form of capital within the last half century. In contradistinction to earlier forms, this form of capital, embodied in what is popularly known as 'multinational companies', distinguishes itself by the fact that it plans for and organises its process of valorisation over the entire globe, buying labour-power, raw materials and other inputs, carrying out production and selling its commodities wherever it is most profitable to do so within a single all-encompassing strategic plan. The obverse of this is that the interdependent activities of the sub-units of mega-capital are spatially separated and diversified into a great number of regions and single countries. Thus a fragmented world economy, with innumerable barriers in the way of flows of money, commodities and productive capital is, by its very nature, inimical to the interests of this form of capital and contradicts and constricts its free development. Hence the intense pressure exercised by mega-capital, as the most internationalised form of capital, to break up and dismantle what appears to it as rigid barriers that stand in the way of its unfettered circulation and profitable valorisation. Mega-capital, in collusion with financial capital in search of the highest return on monetary investment, is thus the major moving force behind the rapid adoption of neoliberalism ('free market' policies), and 'globalisation' as a specific variant of neoliberalism, as the dominant strategy of the international bourgeoisie over the last two decades of the twentieth century. In the last instance, neoliberalism can best be summed up as the attempt by mega-capital to create a world in its own image.

However important it is to lay bare the social force behind 'globalisation' and neoliberalism, a vulgar (i.e. non-Marxist) understanding of the category 'capital' may still lead to a kind of conception where the adoption of the new strategy of 'globalisation' can be seen, in pure functionalist tradition, as the adaptation of the superstructure of economic policy to the shift of the fundamental structures of world capitalism. This kind of conception would not only hide from the view the myriad contradictions, hesitations and frictions within the process of adaptation in question, converting it instead into an imaginary smooth process, but much more importantly perhaps, would conceal the class nature of the new strategy, the very essential fact that the adoption of the neoliberal cum 'globalisation' strategy is in effect a class assault by the international bourgeoisie against the international proletariat and the working masses at large. For 'capital' is not simply a sum of money in search for self-expansion; its self-expansion is at bottom tributary to the extraction of surplus labour from the direct producers, primarily but not exclusively the proletariat. It is not a thing but a social relation. And whenever it is a question of making capital more profitable, the reverse of the coin is to change the balance of forces between capital and the working class in favour of the former. Hence, to the extent that neoliberalism and policies in the service of 'globalisation' cater to the needs of the worldwide maximisation of profits for mega-capital, they are, *ceteris paribus*, an assault on the power, however limited, of the working class, and concomitantly of other classes and layers of direct producers, to protect themselves from further encroachment by capital.

Here it would be in order to bring into the analysis the second factor that has gone into the making of neoliberalism and the strategy of 'globalisation'. With the onset of the depressive phase of the long wave of capitalist development in the mid-1970s, relations between the classes changed dramatically. Faced with the fall in the average rate of profit, itself the decisive cause of the depressive wave, capital gradually moved to attack the positions that had been gained, albeit to an unequal degree in different countries, by the working class and the large labouring masses of all countries in order to raise the rate of surplus-value and hence of profit and thereby lay the ground for renewed stable capital accumulation. In all major crises, the space for compromise between the contending classes narrows down and the antagonistic nature of the relations between the classes is revealed for all to see. Hence the ruthless drive of capital to remove forms of protection for the working classes that had, for reasons we cannot go into here, accumulated over the decades. From partial tolerable concessions, at times acting as partial guarantees for its class rule, these had now, with the turn in the situation, become so many barriers to be overcome.

Workers employed by the public sector formed the backbone of the trade union movement in every country without exception; hence the public productive sector had to be destroyed through privatisation. (There were, of course, other reasons why the bourgeoisie pushed for privatisation.) Public services (the so-called 'welfare state') created solidarity among the great masses of people and inhibited competition between workers and so had to be dismantled through a combination of budgetary cuts, commodification of services and privatisation. The same went for certain municipal services, which were abandoned to the pressure of the market through 'private–public co-operation' and so-called 'governance'. Hard-won legal rights in industrial relations were attacked through forms of 'atypical' and 'contingent' work and the new reality of 'flexible work' translated into labour laws wherever capital managed to get the upper hand in the legislative process. The overall objective was to dismantle the trade union movement, legal protection for labour, social protection for the great masses, the state productive sector and anything else that acted to partially counter the forces of the market so that competition would be driven up, worker would be pitted against worker and the working class would become atomised and defenceless.

It is in the context of this wide array of measures to create competition between individual workers and groups of workers that the true meaning of 'globalisation' can be understood in its full import. 'Globalisation' is the strategy that aims to pit national sections of the international working class against each other. 'Globalisation' is the drive initiated by the international bourgeoisie to create a race to the bottom by re-establishing the full force of competition between countries and their working classes and masses. It is, then, true that 'globalisation' is an attack on the nation-state, but only from a certain angle. 'Globalisation' tries to dismantle every facet of the existing nation-states that, over a certain period, had come to act as a bumper mechanism to tame the wild forces of market competition and create a defence for the working class and the masses at large. But 'globalisation' exercises, and can only exercise, this impact on nation-states with the active consent and participation of the ruling classes of each state in question, even in those countries dominated by imperialism. For this kind of change acts not only in favour of the bourgeoisie of the imperialist countries; it also changes the domestic balance of forces within the dominated country in favour of the ruling classes at the expense of the working masses. Imperialist super-exploitation is concomitantly reinforced.

Where 'globalisation' theory goes astray is to present this erosion in certain facets of the nation-state as an undifferentiated general process of obsolescence for the nation-state as a whole. The picture that emerges obfuscates the fact that all so-called nation-states actively pursue policies that favour the capitalist class, both international and domestic. 'Globalisation' theory also triumphantly declares as consummated a process that is progressing in a very contradictory manner, with immense frictions, sometimes moving forward in great leaps and bounds, but at other times proceeding in a very hesitant manner, even at times halted by forces of various kinds. It is here that one can discover the real ideological function of the theory and ideology of 'globalisation': by declaring general, completed and irreversible a process that is only partial and only at its initial stages, 'globalisation' theory and ideology act to disarm the great masses of working people and dissuade them from entering into struggle against what is in fact of matter a capitalist assault on their positions.

This, though, is not the only factor that works to weaken the mass struggle against 'globalisation' and neoliberalism in general. Here the third of the world-historical factors we are discussing has played an equally pernicious role. The collapse of the bureaucratic workers' states in Central and Eastern Europe in 1989 and the dissolution of the Soviet Union in 1991, the ensuing rampant process of the restoration of capitalism over this whole area, along with creeping capitalist restoration in the People's Republic of China, have taken their toll on the workers' movement and the struggle of the masses in various ways. On the one hand, these events have reinforced the capitalist assault on everything that belongs to the public domain; on the other hand, they have destroyed, or at least tremendously weakened, the hopes and aspirations of the great masses of people for a different and better future. We will have to return to other aspects of the significance of the collapse of the bureaucratic workers' states in the next section on the NWO.

We can now draw a partial balance sheet on the basis of our discussion of the myth and reality of 'globalisation'. The bourgeois liberal theory of 'globalisation' posits the onset of a new stage in the development of the world economy beyond imperialism that is indissociably linked to the demise of the nation-state. To that extent, 'globalisation' theory is in fact dealing with myths. It is for this reason that, all throughout this chapter, the term 'globalisation' has been written in inverted commas. The critics of the bourgeoisie and its policies should not, in my opinion, treat 'globalisation' as a legitimate theoretical concept that depicts an objective process. The time-tested Marxist concept of the *internationalisation of capital* is a much better choice to describe what is happening in this area.

On the other hand, it is certainly true that, with the purpose of creating an untamed competition between the national sections of the international proletariat and other labouring masses, the international bourgeoisie is trying to dismantle those facets of the existing nation-states that, under the conditions of a prior period, acted as buffer mechanisms of protection for the working masses. This is part and parcel of the neoliberal strategy and, to that extent, is a reality. In order to distinguish the myth from the reality, the latter may conveniently be called globalism. 'Globalisation', then, is a false theoretical concept that acts as one of the dominant elements within present-day bourgeois ideology. The strategy of *globalism*, on the other hand, is a living material force to be fought in practice.

## THE NEW WORLD ORDER:
## THE UNFETTERED CIRCULATION OF IMPERIALIST ARMIES

It is of the utmost importance for opponents of imperialism to understand the strategic orientation that is encapsulated in the concept New World Order (NWO). Sufficient evidence has gathered now over the decade of the 1990s and the early years of the new century to provide the material on the basis of which one can attempt to present a more comprehensive analysis of the political and military strategy represented by the NWO. The following does not, of course, pretend to be an exhaustive analysis of what is a process in becoming, but merely tries to provide certain decisive elements that go into the making of the NWO.

### The role of the clique in history

We should, however, first deal with the dominant explanation of US policy, at least for the period after September 11. In the introduction to this chapter mention was made of the analysis, widespread on the international left, that explains the catastrophic course of action adopted by the US administration after September 11 on the basis of the political orientation of the clique of neo-cons who have assumed power under George Bush junior. It is first to this explanation that we turn.

Many a thinker on the left, from Marx through Plekhanov down to Mandel, has studied the role of the individual in history. The axiomatic statement by Marx that 'men make history' (assuming that the concept includes women as well) rules out immediately any kind of mechanistic vision of history within which the will and consciousness of the actors are disregarded. Hence if all human beings make history, there is no reason to exclude the impact that certain individuals or, *a fortiori*, cliques can make. No one would doubt that individuals such as Napoleon Bonaparte or Stalin or Hitler, to cite some of the most obvious examples, have left the imprint of their personality on the course of human affairs for decades, if not centuries, to come. Given that George W. Bush is less than an individual to make this kind of impact, the present theory naturally concentrates on the clique acting behind his presidency. And it is certainly true that Vice-President Cheney and his cohort have played a significant role in the adoption of the present policies of the US administration.

As in every discussion on the importance of individuals or groups of individuals for the course of history, the debate here is not whether they *can* have an impact, but why and under which circumstances they have been formed in the way they have and have been able to exert the impact that they have. It is here that the superficiality of the argument reveals itself. This argument typically stresses, in one-sided fashion, that the intellectual roots of many members of the group can be traced to Leo Strauss, a pro-Nazi thinker, but hardly dwells on the specificity of the post-Soviet epoch, which made possible the formation of a group that defends such an extremely aggressive foreign and military policy for the US. And whenever a material explanation is sought for why these people hold these particular ideas, it is always with reference to their personal links to a company like Halliburton or the oil and armaments industries that the answer is provided. This means that if you leave the analysis at this stage, as many analysts do, it is not a case of an individual or a clique being important in the making of history, but a case of history being shaped *exclusively* by, and in the interests of, these people.

There are many questions that would allow us to exit this closed circle. To cite only a few: Since the views of this clique were known clearly to the US ruling class, why was it that at least major dominant sections of this class preferred to support them at the expense of bringing a personality as inept as Bush junior to the helm of the most powerful state on earth? After all, isn't it a mundane fact that all leaderships have a certain political orientation and they are either brought to power or rejected on the basis of these ideas? Isn't the question of why this clique was brought to power as important as, if not more so than, the question of why its members have the ideas that they do? When we turn to these more pertinent questions, the important but minor role of the neo-cons recedes to the background and the front stage is taken by the deeper-lying factors at play within the US system of power and the world situation at large.

Not only does the one-sided fixation on the neo-cons hide from view these deeper forces, it also consigns to oblivion the essential continuity between the overall strategic orientation of the 1990s, the Clinton era, and the present period. It becomes impossible to understand the internal coherence of the series of wars from the Gulf War of 1991 through Bosnia and Kosovo to the more recent wars of Afghanistan and Iraq as decisive episodes of the construction of the NWO. The inner connection between the different forms of revival of the categories of colonialism (e.g. 'protectorate' in the case of Kosovo and outright colonialism in the case of Iraq) is lost from sight. It becomes a riddle why Bush junior, who came to power on a platform that explicitly rejected 'nation-building', criticising the Clinton administration for pursuing that policy, had to adopt the same stance once in power or how Tony Blair can make such close buddies with two presidents whose policies are supposedly worlds apart.

In what follows, we will attempt to draw attention to the more systemic aspects of the NWO.

## The political superstructure of globalism

We have seen that for mega-capital, the hegemonic component of capital at the dawn of the twenty-first century, the space of valorisation extends over the whole surface of the planet, covering all regions and countries where it does not confront insuperable barriers to its movement. Both the consolidation and the further extension of this geographic expanse require a political superstructure adequate for the task of ruling the world on behalf of the interests of mega-capital. The common interests of this dominant fraction of world capital logically necessitate the assumption of the tasks of economic regulation by international instances on an ever-increasing scale. On the other hand, nation-states continue to be the repository of both class domination and inter-capitalist rivalry. Thus capital can neither dispense with nor create a world government. There is no easy solution to this contradiction. In the absence of a definitive solution, the world bourgeoisie has recourse to a panoply of international organisations that carry out certain tasks of a world government in primitive fashion. These organisations are controlled behind the scenes by the imperialist coalition, above all the North Atlantic coalition, often euphemistically dubbed the 'international community'.

Among these international organisations, three categories stand out for the real power they wield, towering above those with limited emergency functions, such as the UNHCR or the Red Cross, and those with consultative and research functions, such as the ILO and the WHO. Among those organisations where real power is vested, there is first the troika of economic and financial organisations, that is, the IMF, the World Bank and the WTO. These seemingly neutral and technical organisations are in fact political through and through. To take the IMF as the outstanding representative of so-called market rationality, the recent examples of loans to Pakistan and Turkey in

2001 and to Brazil in 2002 for blatantly political purposes, while Argentina was left on its own to crumble under the weight of its economic woes, show amply that these institutions are under the tight control of the imperialist powers, the US above all. This should dispel any illusions as to the dispersion of sovereignty among a hierarchy of institutions under the NWO, illusions harboured, for instance, in Hardt and Negri's *Empire*.

While the economic troika fulfil in a partial and one-sided manner the tasks of an economic administration, the UN serves as a political body where grievances are heard, a quasi-parliament at the international level, so to speak. Here again, it must be noted immediately that the General Assembly has from the beginning been a 'talking shop', while any real power in international affairs is vested in the Security Council, in which the five permanent members that wield the power to veto any decision are clearly 'more equal than the others'. The UN, just like many of the other international institutions in question, predates the NWO, and, in its earlier epoch, acted as a forum for political (and ideological) struggle between the two sides of the Cold War, with the group of the non-aligned exerting additional pressure. However, with the end of the Cold War, it has now become an instrument used at will by the US and its allies whenever convenient. It also acts, along with the World Bank, as a forum where, especially during the interminable series of international conferences on hunger, the environment, housing, women's oppression etc., the grievances of NGOs and INGOs are vented, producing volumes of solemn resolutions subsequently left to the criticism of the mice.

By far the most important international organisation of the NWO is, of course, NATO. This military arm of Western imperialism, built against the Soviet Union, became the subject of heated debate in the aftermath of the collapse of the latter. The debate ended in 1999, when NATO waged its first-ever war in Kosovo and when the Washington summit that gathered on the heels of the war defined a new concept for the organisation. NATO has been renovated to act as the joint military command of the imperialist coalition and, unless and until imperialist rivalries sharpen to the point where EU countries make a definitive break with the hegemony of US imperialism, it will serve as such whenever it is convenient for the US. The recourse, after September 11, to Article 5 of the North Atlantic Treaty, the article that stipulates that any attack on one of the allies will be considered as an attack on all, has confirmed the fact that NATO has been transformed so as to be functional in the construction of the NWO.

One final point should be carefully noted. With the exception of the World Trade Organisation, itself the inheritor to the loose structure around GATT, all these international organisations are the products of the balance of forces towards and after the end of the Second World War. In that sense, there is a certain continuity between the NWO and the period of the Cold War that preceded it. These organisations are certainly much more in the forefront of world politics today than before and, more importantly, are being gradually transformed so as to satisfy new needs and requirements. But this does not obliterate the fact that they are products of an earlier period, and in that sense the question is posed whether any reform will conclusively render them adequate to the needs of the NWO.

There are other, newer aspects of NWO, foremost among which are the denigration of national sovereignty, the revival of colonialism and the widening network of US bases around the world. These will be taken up in subsequent sections.

However, before going into these, we first have to look at another dynamic behind the NWO.

### Repartition of the world

The NWO is thus the political superstructure of the new system globalism is trying to establish. However, this political superstructure is being constructed within a definite historical context. And that context is determined to its very core by a world-historical development: the demise of the bureaucratic workers' states. Hence, the NWO is also an attempt to realign international relations of power so as to fill in the vacuum created by the dissolution of the Soviet Union.

The collapse of the bureaucratic workers' states in Europe and the mutation of those in Asia have opened up a totally new situation in modern history. When Lenin wrote his *Imperialism* in 1915–16, he noted: 'the territorial division of the whole world among the biggest capitalist powers is completed'.[2] And so it was, if one includes within the concept 'division' not only colonies in the strict sense of the term, but also semi-colonies and spheres of influence. A development that started with the October Revolution of 1917 and continued after 1945 changed this situation in the sense that certain territories where capitalism was abolished withdrew in a relative sense from the world economy and tried to construct their economic development in an insulated manner. It is true that from the 1960s on, there was an increasing tendency for these bureaucratic workers' states to set up closer ties with the capitalist world economy. However, the real change in the situation came about after the collapse of the Berlin Wall and the dissolution of the Soviet Union. The process of capitalist restoration that these events set off brought forcefully on the agenda a new question of gigantic proportions: the full reintegration of these territories into the circuits of world capital. A parallel process was going on concerning China, where political continuity was coupled with a creeping restoration of capitalism and an increasing integration with world capitalism. So in a very real sense, this development takes us back, under radically new conditions, to the last quarter of the nineteenth century, before 'the territorial division of the whole world among the biggest capitalist powers [was] completed'. Given the chaotic process of the restoration of capitalism in the former republics of the Soviet Union, one can justifiably talk about the 'Wild East', using the historical analogy, *mutatis mutandis*, of the expansion, in the nineteenth century, of US capitalism into the 'Wild West'. Imperialism is thus confronted with the task of assimilating a vast expanse of territory, practically extending from Berlin to the China Sea.

But this is not all. The collapse of the Soviet Union has also created a political vacuum in many areas of the world where different governments had set up alliances with the Soviet Union in order to counterbalance the pressure of imperialism. The Middle East is the foremost example, but the Indian subcontinent and several regions in Africa, not to mention the isolated case of Cuba, also fall into this category. It is thus no coincidence that Bush senior chose a war in the Middle East as the gambit of the new strategic orientation labelled the NWO.

Both the assimilation of the bureaucratic workers' states and the filling in of the vacuum left behind by the collapse of the Soviet Union pose two distinct questions. On the one hand, there is the task of establishing a stable set-up in these regions, which will work to consolidate and make irreversible capitalist restoration in the former case and provide for conditions that will guarantee the valorisation of capital without major anti-systemic upheavals in the latter. This task is obviously in the interest of the imperialist world system in general, without distinction as to the particular interests of the various imperialist powers. It can thus be carried out jointly. On the other hand, there is also the question of who gets how much and who gets to control the new overall set-up. Will it be American capital that will receive the lion's share in the vast markets of the former 'Eastern Bloc' and China, or German or Japanese? Will it be American and British oil companies that will profit from the oil wells of Iraq and Iran and the untapped energy resources of the Caspian basin, or French and Italian? As opposed to the dynamics of unity the first task creates, this second question, by its very nature, sets in motion a tendency for competition and rivalry.

This rivalry is exacerbated by the fact that the collapse of the Soviet Union has lifted the pressure of this mighty common foe on the imperialist coalition and thereby raised the lid on the competition between the different imperialist powers. The onset of the depressive phase of the long wave of economic development since 1974–75 has also contributed to the intensification of competition between the capitals of the triad of the US, Western Europe and Japan. The deepening unification of European imperialist interests within the European Union has added clout to European imperialist capital, which can now stand up against US capitalist interests in many a part of the world. Before it slipped in the early 1990s into what seems to be a perpetual crisis, Japan was of course the rising imperialist power. It is still too early to count it out of the race. But the recent competition is really between the US and the EU. The euro has been conceived as a rival world currency challenging the supremacy of the dollar. The European Security and Defence Initiative is an attempt on the part of European imperialism to break free from its military subservience to US imperialism. There are certainly immense obstacles that confront the EU in its quest to achieve equal status with the US, be it economically, politically or militarily. The effort is nonetheless there, and the rivalry is visible in different parts of the world such as Latin America (since the nineteenth century a hunting ground for the US, but where now Spain, followed by the other Europeans, has gained a serious foothold), Africa (traditionally a European sphere where the US is now increasing its clout) or even the Middle East.

It is the interpenetration of these dual tendencies, one working towards the unity of imperialist interests and the other towards confrontation between them, that provides the key to the uneasy and contradictory alliance between the imperialist states throughout the 1990s and the early years of the new century. In all major episodes of the construction of the NWO, frictions, albeit of varying degree, were visible between the US and one or more European powers. With the exception of the last war on Iraq, though, this went hand in hand with a military alliance in practice. And even with respect to the last war, the UN Security Council resolution after the war legitimising the occupation of the country and giving a free hand to the occupying forces was a stamp of approval *post factum* given to the US–UK alliance by France and Germany (as well as Russia and China). It is this contradictory process of unity and division between the imperialist forces that will stamp with its mark events in many regions of the world during the construction of the NWO, whose final shape will only become clear as a result of the interaction of these two tendencies.

It is essential to remind ourselves at this point that for the mass movement it would be suicidal to lay its hopes in the European powers on the pretext that the EU represents a more 'social' and peaceful model of capitalism. Euro-nationalism of the left, which was quite powerful in the 1990s owing to the supposed virtues of the EU, seems to be making a comeback in the aftermath of the Iraq War. Two remarks are pertinent in this respect. On the one hand, even if we leave aside the special cases of Britain and the newcomers of Eastern Europe, Italy, Spain and Portugal are as much part of the EU as France and Germany. Their support to US belligerence in Iraq is testimony that it was not the 'values' represented by Europe but pure perception of national interests that guide each and every one of the member states of the EU.

On the other hand, even if we could assume for a moment that the whole of the EU stood up in unison against the US war drive, this would not in the least alter the fact that supporting the EU would be suicidal for the mass movement. The reason is not difficult to detect. If France and Germany, after so much tension and contradiction before the war, finally bowed before the US victory in Iraq afterwards, this was because the EU, all forces combined, is a military midget when compared with the might of the US armed forces. Hence for the EU to balance US power, the European states would have to initiate a comprehensive campaign to build up their armed forces and their military industries. This would necessarily mean a militaristic drive that would moreover imply further severe erosion of social services in the EU on top of the creeping impact of Maastricht and Amsterdam.

We may then conclude that, whatever the importance of the contradictions between the imperialist powers, it would be folly for the mass movement to side with one or the other of these powers in its quest for a world free of exploitation and war.

## The US military as world police

Armed with an understanding of the twin tendencies of imperialism at the present, one driving towards unity and the other towards division between the imperialist powers, we can now proceed to look at the specifically new aspects of the politico-military structure of the NWO. For this, we have to go back to the major international organisations that form the backbone of imperialist policy in this epoch.

We should start out by emphasising once again that none of the three categories of international organisations (i.e. the economic–financial troika, the UN and NATO) are neutral institutions rising, even in a relative sense, above the *mêlée* of interactions within the existing international system of nation-states. They are all instruments used by the imperialist coalition, and above all the US, whenever circumstances are conducive to present them as more neutral and technical institutions striving to establish international stability and law. We stress 'when circumstances are conducive'. Witness the very different paths chosen by the US in its four major wars of the NWO era: the Gulf War of 1991 was sanctioned by the UN; the Kosovo War was decided and waged as a NATO war; the Afghanistan War, despite the clear declaration of NATO members concerning Article 5, was based on a shifting series of alliances formed by the US; finally, the recent Iraq War simply by-passed both the UN and NATO, to be waged on the basis of the so-called 'coalition of the willing'. Illusions about these institutions being loci of power even relatively autonomous from the US and the EU countries are extremely pernicious for the opponents of imperialism and will lead to dead-end strategies of working exclusively in and through these institutions and accepting them as legitimate institutions for a different set-up of the future.

Having established this, we can now observe that US war strategy in this era can be visualised in the shape of concentric circles. In the outer layers lie the different alliances that the US has been able to concoct for the particular war in question. But at the very centre is the invariable factor: the US military (so far hand in hand with Britain in all four episodes). The US military is the indispensable hard core of the military might of imperialism in the present epoch. The proliferation of US military bases into all corners of the world, including for the first time into Eastern Europe and the Balkans, the Caucasus and Central Asia, and soon Africa, is but an expression of the fact that the US intends to transform its military into the police force of the whole earth. Most significant in this respect is the setting up of US bases in Afghanistan, Uzbekistan and Kyrgyzstan in addition to US military involvement in the Philippines, Georgia, Yemen and Indonesia after the war in Afghanistan. This is the first time in modern history that Western capitalism has secured a military foothold in Central Asia and the first time imperialist troops have established a consented presence on the former territory of the October Revolution.

This is not simply a quantitative progression of already existing tendencies. Nor is it fortuitous. It derives from the very logic of the NWO, both as the superstructure of globalism and as repartition of the world among imperialist powers. We have already seen that the dominant fraction of capital at the present stage, i.e. what we have termed mega-capital, tends to unify the world economy and accordingly needs the task of economic regulation to be carried out at the world scale. To the extent that capital is internationalised, a world government is the logical counterpart in the political sphere. However, the very nature of imperialism also fractures international capital into so many national units (supranational in the case of the emerging behemoth, the EU), among which rivalry and competition holds sway as well as common interests. This makes the establishment of a world state impossible, under the given constraints of the world system. At the economic and purely political levels, an uneasy set-up that functions as a primitive world government but is constantly torn between the two poles of this contradiction is possible. However, military domination of the world in the name of the international bourgeoisie admits of no such dispersion of power between the contending forces. The US military, then, aspires to be the military arm of the world government needed by mega-capital. Since that world government itself is absent, and impossible to realise, the US state takes it upon itself to regulate the world militarily.

We see here the contradiction between the two tendencies reproduced at a new level. Since, according to the time-tested maxim of von Clausewitz, 'war is the continuation of politics by other means', the contradiction between unity and division becomes one between the military unity of imperialism and the political fragmentation of imperialist power, vested, as political power is, in the different nation-states (and only ideally in the rising proto-state in the case of the EU). Within the limits of the system of imperialism, this contradiction can only be resolved in one of two manners: either the imposition of the will of the US state on all others, the logical implication of which is the colonisation of the whole world by the US, or a radical change in the balance of forces between the different imperialist powers.

It goes without saying that the first alternative is impossible at this stage of world development even for the mighty US state. The question, then, is whether the radically altered balance of forces between the contending imperialist powers can be attained without war between them. If we are to draw the lessons of the twentieth century, then it would be wise not to rule out an eventual confrontation between the imperialist countries, in particular between Europe and the US.

We should also note that whatever alternative route through which this contradiction is resolved, we are left face to face simply with different versions of barbarism.

## The national question as an instrument of the NWO

### Inroads into national sovereignty: The Annan doctrine

The NWO has proved to be a New War Order. Leaving aside 'minor' military interventions by the US and its allies, the Iraq operation was the fourth major war since the proclamation of the NWO, that is, within the space of a mere twelve years. This has been called the 'new interventionism'. It is important to stress that there is a developing tendency to justify this new interventionism in legal and moral terms.

As we have seen, globalism asserts the demise of the nation-state. This ideological statement is given a semblance of truth by the imperialist drive to unify the whole world into a single domain without any barriers for the circulation of capital. So it was obvious from the very dawn of the rise of globalist ideology that this outlook would result in the denigration of the concept of 'national sovereignty' as a principle that, at least nominally, regulates the arena of international politics. The discussion around an international law of intervention was indeed the rising trend throughout the 1990s and reached its apogee during the Kosovo War, with shrill voices haughtily proclaiming that humanitarian intervention is a principle superior to national sovereignty. (Not one among these voices explained why humanitarian compassion did not move the so-called 'international community' to intervene in even greater human tragedies such as those that unfolded in Rwanda, in Palestine, in the Kurdish regions of Turkey or other hot spots that arose around the world within the space of the same decade.) But no-one yet dared suggest that the whole structure of UN activities be changed accordingly, remembering that the very backbone of the UN Charter is this vilified notion of national sovereignty. Even after the Kosovo War, Tadeusz Mazowiecki, former Polish premier and UN representative in Bosnia in the period 1992–96, for instance, excluded a revision of the UN Charter even as he explicitly defended the promotion of a law of intervention in order to 'protect minorities'.

This task was finally shouldered by Kofi Annan. The UN secretary-general, during his opening speech to the General Assembly at the beginning of the fall 1999 session, that is to say right after the Kosovo War, propounded a doctrine that resounded as an open invitation to imperialist interventionism of the kind witnessed during the Gulf War and the Kosovo War. This is why the 'Annan doctrine' is so 'revolutionary' in its outlook and fell like a bomb when it was first uttered. The gist of the doctrine is simple: globalisation and international co-operation have made the defence of national sovereignty in its earlier version obsolete and have strengthened the 'sovereignty of the individual'. It follows that in cases where a state violates human rights, the 'international community' has the 'right to intervene', militarily if need be, in the internal affairs of that state. Moreover, Annan opines that 'the United Nations Charter does not forbid the recognition of the existence of cross-border rights', by which of course he means the right to intervene. Clinton, in his address to the General Assembly, approved of Annan's approach, but understandably warned that the principle could probably not be applied universally. It is not difficult to discover the secret of Clinton's reserve: why would US imperialism incite the UN to 'intervene' in the affairs of its loyal allies? No wonder then that countries such as China or Cuba, indeed the whole world outside the domain of imperialist countries, should regard the Annan doctrine as legitimising a rehashed version of the 'gunboat policy' of British imperialism in the nineteenth century.

The debate has since subsided, as the strong reaction to this gambit prevented the advocates of the new interventionism from proceeding in a swift manner. However, whether a new legal doctrine making inroads into national sovereignty is developed or not, the practice has since continued. What distinguishes the Gulf War from later ones is that the former was waged in the name of saving a nominally independent country (Kuwait) from the invasion of another (Iraq). The Kosovo War declared its objective as the restitution of the rights of Kosovar Albanians and not (as was really the case) as, for instance, punishing or ousting the Milosevic administration. Since September 11 we have moved even further: 'retribution' and 'regime change' now serve in unabashed fashion as the rationale.

*The abuse of national grievances*

In the most hypocritical fashion, even as they denigrate national sovereignty, the proponents of the NWO also exploit the grievances of nations and ethnic groups oppressed by the foes of imperialism. The experience of the last decade shows that this has become a privileged weapon of imperialism.

In the first three of the four major episodes of the construction of the NWO, the Gulf and Kosovo wars and the recent war on Iraq, the legitimate aspirations of nations oppressed by the state that was the target of imperialism were manipulated cynically by the latter, with the complicity of the existing leaderships of the oppressed nations in question. In the case of the Gulf War, it was the Kurds whose suffering was the basis for US imperialism to chop off a whole section of Iraq's territory from the jurisdiction of that country (the region above the notorious 36th parallel). As for the Kosovo War, the bombing of Yugoslavia along with Kosovo itself was justified on the basis of the oppression to which the Milosevic administration subjected the Kosovar Albanians. Finally, in the Iraq War the Kurds were the only allies of the US inside Iraq itself.

There is, however, nothing new or original here. It has been a time-tested tactic for imperialism to exploit the grievances of nations and nationalities oppressed by its foes. The British were masters at it. A very appropriate example is the 'liberation' of the Arab world from Ottoman yoke during and in the aftermath of the First World War. This resulted in the formation of a series of British and French colonies and puppet regimes in the Middle East. However, Wilson's advocacy of the right of nations to self-determination did not apparently apply to the Arabs or for any of the other 'native' peoples. The plight of the Arab Middle East continued between the two wars and came undone only with the overall turn of the tide against colonialism. The case of Palestine, of course, was, until recently, the tragic exception. This nation, after having 'liberated' itself from Ottoman rule in the aftermath of the First World War, had then to go through a period of British colonial rule between the two wars, but, as opposed to the other nations of the Arab Middle East, fell prey to the creation of a settler colonial state, Zionist Israel, after the Second World War. So almost a century after imperialism promised the Palestinian people its freedom, this people without a home is still living under the colonial yoke of a foreign state. If we are to learn lessons from history, the wise conclusion to draw is that imperialism is no reliable friend of the liberation of oppressed nations and nationalities.

This should in no way blind us to the plight of nations and peoples that are oppressed by the existing nation-states in the Third World. The emancipation of such peoples, however, will not come through the hypocritical policies of imperialism, which cynically manipulates legitimate grievances to its own end and frequently betrays the cause that it has supported so strongly once circumstances change and the rights of the oppressed people in question become a burden for its new status quo.

## The revival of colonialism

Finally, the new interventionism of the NWO strategy clearly reveals a developing trend: that of the formation of what could be labelled 'international' or 'multilateral' colonies. In the age of classical colonialism, the central purpose of the colonial powers was to secure for themselves the economic benefits to be acquired from the colonised territory. (There were of course also cases of colonisation for purely political and military reasons). So the principle behind classical colonialism was monopolistic. The new trend has been, until the Iraq war, to establish colonies or semi-colonies of the 'international community'.

The clearest cases are those of Bosnia and Kosovo. The administration that was formed in Bosnia on the basis of the much-acclaimed Dayton Accords can be called by no other name than a 'colony'. At the summit of the 'state' established by the Dayton Accords is a high commissioner, who wields powers similar to colonial administrators, including the annulment of elections and the removal from their posts of high-level civil servants. The police force is recruited from abroad and functions under the jurisdiction of the high commissioner. Bosnia is militarily under the occupation of NATO-led forces. Economic life, too, is under the iron fist of imperialism. In line with the Dayton Accords, the governor of the central bank was appointed by the IMF, that latter-day agent of disguised colonialism. To add insult to injury, the central bank was deprived of the routine powers of a normal central bank: according to the Dayton Accords, the bank could not, for a transitional period, extend credit through the creation of money, but was authorised solely to act like a currency board.

That this kind of multilateral colonialism was the rising trend of the day was demonstrated even more convincingly by what happened in Kosovo in the aftermath of the war. In fact, even at the beginning of the war, Kosovo's future was characterised as a UN 'protectorate', a status just short of full colonisation but one that nonetheless has nothing to do with an independent state. In the light of this, the hypocrisy of Resolution 1244 of the UN on Kosovo, where the latter is characterised as an 'international protectorate' but the supposed sovereignty of Yugoslavia over the entirety of its former territory is recognised, is all the more glaring. Kosovo today, just like Bosnia its predecessor, is ruled by a high representative appointed by the instances of the European Union, subjected to military occupation under NATO command, with a police force recruited internationally. Bernard Kouchner, the first high representative, made the Deutschmark the 'national' currency and, most appalling of all, represented Kosovo in international meetings, such as the one on the Balkan Stability Pact.

The case of Afghanistan after the war partially confirms this trend. Months after the war was over, General Tommy Franks, commander of the US forces in the region, declared openly that US troops were there to stay for many years to come.

With Iraq the tendency for the revival of colonialism has become, if anything, more marked. Even with the establishment of the so-called 'Interim Governing Council', composed of representatives of different Iraqi factions, the US occupation administration under Paul Bremer in Iraq is no different from the British mandate administration set up under the notorious colonial administrator Sir Percy Cox in Iraq in the 1920s, after the British wrested the Arab Middle East from the Ottomans during the First World War. In effect, notwithstanding the military presence of close to a score of US allies on Iraqi soil and the planned inclusion of still others, the regime in Iraq is much closer to classical colonialism than the multilateral colonies of Bosnia and Kosovo, in that US power is hardly constrained even nominally by UN resolutions.

## THE DYNAMICS OF CONFLICT OVER EURASIA

Every historical epoch delineates new geographical areas of a special internal coherence, real or imagined, vis-à-vis the world system. The geographical concept of the Middle East, to cite the most obvious example, is a recent creation of Western imperialism, designed to supersede the earlier notions of the 'Orient' and the more recent 'Near East'. The coherence of the Middle East was (and still is) defined by the overwhelming weight of the region in world oil production and by the importance of the Israeli-Arab conflict. The clearest recent example is the new terminology applied to the Balkans, 'South-Eastern

Europe', in order to divest that region of its historical specificity and assimilate it into the emerging European behemoth.

The term Eurasia has a long history behind it, but was usually used to denote the essential unity of the two continents Europe and Asia, spread as they were in contiguous manner across the gigantic land mass that stretches from the Atlantic on the West to the Pacific on the East. The new meaning that is nowadays attached to the term is directly related to the dissolution of the Soviet Union. This historical event has, for the first time since the early to mid-nineteenth century, brought to the world stage a series of independent nation-states in areas that were only until a decade ago part of the Russian, and later the Soviet, state. The majority of these states share, moreover, certain economic, political, ethnic and religious characteristics. In a narrow sense, then, Eurasia is now defined as the Caucasus and Central Asia. However, for reasons we will shortly go into, Eurasia is more usefully defined as the whole area that extends from the Balkans through Russia, Turkey and the Middle East all the way to Central Asia or, to paraphrase a former president of Turkey, Suleyman Demirel, as the area that extends 'from the Adriatic to the Great Wall of China'.

The attentive reader will immediately have noted that all the great upheavals and major wars of the epoch of the NWO (the Gulf War, the ethnic wars of Yugoslavia and the Kosovo War, the Afghanistan War, the second Intifada, the recent Iraq War etc.) have taken place either within the borders of Eurasia thus defined or in its immediate periphery. The reason for this should be clear: it was established above that the NWO is in fact an attempt by imperialism, primarily the US, to create a realignment of the relations of power in the face of the vacuum engendered by the collapse of the second superpower, the Soviet Union. Eurasia is the epitome of such regions where this kind of power vacuum appeared after the fall of the Berlin Wall.

### The importance of Eurasia

However, simply to state that there is a power vacuum is not sufficient to understand why there has been so much turmoil in the region and why after 11 September it has become the epicentre of the upheaval in world politics. There are several factors that give Eurasia the special importance it has attracted from imperialism.

The first of these characteristics is related to the new geography of energy resources (petroleum and natural gas) established by the emergence on the world market of the Caspian basin region after the dissolution of the Soviet Union. Some of the new independent Turkic republics of the Caucasus and Central Asia (primarily Azerbaijan, Kazakhstan and Turkmenistan) wield abundant energy resources, in addition to the gold and other mineral reserves of the entire region. Given the fact that Azerbaijan neighbours Iran, a major oil producer of the Middle East, we are witnessing the formation of *a new unified energy-producing region* that extends all the way from Saudi Arabia and the Persian Gulf in the south to Kazakhstan in the north. It is significant, in this context, that the concept of the Middle East has lately, in daily political discourse, been reduced exclusively to the Israeli-Palestinian conflict, with such bizarre turns of the phrase as 'the question of the Middle East should be solved before any attempt is made to sort things out in Iraq', as if the latter country itself were not an integral part of the Middle East. The concept of the 'Greater Middle East', recently brought into circulation at an official level and covering the Caucasus as well as the Middle East proper, once again attests to the fact that not only national but regional borders too are being redrawn.

The exact amount of oil and gas reserves of the Caspian basin seem to be open to debate as figures fluctuate quite widely according to different estimates. However, most reliable sources concur on the importance of these reserves. The International Energy Agency cites proven reserves of between 15–40 billion barrels, with an additional 70–150 billion barrels of possible reserves. These figures are not incompatible with the estimate given by the US Energy Administration Agency of total reserves between 179 and 195 billion barrels and the figure of 200 billion barrels of total reserves calculated in a report prepared by former US national security adviser Rosemarie Forsythe. On the other hand, overall natural gas reserves of the Caspian basin countries are estimated by the US Energy Administration Agency as between 565 and 665 trillion cubic feet. Petroleum is abundant in Kazakhstan and Azerbaijan, while Turkmenistan, which also has some oil, ranks first in natural gas (30 per cent of world reserves), trailed by Kazakhstan, Uzbekistan and Azerbaijan, in that order. Such high and untapped reserves naturally whet the appetite of the big oil corporations and incite imperialist powers and regional states to intervene both on behalf of their respective corporations and for strategic reasons.

However important this economic factor may be, though, the region's importance for the international power game cannot be reduced to it. The region presents an immense importance from the geopolitical and geostrategic points of view for future struggles over the whole of the Asian land mass in general. It is an open secret that, in Asia, US imperialism views Russia and China as potential threats. There are two distinct aspects to this perception. On the one hand, these are both countries thrown into socio-economic turmoil by the process of capitalist restoration. It is an urgent priority for the US and for imperialism to ensure, in the face of the immense hardships suffered by the working people of these countries, that this process and the accompanying one of the integration of these countries into the capitalist world economy be carried through to their logical conclusion. It is not to be doubted that should there be a move toward an interruption of these processes, whether through a mass uprising or a machination from the top, imperialism will throw its whole weight behind the restorationist camp and even, in the extreme case, intervene militarily. China poses an even greater threat from this point of view, since capitalist restoration there is taking place not under the political guidance of an openly restorationist regime, but co-exists uncomfortably with the political superstructure of the bureaucratic workers' state. This creates a potentially explosive situation. The contradiction has to be solved, but how it will be solved is not clear at all.

The second aspect has to do with the sheer weight exercised by these two states on the affairs of the region, for historical, economic, political and military reasons. In other words, even if the process of capitalist restoration is carried through to its logical conclusion in both of these countries, they, and again especially China, with its 1.2 billion-strong population, its vibrant economy and its growing military power, will be considered by the US, and imperialism in general, as formidable rivals to be kept under control.

This, then, is the second reason why Central Asia and the Caucasus hold great importance for the future of struggles over Asia. The countries of Central Asia provide an excellent geographic location for military operations against either country. This is why the military bases that the US built during the Afghanistan war in Uzbekistan, Kyrgyzstan and Afghanistan itself are of such immense importance. But given the fact that both Russia and China are nuclear powers and notwithstanding the development of the National Missile Defense (NMD) programme, a direct war of aggression on either country can only be considered as a measure of last resort. It is precisely here that the peculiar characteristics of the Eurasian region come into play.

In the vast geographic space that extends from the Balkans to the frontiers of China (and beyond, if one includes this country's controversial province of Xinjiang, alias eastern Turkistan), history has for centuries unfolded as successive cycles of confrontation between two major ethnic families (the Slavs and the Turkic), along with the numerically smaller but significant Persians, and two religions (the Orthodox variant of Christianity and Islam). The Caucasus, both within the Russian Federation and in Transcaucasia in the south, is an ethnic cauldron, where hundreds of small nationalities exist side by side and intermingle, ready to erupt any moment into mutual carnage. As for the Turkic republics of Central Asia (and Tadjikistan), they lived grudgingly under Russian rule from the mid-nineteenth century until very recently. Finally, a host of Turkic republics of different sizes exist inside the Russian Federation itself, even in zones remote from the Caucasus.

Given this overall picture, it would be wise to remember the characteristic features of the NWO strategy depicted earlier. The exploitation of national grievances for manipulative purposes, the utter disdain for national sovereignty (the 'Annan doctrine'), the new tendency to set up international colonies – all the typical instruments of this strategy will be able to find ample material to draw upon in this region full of explosive ethnic and religious tensions. It is into this vast geographic space of smouldering ethnic tensions that US imperialism and its allies have made their entry through the Afghanistan War. It is no wonder then that, in his influential book, *The Grand Chessboard*,[3] Zbigniew Brzezinski, one of the foremost representatives of the US foreign policy establishment, has recourse to so many ominous characterisations to describe the present situation in the area: this 'volcanic region' that Brzezinski aptly dubs 'the Eurasian Balkans', is, in his opinion, 'likely to be a major battlefield', and the US and the so-called international community 'may be faced here with a challenge that will dwarf the recent crisis in the former Yugoslavia'.

This comparison is not fortuitous. Yugoslavia served, among other things, as the testing ground for the policies to be followed in Eurasia. We should then turn to this example in order to draw lessons for the future.

### Yugoslavia as harbinger

There is a simple fact that most commentators, their attention fixed on inter-ethnic struggles, forget to mention when discussing the decade-long convulsions and wars that shook former Yugoslavia. That country, whatever its many specificities, was a link in the chain of a series of states where capitalism had been abolished until the restoration process was set in motion by the momentous events of the late 1980s and early 1990s. The catastrophe that descended on Yugoslavia also happened to coincide with the proclamation of the NWO in 1990, at the threshold of the Gulf War. The coincidence is not spurious and it is imperative that both facts be taken into consideration if one wants to reach a sound analysis of the break-up of former Yugoslavia, of which the Kosovo War is a specific phase.

Yugoslavia's ordeal can only be understood within this overall context. The country was a link in the chain of the Central and Eastern European bureaucratic workers' states as a whole, but given its deep-rooted historical specificity had not collapsed in the same manner and with the same speed as the others. Moreover, it was the single most important regional power in the Balkans vis-à-vis NATO members Greece and Turkey and a country that had successfully defied Nazi occupation during the Second World War. And, for reasons of ethnic and religious affinity, it was at least a potential ally of Russia, the ever-feared potential rival of the imperialist West. This is why, led by Germany, Austria and the Vatican, the West immediately gave diplomatic recognition to the secessionist states of Slovenia and Croatia in 1991 and also why the United States encouraged the Bosnian Muslims to adopt an intransigent position in 1992, both political acts that fanned the flames of ethnic war in Yugoslavia between 1991 and 1995. The ensuing dissolution, in matter of fact the dismemberment, of Yugoslavia and the penetration of NATO along with the European Union into the vacuum thereby created has resulted, above all, in a consolidation of the newly acquired power of imperialism in that region.

But even a rump Yugoslavia was a threat to the durability of an arrangement guaranteeing capitalist stability in the Balkans. Within the multi-pronged strategy of imperialism aiming to assure the durability of capitalist stability in the Balkans and beyond, the dismemberment of Yugoslavia was an important element. Kosovo was thus a new phase in the creation of mini-states where once rose Tito's powerful Yugoslavia. Everything from sudden US support in 1998 to the KLA, an organisation once classified as 'terrorist' by the very same State Department, to the ultimatum of Rambouillet, which any child could predict would have been rejected by the Milosevic administration, shows that the road that led to the Kosovo War was meticulously and systematically paved by American policy.

The foregoing is not to deny that there existed forces within former Yugoslavia that worked towards the break-up of the country. There certainly were, and imperialism could surely not have provoked the carnage that took place without these being present in the first place. However, that story itself has been told so one-sidedly that to untangle all the distortions would take us far from the aim of this chapter. Suffice it to say that a host of factors ranging from IMF-imposed economic austerity through uneven development of the republics in a country that had been organised along a more decentralised manner than the classical Soviet-type state to the rabid nationalism propagated by the ruling bureaucracies (certainly Milosevic was not unique in this respect) played its part in the unfolding tragedy. From the standpoint of an analysis of the strategy of imperialism, though, what is decisive is that these were put to use with the aim of dismembering Yugoslavia.

If the foregoing analysis is right, one should then stop to pose the following question: If former Yugoslavia, important as it was on the scale of the Balkans, was considered to be a menace for capitalist stability, how would Russia and China, giants not only on the Asian but on a world scale, fare as a threat?

The next question immediately suggests itself: what would be the difference between a war on Russia or China and the Third World War?

### CONCLUSION: GLOBALISM AND THE NWO
### AS INHERENTLY CRISIS-PRONE PROCESSES

The argument presented in this chapter seems sufficient to reach a very simple conclusion: For the working masses of the world, globalism and the NWO, by their very nature, promise nothing but increased poverty and the threat of war on a great scale. The important point here lies in the phrase 'by their very nature'. For 'globalisation' is too often criticised, both within the international trade union movement and the anti-globalisation movement, with respect to its consequences, but these consequences are hardly ever related to the strategy of globalism *per se*. As for the rising threat of war, too clear to be ignored after September 11, too many critics of US policy have talked about mistakes or intransigence on the part of one administration or another, while refusing to see through the logic of the NWO strategy itself.

Behind these attitudes lies a conception that perceives 'globalisation' as inevitable and irreversible. This is precisely the idea that this chapter wishes to demolish. On the one hand, 'globalisation' should not be conflated with the progressive integration of the world in the economic, political and cultural spheres. 'Globalisation' is only one modality through which such integration can be brought about. It is a form of international integration that is predicated on the voraciousness of capital for profit, on the unfettered play of market forces, on the dictates of the imperialist powers, hence overall on the law of the strongest. 'Globalisation' is not any kind of integration; it is neoliberal integration. Hence to ask for an 'alternative globalisation' is to remain on the terrain defined by the strategy of mega-capital and the imperialist states. 'Globalisation with a human face' is a contradiction in terms.

Not only is 'globalisation' (and the NWO as its political superstructure) not inevitable, but it is ridden with such contradictions that it is likely to collapse in the not too distant future. Here we can only point to these, leaving an elaboration to other occasions. There are at least three sets of such contradictions. First is the series of contradictions of the world economy specific to the age of 'globalisation'. Capital roams the world freely as if it were a 'smooth' space of valorisation, but national spaces have their specificities, which, too often ignored, become so many bases of crisis, which then spills through a 'contagion effect' into other economies, threatening the whole world economy. Against the background of the depressive phase of the long wave that the capitalist world economy is going through and the sea of debt and overcredit in which all economic units are floating, this dialectic of the national and the international creates a constant threat of financial collapse and a depression of the classical type. That this is so is amply shown by the evolution of the successive crises of Mexico (1994–95), Asia (1997–98), Russia (1998), Brazil (1998–99), Argentina and Turkey (2001–02), the generalised recession of 2001–02 and the present stage of impending deflation. Were the virtuality of such a generalised financial collapse to come about, it is beyond doubt that the world economy would again be fragmented into mutually hostile blocs, which would mean the total demise of the strategy of 'globalisation'.

Secondly, the many different factors pointed out above that lead to a rise in the rivalry between different imperialist powers might engender a dynamic of cut-throat competition and even outright hostility between the contending parties. It is obviously too early to imagine an open break of the EU or of Japan from the US. But the tension, especially between the US and the rising giant that is the EU, constantly surfaces in economic, political, cultural and even the military spheres. We should remember that in the period leading up to the Iraq war three institutions of the Western alliance, the UN, NATO and the EU, were shaken to their roots as a result of this kind of tension. Given the experience of the twentieth century, it would be folly to rule out conflict between the various imperialist powers once the conditions mature. A generalised depression, if it comes about, will, of course, hasten the process immensely. But even short of this kind of open conflict between the major powers, the argument presented here has tried to show that war and militarism are part and parcel of the NWO. This is what makes Eurasia (and China) the probable epicentre of world politics in the next two decades, despite other types of simmering tensions in other parts of the world such as Latin America, South-East Asia, Southern Africa and Western Europe.

Finally, capital's assault on all the hard-won rights and gains of the working masses in the imperialist countries, in those where the restoration of capitalism is being played out and in the Third World is bound to create a backlash against both impoverishment and the miseries of war. We should perhaps even say 'was', since all the indications are gathering that a sustained movement against the consequences of 'globalisation' and the NWO has already started, in uneven fashion it is true, in many parts of the world. These take two distinct forms. On the one hand, there are those struggles that are confined to single countries, among which the French strikes of 1995, workers' struggles in South Korea, the mass struggles in Ecuador, the general strikes in Greece, Italy and Spain, and above all the revolutionary days of December 2001 in Argentina stand out. That 'contagion' is not confined to the crisis tendencies of capital but also to class struggle has amply been shown by the mass movements of Latin America (Venezuela, Bolivia, Peru, Paraguay, Uruguay etc.) in the course of 2002–03 and the general strikes in France and Austria in 2003. There is, next, the series of international actions that started with Seattle in 1999 and continued with Prague, Genoa, Evian and also with the World Social Forums in Porto Alegre and Mumbai. The demonstrations during EU summits (Nice, Gothenburg, Laeken, Barcelona, Seville, Thessaloniki etc.) partake of both types of movement in that they bring together the working masses and the youth of different nations but nonetheless are limited in scope in their demands, focused as these are on EU policies. Despite the state of the socialist movement in the wake of the collapse of the bureaucratic workers' states, which creates so many obstacles in the way of a victory for the masses, it would be unwise to rule out a breakthrough in the future by the working class and the masses. This would again change the conjuncture entirely and signify the beginning of the end for 'globalisation' and the NWO.

It is certainly true that none of this may happen, that the international bourgeoisie may be able to weather the deep-seated contradictions that flow from the structure of the capitalist world economy, inter-imperialist rivalries and class struggles and that globalism and the NWO strategy have the upper hand for the foreseeable future. To grant that possibility, though, is worlds apart from saying that it is inevitable. Of course, the movement should start out by partial demands and fight for reforms in the system. What is suicidal, though, is not to start there, but to stop there. It is time for us to overcome the trauma of the defeat of the first wave of the socialist experience, draw the lessons of that experience and start thinking about and planning for a world that is really and truly 'another world'. For such a world is indeed possible and, what is more, necessary.

### NOTES

1. Michael Hardt and Antonio Negri (2001) *Empire* (Cambridge, MA: Harvard University Press).
2. Vladimir Il'ich Lenin (1975) *Imperialism. The Highest Stage of Capitalism* (Moscow: Progress Publishers), p83.
3. Zbigniew Brzezinski (1997) *The Grand Chessboard* (New York: Basic Books).

# 6

# The Crisis of Global Capitalism: How it Looks from Latin America

*Bill Robinson*

## CRISIS AND THE RESTRUCTURING OF WORLD CAPITALISM

The downturn in the world economy that began in the closing years of the twentieth century heralded a crisis that, in my view, was more than merely cyclical. The turn-of-century turmoil may turn out to be opening scenes in Act II of a deeper restructuring crisis that began nearly three decades earlier. Mainstream business cycle theories are keen to identify periodic swings from expansion to recession in the market economy. But world-system and other Marxist-inspired theories have long pointed to the deeper cycles of expansion and contraction in world capitalism. Cyclical crises eventually usher in periods of restructuring. These restructuring crises, as scholars from the French regulation, the US social structure of accumulation, the world-system, and critical Marxist schools have shown, result in novel forms that replace historical patterns of capital accumulation and the institutional arrangements that facilitated them.[1] The post-Second World War expansion – the so-called 'golden age' of capitalism – entered into crisis in the 1970s, precipitating a period of restructuring and transformation that led to a new mode of global capital accumulation now known as neoliberalism. The theoretical rationale for this model was first sketched by Friedrich Hayek and the 'Austrian school' of economics and later refined by Milton Friedman and other neoclassical economists from the monetary school at the University of Chicago (known as the 'Chicago boys').[2] It was implemented experimentally in Chile following the 1973 *coup d'état* that brought the Pinochet dicatorship to power. But it was the Reagan and Thatcher regimes of the 1980s that catapulted neoliberalism to centre stage of world capitalism, and the International Financial Agencies (IFAs) that imposed the model of much of the Third World in the 1980s and 1990s through structural adjustment programmes, in what came to be known as the 'Washington Consensus'.[3]

I have been researching and writing since the early 1990s on globalisation and crisis, and the conclusions of my earlier work can be summarised as follows. The crisis that began in the 1970s could not be resolved within the framework of the post-1945 Keynesian social structure of accumulation. Capital responded to the constraints on accumulation imposed by this earlier model of nation-state redistributional projects by 'going global'. What was international capital in the preceding epoch metamorphosised into transnational capital, which became the hegemonic fraction of capital on a world scale in the 1980s. Transnationalised fractions of capitalist classes and bureaucratic elites captured state power in most countries of the world during the 1980s and 1990s and utilised that power to undertake a massive neoliberal restructuring. Free trade policies, integration processes and neoliberal reform – including the whole gamut of well-known deregulation, privatisation and fiscal, monetary and austerity measures – opened up the world in new ways to transnational capital. For instance, deregulation made available new zones to resource exploitation, privatisation opened up to profit making public and community spheres, ranging from healthcare and education to police and prison systems. New information technology and novel forms of organisation (e.g. flexible accumulation) also contributed to renewed accumulation. The correlation of social forces worldwide changed in the 1980s and early 1990s against popular classes and in favour of transnational capital. The latter used the new-found structural leverage that global mobility and financial control provided to impose a new capital–labour relation, based on diverse categories of 'contingent' or deregulated employment ('casualised' and 'informalised' labour). Income shifted from working and poor people to capital and to new high-consumption middle, professional and bureaucratic strata that provided a global market segment fuelling growth in new areas. All this reverted – temporarily – the crisis of stagnation and declining profits of the 1970s.

These propositions have been broadly discussed and debated in my own previous work on globalisation and more generally in the interdisciplinary literature on global political economy.[4] The ambition of the present chapter is to examine the experience of one particular region, Latin America, in the crisis and restructuring of world capitalism in the late twentieth and early twenty-first centuries. We are in the Autumn of neoliberalism in Latin America and in global society, and what comes next may be seen as a new moment in the restructuring crisis that began in the 1970s. The remainder of this section summarises my propositions on globalisation as a new epoch in world capitalism. The next section, the empirical and analytical core of the chapter, examines Latin America's experience in the world capitalist crisis, with particular emphasis on the neoliberal model, turn-of-century social conflicts that engulfed the region, and the rise of a new resistance politics. The last section returns, by way of conclusion, to the broader issues of crisis and restructuring in world capitalism raised above.

## From nation-state to global capitalism

The restructuring crisis that began in the 1970s signalled the transition to a new transnational stage of world capitalism. The capitalism system has gone through previous mercantile, competitive industrial and 'monopoly' (or corporate) epochs in its evolution. An *epochal shift* captures the idea of changes in social structure that transform the very way that the system functions. Globalisation as a fourth epoch in world capitalism is marked by a number of fundamental shifts in the capitalist system.

One of these is *the rise of truly transnational capital*. The production process itself has progressively transnationalised. National circuits of accumulation have increasingly been reorganised and integrated into new transnational circuits. The concepts of flexible accumulation and network structure capture the organisational form of these globalised circuits. Another feature of global capitalism is *the rise of a transnational capitalist class* (TCC), a fraction grounded in global markets and circuits of accumulation over national markets and circuits.[5] Transnational class formation also entails the rise of a global proletariat. Capital and labour increasingly confront each other as global classes. A third is the rise of a *transnational state* (TNS) apparatus, a loose but increasingly coherent network comprised of supranational political and economic institutions and national state apparatuses that have been penetrated and transformed by transnational forces. The nation-state may be around for a long time to come but the nation-state system is no longer the organising principle of capitalism. National states as components of a larger TNS structure now tend to serve the interests of global above national accumulation processes. The TNS has played a key role in imposing the neoliberal model on the old Third World and therefore in reinforcing the new capital–labour relation.

A fourth shift, accordingly, is *from nation-state to transnational hegemony*. Hegemony in the global capitalist system is exercised not by a nation-state but by a new transnational elite.[6] In contrast to the predominant story-line of a resurgent US empire, I suggest that empire in the twenty-first century is not about a particular nation-state but about an ascendant empire of global capital. This empire of capital is headquartered in Washington. But this does not mean that US imperial behaviour seeks to defend 'US' interests. As the most powerful component of the TNS, the US state apparatus defends the interests of transnational investors and the overall system. Military expansion is in the interests of transnational corporations (TNCs). The only military apparatus in the world capable of exercising global coercive authority is the US military. The beneficiaries of US military action around the world are not 'US' but transnational capitalist groups. This is the underlying class relation between the TCC and the US national state. For evident historical reasons, the US military apparatus is the ministry of war in the cabinet of an increasingly globally integrated ruling class, a ministry with considerable autonomous powers. Militaries typically acquire tremendous autonomous powers in times of escalating wars and conflict, especially in undemocratic systems such as the current global capitalist system.

Yet another element of change is *novel relations of inequality* in global society.[7] Unequal exchanges – material, political, cultural – are not captured so much in the old concept of the *international* division of labour as the *global* division of labour. A global division of labour suggests differential participation in global production according to social standing and not necessarily geographic location, and accounts for sweatshops in East Los Angeles and northern Honduras, as well as gated communities in Hollywood and Sao Paulo. Inequality is the permanent consequence of capitalist social relations, and as capitalism globalises the twenty-first century is witness to new forms of poverty and wealth. Globalisation renders untenable a sociology of national development since it undermines the ability of national states to capture and redirect surpluses through interventionist mechanisms that were viable in the nation-state phase of capitalism. Neither 'socialism in one country' nor 'Keynesianism in one country' can be sustained any longer.

The empirical evidence of the growing gap between North and South is well known, but so too is that indicating a dramatic widening of the gap between the rich and the poor within countries. There remain very real regional distinctions in the form of productive participation in the global economy, as we shall see here in the case of Latin America. But processes of uneven accumulation increasingly unfold in accordance with a social and not a national logic. The material processes associated with what we call development are in essence social rather than geographic, spatial or territorial. Transnationality is a *social* category and development should be seen not in terms of nations but in terms of social groups in a transnational setting. In the epoch prior to globalisation core affluence and the attenuating effects it had on social polarisation were made possible by the core's relation to a spatially defined periphery. As accumulation processes globalise they are no longer co-extensive with specific national territories and they tend to stratify people along new transnational social lines. Under global capitalism the historic affinities between capital accumulation, states conceived of in the Weberian sense as territorially based institutions, and social classes and groups tends to dissolve. The persistence, and in fact *growth,* of the North–South divide remains important for its theoretical and practical political implications. What is up for debate is whether the divide is something innate to world capitalism or a particular spatial configuration of uneven capitalist development during a particular historic phase of world capitalism, and whether tendencies towards the self-reproduction of this configuration are increasingly offset by countertendencies emanating from the nature and dynamic of global capital accumulation.

I cannot pursue the matter further here. Suffice it to conclude this section with the observation that the empire of global capital has barely emerged, and yet already it faces twin structural and subjective crises; one of overaccumulation and the other of legitimacy. Globalisation resolved some problems for capital but the underlying laws of capitalism remain in place and continually assert themselves. The breakdown of nation-state based redistributional projects may have restored growth and profitability but it also aggravated the tendencies inherent in capitalism towards overaccumulation by further polarising income and heightening inequalities worldwide. It was, I believe, overcapacity that lay beneath the Asian crisis of 1997–98 and it is overaccumulation that underpinned the world recession of the early twenty-first century. The unfolding crisis in the world economy may turn out to be neither a recurring business cycle nor the opening salvos of a new restructuring crisis. Hardly had the neoliberal model triumphed in the 1980s and 1990s than it began to appear as moribund. I suggest here – not as a conclusive affirmation but as a working hypothesis – that neoliberalism may prove to be a parenthesis between old nation-state accumulation models and a new global social structure of accumulation whose contours are not yet clear.

## LATIN AMERICA FACES THE GLOBAL CRISIS

Latin America has been deeply implicated in the restructuring crisis of world capitalism. The mass movements, revolutionary struggles, nationalist and populist projects of the 1960s and 1970s were beaten back by local and international elites in the latter decades of the twentieth century in the face of the global economic downturn, the debt crisis, state repression, US intervention, the collapse of a socialist alternative, and the rise of the neoliberal model (the diverse popular projects and movements had their own internal contradictions as well). Economically, Latin American countries experienced a thorough restructuring and integration into the global economy under the neoliberal model. But by 2000 the model was in crisis in the region, unable to bring about any sustained development, or even to prevent continued backward movement. Politically, the fragile polyarchic systems installed through the so-called 'transitions to democracy' of the 1980s were increasingly unable to contain the social conflicts and political tensions generated by the polarising and pauperising effects of the neoliberal model. But the restructuring of world capitalism, its new transnational logic and institutionality, the polarisation between the rich and the poor, and the escalation of inequalities, marginalisation and deprivation taking place under globalisation, have profoundly changed the terrain under which social struggle and change will take place in Latin America in the present century.

### Neoliberalism and stagnation in Latin America

As transnational capital integrates the world into new globalised circuits of accumulation it has broken down national and regional autonomies, including the earlier pre-globalisation models of capitalist development and the social forces that sustained these models. Through internal adjustment and rearticulation to the emerging global economy and society, local productive apparatuses and social structures in each region are transformed, and different regions acquired new profiles in the emerging global division of labour. Economic integration processes and neoliberal structural adjustment programmes are driven by transnational capital's campaign to open up every country to its activities, to tear down all barriers to the movement of goods and capital, and to create a single unified field in which global capital can operate unhindered across all national borders.[8]

In Latin America, the pre-globalisation model of accumulation based on domestic market expansion, populism and import-substitution industrialisation (ISI), corresponded to the earlier nation-state phase of capitalism. This was a particular variant of the model of national capitalism that prevailed for much of the twentieth century. Regulatory and redistributive mechanisms provided the basis for the post-1945 national economies around the world, whether the Keynesian 'New Deal'/social democratic states in the First World, the developmentalist states of the Third World, and the socialist-oriented redistributive states of the Second World. In Latin America, the pre-globalisation model put into place national circuits of accumulation and expanded productive generate in the post-1945 years. Surpluses were appropriated by national elites and transnational corporations but also redistributed through diverse populist programmes, ranging from packets of social wages (social service spending, subsidised consumption, etc.), expanding employment opportunities and rising real wages. But the model became exhausted and its breakdown, starting in the late 1970s, paved the way for the neoliberal model based on liberalisation and integration to the global economy, a 'laissez-faire' state, and what the current development discourse terms 'export-led development'.[9] Table 6.1 provides one indicator of this process of increasing outward orientation of Latin American countries in the final decade of the twentieth century.

The dismantling of the pre-globalisation model and its replacement by the neoliberal model threw Latin American popular classes into a social crisis that hit hard in the 1980s, Latin America's 'lost decade', and has continued into the twenty-first century. During the 1980s, other regions, particularly East Asia, North America and Europe, became the most attractive outlets for accumulated capital stocks. Latin America stagnated in absolute terms and experienced backward movement when seen in relation to other regions in the world economy. The region experienced a contraction of income and economic activity. Its share of world trade dropped by half from 1980 to 1990, from about 6 per cent to about 3 per cent.[10] In the 1980s it became the region with the slowest growth in per capita income, behind other Third World regions and behind the world as a whole, as indicated in Table 6.2. Of course, these nation-state indicators need to be approached with caution, as they often conceal more than they reveal. Nonetheless, these sets of data underscore the region's troubled integration into the emergent global economy.

*Table 6.1*    Trade in goods as % of GDP, Latin America and selected countries

|  | 1989 | 1999 |
| --- | --- | --- |
| Latin America and Caribbean | 10.2 | 18.2 |
| Argentina | 5.1 | 10.9 |
| Brazil | 6.3 | 8.4 |
| Chile | 24.0 | 23.7 |
| Colombia | 6.7 | 9.3 |
| Costa Rica | 19.9 | 40.6 |
| Dominican Republic | 21.4 | 29.0 |
| Ecuador | 15.5 | 20.1 |
| Guatemala | 11.5 | 16.6 |
| Honduras | 18.4 | 26.9 |
| Mexico | 14.1 | 35.6 |
| Peru | 7.5 | 12.2 |
| Venezuela | 22.6 | 26.6 |

*Source*: World Bank[11]

*Table 6.2*    Comparison of growth by regions (% average annual growth rate)

|  | 1965–80 | 1980–89 | 1990–2000 |
| --- | --- | --- | --- |
| World | 4.1 | 3.1 | 2.6 |
| Latin America | 6.1 | 1.6 | 3.3 |
| Sub-Saharan Africa | 4.2 | 2.1 | 2.4 |
| East Asia | 7.3 | 7.9 | 7.2 |
| South Asia | 3.7 | 5.1 | 5.6 |
| OECD members | 3.8 | 3.0 | 2.4 |

*Source*: World Bank[12]

What accounted for this *apparent* stagnation and marginalisation? In fact, the data indicates that Latin America did not stop producing wealth for the world capitalist system as it integrated into the global economy. On the contrary, the volume of Latin American exports to the world increased significantly throughout the 1980s and 1990s. As Table 6.3 shows, between 1983 and 1998, the volume of the region's exports *rose* by an annual average of 15.1 per cent yet the value of these same exports actually *decreased* by an annual average of 0.1 per cent. In other words, Latin Americans have worked harder and harder, increasing the wealth they have produced for the global economy. Yet the income they have received from that work has decreased as they have become more impoverished and exploited.

*Table 6.3* Volume and unit of value of Latin American exports (average annual % growth, in batch years)

|           | Volume | Unit value |
|-----------|--------|------------|
| 1983–85   | 16.2   | −9.9       |
| 1986–88   | 17.7   | −5.9       |
| 1989–91   | 13.7   | 5.2        |
| 1992–94   | 22.3   | 3.3        |
| 1995–97   | 11.5   | 8.4        |
| 1998–2000 | 8.9    | −0.7       |
| 1983–2000 | 15.1   | 0.1        |

*Source:* Compiled from ECLAC

This steady deterioration of the terms of trade is a consequence of Latin America's continued overall dependence on commodity exports. Venezuela and Ecuador depend almost entirely on oil exports, Chile remains dependent on copper prices, Brazil and Argentina on a variety of low-tech and basic agricultural exports, Peru on its mining sector, Central America on traditional agro-exports, etc. This situation has been aggravated by neoliberal adjustment, which has shifted resources toward the external sector linked to the global economy, and by the region's extreme dependence on global capital markets to sustain economic growth. This continued dependence on commodity exports is a structural asymmetry, but it should be interpreted in terms of emergent transnational class relations rather than outdated dependency theories or strictly along North–South lines, as I will discuss below. What this situation does present is a worsening of the development (or social) crisis for the poor majority in Latin America and should not be confused with the region's contribution to global capital accumulation. The region has remained a net exporter of capital to the world market; a supplier of surplus for the world and an engine of growth of the global economy. Table 6.4 shows that Latin America was a net exporter of $219 billion in capital surplus to the world economy during the 'lost decade' of 1982 to 1990, and then became a net importer from 1991 through to 1998. But starting in 1999 the region reverted once again to an exporter of capital.

Table 6.4    Net capital flows, net payment on profits and interest, and net resource transfer (in $ billion)

|  | Net capital flows | Net payments profit/interest | Net transfer |
|---|---|---|---|
| 1982–90 | 99 | 318 | −219 |
| 1991–95 | 266 | 174 | 92 |
| 1996 | 65 | 43 | 22 |
| 1997 | 81 | 48 | 33 |
| 1998 | 78 | 51 | 27 |
| 1999 | 47 | 52 | −5 |
| 2000 | 53 | 53 | 0 |
| 2001 | 50 | 55 | −5 |
| 2002 | 13 | 53 | −40 |

Source: ECLAC (2000, 2001, 2002)[13]

What transpired was a massive influx of transnational capital into the region in the 1990s. This, combined with the renewal of growth for much of the decade, led transnational functionaries from the supranational economic planning agencies (World Bank, IMF, etc.) and local elites to argue that Latin America's development crisis had come to an end. But the vast majority of the inflow of capital was a consequence not of direct – that is, greenfield – foreign investment as much as from diverse portfolio and financial ventures, such as new loans, the purchase of stock in privatised companies and speculative investment in financial services, such as equities, mutual funds, pensions and insurance.[14] While this topic requires further elaboration not possible here, Table 6.5 gives an indication of just how central the purchase of stock in privatised enterprises and speculative finance capital has been to the inflow of resources in the 1990s, resulting in the transnationalisation of the production and service infrastructure that had been built up through the previous development model.

This dominance of speculative financial flows over productive capital reflected the hegemony of transnational finance capital in the age of globalisation and its frenzied 'casino capitalism' activity in recent years and gave an illusion of 'recovery' in Latin America, an illusion that was shattered starting with the Argentine crisis that exploded in December 2001. Prior to the Argentine upheaval, the transnational elite believed it had 'resolved' the debt crisis in the 1980s by making the debt serviceable and removing the issue from the political agenda. But given this continued haemorrhage of wealth from the region combined with liberalisation and deeper external integration, the external debt had in fact continued to grow throughout the late 1980s and 1990s, from $230 billion in 1980 to $533 billion in 1994, to over $714 billion in 1997, and near $800 billion in 1999, and its rate of growth again increased in the 1990s (see Tables 6.6 and 6.7).

Table 6.5   Net foreign investment, international bond issues and proceeds from sale of public enterprises, Latin America and selected countries (in $ million)

| | 1991 | 1992 | 1993 | 1994 | 1995 | 1996 | 1997 | 1998 | 1999 | 2000 |
|---|---|---|---|---|---|---|---|---|---|---|
| *Latin America* | | | | | | | | | | |
| Net FDI | 11,066 | 12,506 | 10,363 | 23,706 | 24,799 | 39,387 | 55,580 | 61,596 | 77,047 | 57,410 |
| Int. bond issues | 7,192 | 12,577 | 28,794 | 17,941 | 23,071 | 46,915 | 52,003 | 39,511 | 38,707 | 35,816 |
| Proceeds from privatisation | 16,702 | 14,886 | 10,179 | 8,529 | 3,433 | 11,458 | 24,408 | 42,461 | N/A | N/A |
| *Argentina* | | | | | | | | | | |
| Net FDI | 2,439 | 3,218 | 2,059 | 2,480 | 3,756 | 4,937 | 4,924 | 4,175 | 21,958 | 5,000 |
| Int. bond issues | 795 | 1,570 | 6,308 | 5,319 | 6,354 | 14,070 | 14,622 | 15,615 | 14,183 | 13,045 |
| Proceeds from privatisation | 1,896 | 5,312 | 4,589 | 1,441 | 1,340 | 1,033 | 969 | 598 | N/A | N/A |
| *Brazil* | | | | | | | | | | |
| Net FDI | 89 | 1,924 | 801 | 2,035 | 3,475 | 11,666 | 18,608 | 29,192 | 28,612 | 30,000 |
| Int. bond issues | 1,837 | 3,655 | 6,465 | 3,998 | 7,041 | 11,545 | 14,940 | 9,190 | 8,586 | 10,955 |
| Proceeds from privatisation | 1,564 | 2,451 | 2,621 | 1,972 | 910 | 3,752 | 17,400 | 36,600 | N/A | N/A |
| *Colombia* | | | | | | | | | | |
| Net FDI | 433 | 679 | 719 | 1,297 | 712 | 2,795 | 4,894 | 2,432 | 1,135 | 985 |
| Int. bond issues | – | 8 | 567 | 955 | 1,083 | 1,867 | 1,000 | 1,389 | 1,676 | 1,451 |
| Proceeds from privatisation | 105 | 27 | 4 | 681 | 138 | 1,476 | 3,180 | 470 | N/A | N/A |
| *Mexico* | | | | | | | | | | |
| Net FDI | 4,742 | 4,393 | 4,389 | 10,973 | 9,526 | 9,186 | 12,830 | 11,311 | 11,568 | 13,500 |
| Int. bond issues | 3,782 | 6,100 | 11,339 | 6,949 | 7,646 | 16,353 | 15,657 | 8,444 | 9,854 | 7,547 |
| Proceeds from privatisation | 10,716 | 6,799 | 2,507 | 771 | 8 | 8 | 84 | 581 | N/A | N/A |
| *Peru* | | | | | | | | | | |
| Net FDI | −7 | 150 | 687 | 3,108 | 2,048 | 3,242 | 1,702 | 1,860 | 1,969 | 1,185 |
| Int. bond issues | 8 | 8 | 30 | 100 | 8 | 8 | 250 | 150 | 8 | – |
| Proceeds from privatisation | 8 | 3 | 208 | 317 | 2,578 | 946 | 2,460 | 421 | 462 | 7,395 |
| *Venezuela* | | | | | | | | | | |
| Net FDI | 1,728 | 473 | −514 | 136 | 686 | 1,676 | 5,036 | 4,168 | 1,998 | 3,480 |
| Int. bond issues | 578 | 932 | 3,438 | 8 | 356 | 765 | 2,015 | 2,660 | 1,215 | 489 |
| Proceeds from privatisation | 2,276 | 30 | 32 | 15 | 21 | 2,090 | 1,506 | 174 | N/A | N/A |

Source: ECLAC[15]

Table 6.6   Latin America's external debt (in $ million)

|       | 1980 | 1985 | 1990 | 1991 | 1992 | 1993 | 1994 | 1995 | 1996 | 1997 | 1998 | 1999 |
|-------|------|------|------|------|------|------|------|------|------|------|------|------|
| Debt  | 230  | 374  | 442  | 457  | 475  | 506  | 533  | 653  | 676  | 714  | 786  | 793  |

Source: World Bank (1998–2000), Country Tables, p36.

Table 6.7   Annual growth rate of Latin America's debt

|                    | 1979–81 | 1982–83 | 1984–90 | 1991–93 | 1994–96 | 1997–99 |
|--------------------|---------|---------|---------|---------|---------|---------|
| Percentage growth  | 22.9    | 11.2    | 3.2     | 4.6     | 10.4    | 5.5     |

Source: ECLAC, reports (1985, 1994–95)

Amortisation of the debt has exacted an ever-rising tribute from Latin American popular classes to transnational capital. But once debt repayment pressures reach the point at which default becomes a possibility or a government can no longer contain pressure for it to meet even minimal social obligations the spiral of crisis begins. Local states are caught between the withdrawal of transnational investors and mounting unrest from poor majorities who can no longer bear any further austerity. The slide into crisis began in 2000 when the net outflow of resources once again came to surpass the net inflow. In Argentina, among other countries, for instance, the government could keep the economy buoyed as long as there were state assets to sell off. Once there is no quick money to be made, capital flight can – and has – plunged countries into overnight recession. As Table 6.8 indicates, Latin America began a downturn in 1998. Although the region as a whole showed positive growth in 2000, this is accounted for by high growth rates in a handful of countries, while most stagnated and experienced negative growth.

While there was a resumption of growth, 'recovery' was accompanied by increased poverty and inequality. What is most notable about Table 6.8 is that GDP per capita declined in the 'lost decade', by 0.9 per cent, from 1980 to 1990, and then barely recovered in the 'growth years' of the 1990s, growing by 1.5 per cent from 1991 to 2000. Moreover, if we separate out 1998–2000 from the rest of the 1990s we find that many countries experienced a renewed decline in GDP per capita over the three-year period 1998–2000. For instance, it *dropped* in aggregate by 3.3 per cent in Argentina, by 6.2 per cent in Colombia, by 10.5 per cent in Ecuador, 3.3 per cent in Honduras, 6.1

per cent in Paraguay, 0.1 per cent in Peru, 8.1 per cent in Uruguay and by 8.3 per cent in Venezuela. In other countries, aggregate growth in GDP per capita for this period slowed to a negligible amount, such as 0.9 per cent in Brazil.[16] By 2003 the UN's Economic Commission for Latin America had begun to refer to the late 1990s as Latin America's 'lost half decade'.[17]

Table 6.8    Latin America: Annual growth rates, GDP and GDP per capita, region and selected countries and years

|  | GDP | GDP per capita |
|---|---|---|
| *Latin America* | | |
| 1980–90: | 1.2 | −0.9 |
| 1991–2000 | 3.3 | 1.5 |
| *Argentina* | | |
| 1981–90 | −0.7 | −2.1 |
| 1991–2000 | 4.2 | 2.9 |
| 1998–2000 | 0.2 | −1.1 |
| *Brazil* | | |
| 1981–90 | 1.6 | −0.4 |
| 1991–2000 | 2.6 | 1.2 |
| 1998–2000 | 1.7 | 0.4 |
| *Colombia* | | |
| 1981–90 | 3.7 | 1.6 |
| 1991–2000 | 2.6 | 0.6 |
| 1998–2000 | −0.3 | −2.1 |
| *Ecuador* | | |
| 1981–90 | 1.7 | 0.9 |
| 1991–2000 | 1.7 | −0.4 |
| 1998–2000 | −1.6 | −3.5 |
| *Mexico* | | |
| 1981–90 | 1.9 | −0.2 |
| 1991–2000 | 3.5 | 1.7 |
| 1998–2000 | 5.2 | 3.6 |
| *Venezuela* | | |
| 1981–90 | −0.7 | −3.2 |
| 1991–2000 | 2 | −0.2 |
| 1998–2000 | −0.8 | −2.8 |

*Source:* ECLAC[18]

The debt has had deleterious effects on the living conditions of popular classes and placed Latin America in ever-increasing hock to transnational finance capital. The Argentine crisis was a harbinger for things to come elsewhere. Argentina's debt climbed from $27 billion in 1980 to $63 billion in 1990, and from there steadily upward to $144 billion by 1998. In this same period, Brazil's debt climbed from $71 billion to $232 billion, and Mexico's from $57 billion to $160 billion. Colombia, Ecuador, Peru, Venezuela and the Central American republics were also heavily indebted relative to their economic size. For Argentina, payment *on the interest alone* ate up 35.4 per cent of export earnings in 1998. For Brazil, the figure was 26.7 per cent; for Colombia, 19.7 per cent; for Ecuador, 21.2 per cent; for Nicaragua, 19.3 per cent; for Peru, 23.7 per cent; and for Venezuela, 15.3 per cent.[19] But the debt has also facilitated internal adjustment and a deeper integration into the global economy and cemented the power of the emergent transnational power bloc in the region.

As Table 6.5 shows, Latin America continued to export annually between 1992 and 1994 an average of $30 billion in profits and interests. 'Growth', therefore, simply represents the continued – and increased – creation of tribute to transnational finance capital. Moreover, in the wake of the Asian meltdown of 1997–98, Latin American countries began the slide towards renewed stagnation. This continuous drainage of surplus from Latin America helps to explain the region's stagnation, declining income and plummeting living standards. The poor have to run faster just to remain in the same place. The social crisis in Latin America thus is not as much a crisis of production as it is of distribution. Inequality is a social relation of unequal power between the dominant and the subordinate, we should recall, and more specifically, the power of the rich locally and globally to dispose of the social product.

Globalisation involves a change in the correlation of class forces worldwide away from nationally organised popular classes and towards the transnational capitalist class and local economic and political elites tied to transnational capital. As the logic of national accumulation is subordinated to that of global accumulation, transnationalised fractions of local dominant groups in Latin America have gained control over states and capitalist institutions in their respective countries. These groups, in-country agents of global capitalism, become integrated organically as local contingents into the transnational elite. This is part of the broader process under globalisation of transnational class formation.[20] Latin America's crisis is part of the crisis of global accumulation, which hit Africa also in the 1980s and finally caught up with the 'miracle economies' of East Asia starting with the currency crises of 1997. Under globalisation, the domestic market has been eliminated as a factor in accumulation. The fact that the domestic market is no longer strategic to accumulation has important implications for class relations and social movements. By removing the domestic market and popular class consumption from the accumulation imperative, restructuring involves the demise of the populist class alliances between broad majorities and nationally based ruling classes that characterised the pre-globalisation model of accumulation.

Regional adjustment in Latin America to the global economy has been effected through the neoliberal programme, which is based on creating the optimal environment for private transnational capital to operate as the putative motor of development and social welfare. And where transnational capital alights is determined by the most overall congenial conditions for accumulation and profit-making. Neoliberal states sought to create the best internal conditions to attract mobile transnational capital, including the provision of cheap labour, depressed and lax working conditions; the elimination of state regulations such as environmental controls; little or no taxation; no insistence on transnational corporate accountability or responsibility to local populations, and so on. In integrating their countries into the global economy, local elites in Latin America, and in particular the transnationalised fractions of these elites that came to power in the 1980s and 1990s, based 'development' on the virtually exclusive criteria of achieving maximum internal profitability as the condition sine qua non for attracting transnational capital. Profitability in this regard rested on the provision of cheap labour and access (often state-subsidised) to the region's copious natural resources and fertile lands. For transnationally oriented elites, successful integration into the global economy is predicated on the erosion of labour's income, withdrawal of the social wage, transfer of the costs of social reproduction from the public sector to individual families, and the suppression of popular political demands.

Hence, in the logic of global capitalism, the cheapening of labour and its social disenfranchisement by the neoliberal state became conditions for 'development'. The very drive by local elites to create conditions to attract transnational capital has been what thrusts Latin American majorities into poverty and inequality. These elites, however, have found that their source of power, privilege and wealth was to follow this path of integration into the global economy. As national elites become integrated into a TCC, a new capital–labour relation is born out of the very logic of regional accumulation based on the provision to the global economy of cheap labour as the region's 'comparative advantage'. The intensified hegemony of transnational capital and new patterns of post-Fordist 'flexible' accumulation in the globalised economy has involved a restructuring of the capital–labour relation in Latin America and worldwide. In this new relation, capital has abandoned reciprocal obligations to labour in the employment contract with the emergence of new post-Fordist 'flexible' regimes of accumulation, which require 'flexible' and 'just in time' labour. And states, with their transmutation from developmentalist to neoliberal, have all but abandoned public obligations to poor and working majorities under the emerging globalised social structure of accumulation.

### New dimensions of inequality

Globalisation has brought about a dramatic sharpening of social inequalities, increased polarisation and the persistence of widespread poverty in Latin America (Table 6.9), reflecting the broader pattern of global social polarisation. Between 1980 and 1990 average per capita income dropped by an unprecedented 11 per cent, so that by 1990 most of the region's inhabitants found that their income had reverted to 1976 levels.[21] Poverty levels also increased throughout the 1980s and 1990s. Between 1980 and 1992, some 60 million new people joined the ranks of the poor. The number of people living in poverty went from 136 million in 1980 to 196 million in 1992, and then to 230 million in 1995, an increase from 41 per cent to 44 per cent, and then to 48 per cent, respectively, of the total population.[22] Most telling is the jump in poverty between 1992 and 1995, since by the end of the 1980s Latin America had resumed growth and attracted a net inflow of capital following the stagnation and decline during much of the decade. In the early 1990s, officials from the international financial agencies began to speak of 'recovery', by which they meant that growth (accumulation) had in most countries resumed. The pattern under globalisation is not merely 'growth without redistribution' but the simultaneous growth of wealth and of poverty as two sides of the same coin.

The contraction of domestic markets, the dismantling of 'uncompetitive' national industry, the growth of the informal economy, revised labour codes directed at making labour 'flexible' and austerity programmes have resulted in the informalisation of the workforce, mass underemployment and unemployment, a compression of real wages and a transfer of income from labour to capital. The accelerated informalisation of the labour market in Latin America has been accompanied by the increase of 'labour flexibility' in what remains of the formal sector, with more frequent use of contract work and the use of contingent labour over permanent employment and collective contracts, with a consequent decline in the role of trade unions in the labour market and of working-class negotiating power. These aspects of the new capital–labour relation reflect trends worldwide. Table 6.10 gives one indication of the stagnation, and often decline, in urban wages.

*Table 6.9* Percentage of population living below $2 per day (poverty) and $1 per day (indigence), selected countries and years

|  | % below $2 | % below $1 |
|---|---|---|
| Argentina (1991) | 25.5 | N/A |
| Brazil (1995) | 43.5 | 23.6 |
| Mexico (1992) | 40 | 14.9 |
| Panama (1989) | 46.2 | 25.6 |
| Colombia (1991) | 21.7 | 7.4 |
| Dominican Republic (1989) | 47.7 | 19.9 |
| Ecuador (1994) | 65.8 | 30.4 |
| Guatemala (1989) | 76.8 | 53.3 |
| Venezuela (1991) | 32.2 | 11.8 |
| Chile (1992) | 38.5 | 15 |
| Nicaragua (1993) | 74.5 | N/A |
| Honduras | 75.7 | N/A |

*Source*: World Bank[23]

*Table 6.10* Annual variation in urban minimum wage, selected countries

|  | 1980 | 1985 | 1990 | 1992 | 1994 | 1996 | 1998 |
|---|---|---|---|---|---|---|---|
| Argentina | 17.3 | −32.5 | −69.1 | −21.4 | 38.0 | −2.0 | −8.0 |
| Bolivia | N/A | −59.6 | −14.7 | −5.0 | 10.3 | −4.0 | 15.0 |
| Brazil | 2.6 | 1.7 | −24.9 | −9.1 | −4.4 | 4.3 | 4.0 |
| Colombia | 2.5 | −3.6 | −2.6 | −1.8 | −1.6 | −7.0 | −1.7 |
| Ecuador | 65.5 | −3.8 | −9.3 | 0.1 | 15.9 | 9.7 | −7.1 |
| Mexico | −6.7 | −1.7 | −10.2 | −5.1 | 0.2 | −9.0 | 0.9 |
| Peru | 23.8 | −12.7 | −6.8 | 0 | 29.6 | 3.2 | 10.9 |
| Uruguay | −4.6 | 5.0 | −11.3 | −2.5 | −11.2 | −3.4 | 3.4 |
| Venezuela | 62.8 | 45.6 | −20.7 | 42.5 | 12.0 | −5.4 | −4.0 |

*Source*: ECLAC[24]

Informality is another central feature of the new capital–labour relation worldwide. In Latin America, there has been an explosion of the informal sector, which has been the only avenue of survival for millions of people thrown out of work by contraction of formal sector employment and by the uprooting of remaining peasant communities by the incursion of capitalist agriculture. But informalisation of work, moreover, is part of the transition from Fordist to flexible employment relations, whereby subcontracted and outsourced labour is organised informally and constitutes an increasing portion of the workforce.[25] National and international data collection agencies reports those in the informal sector as 'employed', despite the highly irregular and unregulated nature of the informal sector, characterised by low levels of productivity, below-poverty (and below legal minimum wage) earnings and instability, usually amounting to underemployment. Four out of every five new jobs in Latin America are in the informal sector.[26] In Mexico, a full 46 per cent of the economically active population was in the informal sector in 2003.[27]

Inequality in Latin America, while high historically, has increased throughout the 1980s and 1990s, as Table 6.11 shows. World Bank data for 18 Latin American countries indicates that the Gini coefficient, which measures income inequality (0 is perfect equality and 1 is perfect inequality) rose from 0.45 in 1980 to 0.50 in 1989.[28] Moreover, the richest 10 per cent of the urban population increased its share of income from 30 to 36 per cent of the total in Argentina from 1980 to 1997; from 39 to 44 per cent in Brazil (1979–96); from 35 to 40 per cent in Colombia (1990–97); from 23 to 27 per cent in Costa Rica (1981–97); from 26 to 34 per cent in Mexico (1984–96); from 29 to 37 per cent in Panama (1979–97); and from 29 to 33 per cent in Paraguay (1981–97).[29]

Table 6.11    Per cent of total household income received by top and bottom quintiles (selected countries)

|  | 1980 | | 1989 | |
|---|---|---|---|---|
|  | 20% bottom | 20% top | 20% bottom | 20% top |
| Argentina | 5.3 | 46.6 | 4.1 | 52.6 |
| Brazil | 2.6 | 64.0 | 2.1 | 67.5 |
| Chile | – | – | 3.7 | 62.9 |
| Colombia | 2.5 | 63.0 | 3.4 | 58.3 |
| Guatemala (1987) | 2.7 | 62.0 (1989) | 2.1 | 63.0 |
| Mexico (1984) | 4.1 | 55.9 | 3.2 | 59.3 |
| Peru (1986) | 6.2 | 49.7 | 5.6 | 50.4 |
| Venezuela (1981) | 5.0 | 47.3 | 4.8 | 49.5 |

Source: World Bank[30]

But income inequality is only one dimension, and often not the most important, of social inequality. Added to income polarisation in the 1980s and 1990s is the dramatic deterioration in social conditions as a result of austerity measures that have drastically reduced and privatised health, education and other social programmes. Popular classes whose social reproduction is dependent on a social wage (public sector) have faced a social crisis, while privileged middle and upper classes become exclusive consumers of social services channelled through private networks. Here we see the need to reconceive development in transnational social rather than geographic terms. Global capitalism generates downward mobility for most at the same time that it opens up new opportunities for some middle-class and professional strata as the redistributive role of the nation-state recedes and as global market forces are less mediated as they mould the prospects for downward and upward mobility.

The escalation of deprivation indicators in Brazil and Mexico, which together account for over half of Latin America's 465 million inhabitants, reveals the process of immiseration that most Latin Americans have experienced under global capitalism. Between 1985 and 1990, the rate of child malnutrition in Brazil, where nearly 48 per cent of the country's 160 million people lived in poverty in 1990,[31] increased from 12.7 to 30.7 per cent of all children.[32] In Mexico, where over 50 per cent of the country's 90 million people were in poverty, the purchasing power of the minimum wage dropped 66 per cent between 1982 and 1991. It was calculated that in the mid-1990s it took 4.8 minimum wages for a family of four to meet essential needs, yet 80 per cent of households earned 2.5 minimum wages or less. As a result malnutrition has spread among the urban and rural poor.[33] In Argentina, meanwhile, unemployment rose steadily in the 1980s and 1990s from 3 per cent in 1980 to 20 per cent in 2001, the number of people in extreme poverty from 200,000 to 5 million and in poverty from 1 million to 14 million, illiteracy increased from 2 per cent to 12 per cent and functional illiteracy from 5 per cent to 32 per cent during this period.[34] In fact, the United Nations Development Programme's Human Development Index (HDI), an aggregate measure of well-being based on life expectancy at birth, educational attainment and standard of living (GDP per capita in purchasing power parity) actually *decreased* for many Latin American countries in the 1990s. With 1.0 the highest score and 0.0 the lowest, the index decreased for the following countries in the 1990s: Argentina, Chile,

Uruguay, Costa Rica, Mexico, Panama, Venezuela, Colombia, Brazil, Peru, Ecuador, Bolivia and Guatemala.[35]

## From social explosions to institutional crises: The fragility of polyarchy

By the late 1970s authoritarianism as the predominant mode of social control in Latin America faced an intractable crisis.[36] On the one hand the authoritarian regimes were besieged by mass popular movements for democracy, human rights and social justice that threatened to bring down the whole elite-based social order along with the dictatorships – as happened in Nicaragua in 1979. This threat from below, combined with the inability of the authoritarian regimes to manage the dislocations and adjustments of globalisation, generated intra-elite conflicts that unravelled the ruling power blocs. This crisis of elite rule was resolved through transitions to *polyarchy* that took place in almost every country in the region during the 1980s and early 1990s. Polyarchy refers to a system in which a small group actually rules, on behalf of capital, and participation in decision-making by the majority is confined to choosing between competing elites in tightly controlled electoral processes.

What transpired in these contested transitions to polyarchy was an effort by transnational dominant groups to reconstitute hegemony through a change in the mode of political domination, from the coercive systems of social control exercised by authoritarian and dictatorial regimes to more consensually based (or at least consensus-seeking) systems of the new polyarchies. Emergent transnationalised fractions of local elites in Latin America, with the structural power of the global economy behind them, as well as the direct political and military intervention of the United States, were able to gain hegemony over democratisation movements and steer the break-up of authoritarianism into polyarchic outcomes. The transitions from authoritarianism to polyarchy in Latin America afforded transnational elites the opportunity to reorganise state institutions and create a more favourable institutional framework for a deepening of neoliberal adjustment. With few exceptions in Latin America, the new polyarchic regimes, staffed by state managers tied to the transnational elite (the new 'modernisers' and 'technocrats') pursued a profound neoliberal transformation. The transnational elite demonstrated a remarkable ability to utilise the structural power of transnational capital over individual countries as a sledgehammer against popular grassroots movements for fundamental change in social structures. Indeed, it is this structural power of global capitalism to impose discipline through the market that (usually) makes unnecessary the all-pervasive coercive forms of political authority exercised by authoritarian regimes.

But it is not at all clear in the early twenty-first century if these fragile polyarchic political systems will be able to absorb the tensions of economic and social crisis without themselves collapsing. State repression organised by polyarchic regimes has been used throughout Latin America to repress protest against neoliberal structural adjustment and has claimed thousands of lives. Almost every Latin American country experienced waves of spontaneous uprisings generally triggered by austerity measures, the formation in the shanty towns of urban poor movements of political protest, and a resurgence of mass peasant movements and land invasions, all outside the formal institutions of the political system, and almost always involving violent clashes between state and paramilitary forces and protesters.[37] The social and economic crisis has given way to expanding institutional quandaries, the breakdown of social control mechanisms and transnational political-military conflict. The revolt in Argentina, the struggle of the landless in Brazil, peasant insurrections in Bolivia, an indigenous uprising in Ecuador, spreading civil war in Colombia, *coups d'état* in Haiti, aborted coups, business strikes and street conflict in Venezuela, and so forth: this was the order of the day in the first few years of the present century.[38]

The region seems to be poised for a new round of US political and military intervention under the guise of wars on 'terrorism' and drugs. US hostility to the populist government of Hugo Chavez in Venezuela, and the apparent political alliance for his removal between Washington and the displaced business class, is of particular significance because Chavez may well represent a new brand of populism that could take hold as desperate elites attempt to regain legitimacy. Remilitarisation under heavy US sponsorship was already well under way by the turn of the century, from the $1.3 billion Plan Colombia, to the sale by Washington of advanced fighter jets to Chile's military, the installation of a US military base in Ecuador, the large-scale provision of arms, counterinsurgency equipment and 'anti-terrorism' training programmes to Mexico, new multilateral intervention mechanisms and a new round throughout the hemisphere of joint US–Latin American military exercises and training programmes.[39] It is worth noting that one or another of the hemisphere's governments have labelled as 'terrorist' the Landless Workers Movement of Brazil, the Zapatistas of Mexico, the FARC and the ELN guerrilla movements of Colombia, the indigenous movement in Ecuador, the Farabundo

Marti National Liberation Front in El Salvador, the Sandinistas in Nicaragua and other legitimate resistance movements. The US Central Intelligence Agency identified in 2002 as 'a new challenge to internal security' the indigenous movement that, 510 years after the Conquest began, had spread throughout the hemisphere and has often been at the forefront of popular mobilisation.[40] Colombia may be the most likely epicentre of direct US intervention and a region-wide counterinsurgency war in South America.

This panorama suggests that the state structures that have been set up (and continuously modified) to protect dominant interests are now decomposing, possibly beyond repair. A long period of political decay and institutional instability is likely. But we should not lose sight of the structural underpinning of expanding institutional crises and recall the fundamental incompatibility of democracy with global capitalism. The model of capitalist development by insertion into new global circuits of accumulation does not require an inclusionary social base. Socio-economic exclusion is immanent to the model since accumulation does not depend on a domestic market or internal social reproduction. This is a fundamental structural contradiction between the globalisation model of accumulation and the effort to maintain polyarchic political systems that require the hegemonic incorporation of a social base. The neoliberal model generates social conditions and political tensions – inequality, polarisation, impoverishment, marginality – conducive to a breakdown of polyarchy. This is the fundamental contradiction between the class function of the neoliberal states and their legitimation function.

### Resistance to globalisation in Latin America

For poor majorities a resolution to the crisis requires a radical redistribution of wealth and power, predicated on the construction of more authentic democratic structures that allow for popular control over local and transnational state institutions. However, to what extent social movements and oppositional forces can improve their lot by forcing concessions from global capital and its regional contingents is relative, and should not be counterposed to revolutionary transformation.

As old corporatist structures crack, new oppositional forces and forms of resistance have spread – social movements of workers, women, environmentalists, students, peasants, indigenous, racial and ethnic minorities, community associations of the urban poor. These popular forces helped protagonise a new progressive electoral politics in the early twenty-first century, including the election of Luis Ignacio da Silva (Lula) and the Workers Party (PT) in Brazil (2002), Lucio Gutierrez in Ecuador (2003) with the backing of that country's indigenous movement, the near victory at the polls of the indigenous leader and socialist Evo Morales in Bolivia (2002), and the resilience in office in the face of elite destabilisation campaigns of the government of Hugo Chavez in Venezuela, elected in 1999. These developments suggest that new political space has opened up in Latin America as the neoliberal elite has lost legitimacy.

These popular electoral victories symbolised the end of the reigning neoliberal order but also the limits of parliamentary changes in the era of global capitalism. The case of Brazil is indicative. Lula, denied the presidency in three previous electoral contests but victorious in 2002, took the vote only after his wing of the PT moved sharply towards the political centre. He forged a social base among middle-class voters and won over centrist and even conservative political forces that did not endorse a left-wing programme yet were unwilling to tolerate further neoliberal fallout. The real power here was that of transnational finance capital. Lula promised not to default on the country's foreign debt and to maintain the previous government's adjustment policies. His 2003 budget slashed health and educational programmes in order to comply with IMF dictates that the government maintain a fiscal surplus.[41] What may have been emerging was a elected left populist bloc in the region committed to mild redistributive programmes respectful of prevailing property relations and unwilling to challenge the global capitalist order. Many leftist parties, even when they sustain an anti-neoliberal discourse, have in their practice abdicated earlier programmes of fundamental structural change in the social order itself.

But if transnational capital is able to emasculate radical programmes through structural pressures exerted by the global economy, the popular electoral victories also involved the mobilisation of new collective subjects, the mass social movements, that are unlikely to be cowed by the transnational elite. The demise of neoliberal hegemony unleashes social forces that neither the established order nor left electoral regimes can contain. Events in Venezuela from Chavez's election in 1999 into 2003 may presage a pattern in which the electoral victory of popular candidates sparks heightened political mobilisation and social struggles that may move events in unforeseen directions. The question may be less how much local populism can accomplish in the age of globalisation than how it may be converted into a transborder globalisation from below.

The dominant groups in Latin America reconstituted and consolidated their control over *political society* in the late twentieth century but the new round of popular class mobilisation in the 1990s and early twenty-first century pointed to their inability to sustain hegemony in *civil society*. The renewal of protagonism demonstrated by subordinate groups at the grassroots level has been outside state structures and largely independent of organised left parties. Grassroots social movements have flourished in civil society at a time when the organised left operating in political society has been unable to articulate a counter-hegemonic alternative despite its continued vitality. The failure of the left to protagonise a process of structural change from political society helped shift the locus of conflict more fully to civil society. Latin America seemed to move in the 1990s to a 'war of position' between contending social forces in the light of subordinate groups' failure to win a 'war of manoeuvre' through revolutionary upheaval and the limits to 'power from above'. But as crises of legitimacy, perpetual instability and the impending breakdown of state institutions spread rapidly throughout Latin America in the early twenty-first century conditions seemed to be opening up for a renovated war of manoeuvre under the novel circumstances of the global economy and society.

## CONCLUSIONS: WHITHER THE EMPIRE OF GLOBAL CAPITAL?

Under the emergent global social structure of accumulation the tendency is towards a separation of accumulation from social reproduction. The social reproduction of labour becomes less important for accumulation as the output of each nation and region is exported to the global level. At the aggregate level of the world economy this means an overall system-wide contraction in demand simultaneous to a system-wide expansion of supply. This is the classic overproduction or underconsumption contradiction, the 'realisation' problem, now manifest in novel ways under global capitalism. Zones of high absorption become the pillars of the system, or the 'markets of last resort', in times of economic difficulty, such as the United States in the mid, and especially the late, 1990s, following the 1997 Asian financial crisis (the US current account deficit increased from $47.7 billion in 1992 to $420 billion by the end of 2000[42]). The markets of last resort may help fuel world economic growth even as many regions experience stagnation and crisis. But at the *systemic* level, the reproduction of capital remains dependent on that of labour, as a matter of course, and this represents a contradiction internal to the global capitalist system. Hence, the contradictions that present themselves now in any one zone of the global system, such as in Latin America, are internal to (global) capitalism rather than between capitalism and atavistic elements. The most fundamental social contradiction in Latin America *and* in global society, is this: the model of polarised (flexible) accumulation does not resolve the social contradictions of capitalism, and cannot, and moreover tends to aggravate them. What countervailing tendencies may continue to offset the consequences of this contradiction was not clear in the early years of the present century.

## Global polarisation and the crisis of social reproduction

Under globalisation, national states have progressively lost the ability to capture and redirect surpluses through interventionist mechanisms that were viable in the nation-state phase of capitalism. In redefining the phase of distribution in the accumulation of capital in relation to nation-states, globalisation undermines the distinct redistributive and other mechanisms that acted in earlier epochs to offset the inherent tendency within capitalism towards polarisation. National cohesion becomes fragmented as the locus of social reproduction shifts from the nation-state to global space where market forces are unmediated. The result has been a rapid process of global social polarisation and a crisis of social reproduction. In most countries, the average number of people who have been integrated into the global marketplace and are becoming 'global consumers' has increased rapidly in recent decades. However, it is also true that the absolute numbers of the impoverished – of the destitute and near destitute – have been increasing rapidly and the gap between the rich and the poor in global society has been widening since the 1970s (Tables 6.12 and 6.13 draw on different sources to indicate the widening gap). There has been growing debate on how to measure global inequality, but the growth of inequality itself is not seriously disputed, or is its linkage to globalisation.[43] Broad swaths of humanity have experienced absolute downward mobility. While global per capita income tripled over the period 1960–94, there were over 100 countries in the 1990s with per capita incomes lower than in the 1980s, or in some cases, lower than in the 1970s and 1960s.[44] Expanding poverty, inequality, marginality and deprivation are the dark underside of the global capitalist cornucopia so celebrated by the transnational elite.

Table 6.12    Shares of world income 1965–90

| | Population percent of total world income | | | |
| | 1965 | 1970 | 1980 | 1990 |
|---|---|---|---|---|
| Poorest 20% | 2.3 | 2.2 | 1.7 | 1.4 |
| Second 20% | 2.9 | 2.8 | 2.2 | 1.8 |
| Third 20% | 4.2 | 3.9 | 3.5 | 2.1 |
| Fourth 20% | 21.2 | 21.3 | 18.3 | 11.3 |
| Richest 20% | 69.5 | 70.0 | 75.4 | 83.4 |

Source: Korzeniewicz and Moran (1997)[45]

Table 6.13    Global income distribution, 1988 and 1993

| | Population percentage of world income | | |
| | 1988 | 1993 | Difference 1988–93 |
|---|---|---|---|
| Top 1% | 9.3 | 9.5 | 0.2 |
| Top 5% | 31.2 | 33.7 | 2.5 |
| Top 10% | 46.9 | 50.8 | 3.9 |
| Bottom 10% | 0.9 | 0.8 | −0.1 |
| Bottom 20% | 2.3 | 2.0 | −0.3 |
| Bottom 50% | 9.6 | 8.5 | −1.1 |
| Bottom 75% | 25.9 | 22.3 | −3.6 |
| Bottom 85% | 41.0 | 37.1 | −3.9 |

Source: Milanovic (1999)[46]

As core and periphery come to denote social location rather than geography, affluence in global society is coming to rest on a peripheral social sector that is not necessarily spatially concentrated. Those who have the equivalent of US $5,000 personal income are considered part of the world of 'consumers'. In the 1990s, for the first time in history, absolute numbers of these in the Third World surpassed the First World.[47] There were in 2000 as many as 200 million middle-class Indians, by some measures a middle class larger than that in the United States. India still has many more poor people but polarisation *across* national and regional lines is clearly increasing in sociological importance relative to polarisation *within* nations and regions.

On the one hand, transnationally oriented capitalists and new global middle classes in Latin America and around the world are part of the new global capitalist historical bloc. Latin American and other transnational investors, as they become integrated into globalised circuits, appropriate surpluses generated by Latin American workers and by workers elsewhere in the global economy, from those in Los Angeles to Tokyo, to those in Milan, London, Johannesburg and elsewhere. In Argentina, Mexico, Chile and other Latin American countries local investors joined foreign capital in appropriating public assets as they were privatised. The state has engaged in a pattern of assuming the burden of private sector debt, in effect socialising on an ongoing basis the debt accumulated by private capital. Numerous nodes allow transnational class groups to appropriate the wealth that flows through global financial circuits. The physical existence of these groups in a particular territory is less important than their deterritorialised class-relational existence in the global capitalist system.

The case of Argentina is instructive. Local financial investors were able to turn their Argentine pesos into dollar holdings and convert their private debts into public debt. This was one of many such novel mechanisms through which surpluses are appropriated. Argentine capitalists operated through global financial circuits to appropriate surpluses generated by Argentine labour. In Joseph Halevi's observation:

> In essence, during the last twenty years, the Argentine population has been subject, in sequence, to the following mechanism. The state takes upon itself the burden of the private external debt. The private sector keeps running up additional debt, while the state sells out its public activities through privatization policies, thereby generating profits (rents) for the private corporations whether national or international. The state then unloads the burden of debt onto the whole population, especially the working population.

To this must be added, he goes on to note,

> the export of capital engaged in by the Argentine capital-possessing classes ... The class based connection between international and local finance capital can be seen from the fact that the entire adjustment of the external debt burden was imposed on the real economy, while capital was enticed with promises of easy gains through privatizations, monopolistic rates indexed to the dollar in

the event of devaluation (in utilities for example), and the freedom to exit the country quickly.[48]

On the other hand, transnationally oriented elites and middle strata face an expansive global proletariat. Global inequalities lead to a new 'politics of exclusion' wherever they are found, in which the problem of social control becomes paramount. There is a shift from the social welfare state to the social control (police) state, replete with the dramatic expansion of public and private security forces, the mass incarceration of the excluded population (disproportionately minorities), new forms of social apartheid maintained through complex social control technologies, repressive anti-immigration legislation, and so on. Global polarisation brings with it increasing residential segregation of the rich, protected by armies of private security guards and electronic surveillance, from the cities of Latin America to those of the United States, Europe, Asia and elsewhere. These 'gated communities', variously referred to as 'enclaves', 'citadels' and 'fortresses', are 'part of the trend toward exercising physical and social means of territorial control', the natural products of global inequalities, and have been spreading to all parts of the world.[49]

But gated communities are no guarantee of security for the affluent. The September 11, 2001 attack on the World Trade Center in New York underscored the rise of new modalities of conflict between the weak and the powerful in global society. In the past, the most exploited, oppressed, and dispossessed sectors of humanity, the colonised, were forced by material and spatial reality to limit their resistance to the direct sites of colonial control; they were limited to facing colonisers and imperialists on their own lands. Now acts of rebellion can be waged around the world regardless of space. The spatial separation of the oppressors from the oppressed as epitomised in the old colonial system is vanishing. Global capitalism is too porous for spatial containment. Just as progressive resistance to the depredations of global capitalism – Seattle, Porto Alegre, etc. – is less space-bound and more transnational than in the past, so too is reactionary resistance. In the wake of the attack on the World Trade Center the transnational elite, led by the US state, seemed to regain the offensive momentarily. The 'war on terrorism' provided a convenient cover for the transnational elite to extend its drive to consolidate and defend the project of capitalist globalisation with a new and terrifying coercive dimension. I do not think it an overstatement to suggest that the powers-that-be in the global capitalist order are organising and institutionalising a global police state. But this *new war order* could not resolve the tensions and contradictions of the global capitalist system, and in fact was likely to aggravate them.

## From IMF riots to organised resistance

Giovanni Arrighi has noted that there has always been a considerable time lag in terms of working class response to capital restructuring.[50] Globalisation acted at first as a centripetal force for transnationally oriented elites and as a centrifugal force for popular classes around the world. Working classes have been fragmented by restructuring. Intense competition forced on these classes in each nation debilitated collective action. Sub-processes such as transnational migration and the diffusion of consumer culture provided escape valves that relieved pressure on the system. The popular sectors were *brought together* in earlier periods of world capitalism as inter-subjectivities and mounted collective challenges to the social order. To the extent that the old subjectivities were fragmented and dispersed and new subjectivities had not yet coalesced, capitalist globalisation blunted the collective political protagonism of the popular classes.

The mass social dislocation, evaporating social protection measures, declining real opportunities and spiralling poverty that neoliberalism generated sparked widespread yet often spontaneous and unorganised resistance around the world in the 1980s and 1990s, as epitomised in 'IMF food riots'. But everywhere there were also organised resistance movements, ranging from the Zapatistas in Mexico to the Assembly of the Poor in Thailand, Brazil's Landless People's Movement, India's National Alliance of People's Movements, the Korean Confederation of Trade Unions, and the National Confederation of Indigenous Organizations of Ecuador. At a certain point in the 1990s popular resistance forces formed a critical mass, coalescing around an agenda for social justice, or 'anti-globalisation movement'. By the turn of the century the transnational elite had been placed on the defensive and a crisis of the system's legitimacy began to develop, as symbolised by the creation of the World Social Forum (WSF) in Porto Alegre, Brazil, under the banner 'Another World is Possible'.

Fundamental change in a social order becomes possible when an organic crisis occurs. An organic crisis is one in which the system faces a structural (objective) crisis and *also* a crisis of legitimacy or hegemony (subjective). An organic crisis is not enough to bring about fundamental, progressive change in a social order (indeed, it has in the past led to social breakdown, authoritarianism and fascism). A popular or revolutionary outcome to an organic crisis also requires that there be a viable alternative that is in hegemonic ascendance, that is, an alternative to the existing order that is viable and that is seen as viable and preferable by a majority of society. Global capitalism was not experiencing an organic crisis in the early twenty-first century. Nonetheless, I believe the prospects that such a crisis could develop were more palpably on the horizon at the turn of the century than at any time since perhaps 1968.

Seen from the viewpoint of capital, neoliberalism resolved a series of problems in the accumulation process that had built up in the epoch of Keynesian capitalism but fuelled new crises of overaccumulation and legitimacy. The model is not sustainable socially or politically. Its coming demise may well turn out to be the end of Act I and the opening of Act II in the restructuring crisis that began in the 1970s. As in all historic processes, this act is unscripted. The next step may be a reassertion of productive over financial capital in the global economy and a global redistributive project, just as it may be the rise of a global fascism founded on military spending and wars to contain the downtrodden and the unrepented. Historical outcomes are always open-ended, subject to contingency and to being pushed in new and unforeseen directions. The crisis in no way guarantees the ascendancy of popular oppositional forces. It would be foolish to predict with any conviction the outcome of the looming crisis of global capitalism.

We can note, however, that the ubiquitous search for an alternative economic model is probably the major shared and to some extent unifying agenda of left political parties and popular social movements around the world. The Washington Consensus, it is broadly recognised, had cracked by 2000.[51] But what may replace the neoliberal order, in Latin America and in global society, not only depends on the struggle to *oppose* the neoliberal order but is also inseparable from the struggle to develop a viable alternative and to *impose* that alternative. Precisely because the neoliberal phase of global capitalism may be coming to a close, resistance must move beyond the critique of neoliberalism. The problem of the particular neoliberal model is in the end symptomatic of the *systemic* problem of global capitalism.

Varying degrees of ungovernability and crises of legitimacy characterise country after country in Latin America and in many parts of global society as the dominant groups find it increasingly difficult to maintain governability and assure social reproduction. The crisis and eventual collapse of neoliberalism may create the conditions favourable to winning state power and promoting an alternative. It is not clear, however, how effective national alternatives can be in transforming social structures, given the ability of transnational capital to utilise its structural power to impose its project even over states that are captured by forces adverse to that project. The rise of a global justice movement is the clearest example that popular and oppositional forces had, in fact, begun to transnationalise in the 1990s, moving to create alliances, networks and organisations that transcend national and even regional borders. The real prospects for counter-hegemonic social change in the age of globalisation is a globalisation-from-below movement that seeks to challenge the power of the global elite by accumulating counter-hegemonic forces beyond national and regional borders; to challenge that power from within an expanding transnational civil society and to convert the transnational state into contested terrain.

## NOTES

1.  See, *inter alia*, Michel Aglietta (1979) *A Theory of Capitalist Regulation* (London: Verso); David M. Kotz, Terrence McDonough and Michael Reich (eds) (1994) *Social Structures of Accumulation: The political economy of growth and crisis* (Cambridge: Cambridge University Press); Giovanni Arrighi (1994) *The Long Twentieth Century* (London: Verso); David Harvey (1982) *The Limits to Capital* (Chicago: University of Chicago Press).
2.  See, e.g., Friedrich Hayek (1972) *New Studies in Philosophy, Politics, Economics and the History of Ideas* (Chicago: University of Chicago Press); Milton Friedman (1962) *Capitalism and Freedom* (Chicago: University of Chicago Press); Friedman (1974) *Monetary Correction* (London: Institute of Economic Affairs).
3.  See John Williamson (1993) 'Democracy and the "Washington Consensus"', *World Development*, vol. 21, no. 8, pp1329–36; Williamson (ed.) (1990) *Latin American Adjustment: How much has happened?* (Washington, DC: Institute for International Economics).
4.  The literature on globalisation and global political economy is too vast to reference here. For a collection surveying recent theoretical directions, see Ronen Palan (ed.) (2000), *Global Political Economy: Contemporary theories* (London: Routledge). On my theoretical propositions and empirical studies on globalisation, see, *inter alia*, *A Theory of Global Capitalism: Transnational production, transnational classes, and the rise of a transnational state* (Baltimore: Johns Hopkins University Press, forthcoming); *Transnational Conflicts: Central America, social change and globalization* (London: Verso, in press); *Promoting Polyarchy: Globalization, U.S. intervention, and hegemony* (Cambridge: Cambridge University Press, 1996); 'Globalisation: Nine Theses of Our Epoch', *Race and Class*, vol.

18, no. 2 (1996), pp13–31; 'Social Theory and Globalization: The rise of a transnational state', *Theory and Society*, vol. 30, no. 2 (2001), pp157–200; 'The Transnational Capitalist Class and the Transnational State', in Wilma A. Dunaway (2003) (ed.) *New Theoretical Directions for the 21st Century World-System* (Westport, CT: Greenwood Press).

5. The notion of a TCC is certainly not new nor exclusively my own. See, e.g., Leslie Sklair (2002) *The Transnational Capitalist Class* (London: Blackwell). See Chapter 2 in Robinson, *A Theory of Global Capitalism*, for a review of the literature on the transnationalisation of capitalists.

6. On this point, see William I. Robinson 'From State Hegemonies to Transnational Hegemony: A Global Capitalism Approach', forthcoming in Tom Reifer, *Hegemony, Globalization and Antisystemic Movements*.

7. On this point, see William I. Robinson (2002) 'Remapping Development in Light of Globalization: From a territorial to a social cartography', *Third World Quarterly*.

8. Neoliberalism is the specific mechanism that adjusts national and regional economies to the global economy by creating the conditions, including an appropriate macroeconomic and policy environment, the legal framework, and so on, for internal productive reorganisation and insertion into the global economy. These themes are analysed in Robinson, 'Social Theory and Globalization', William I. Robinson (2001) 'Transnational Processes, Development Studies, and Changing Social Hierarchies in the World System: A Central American case study', *Third World Quarterly*, vol. 22, no. 4, pp529–63. For analysis of neoliberal adjustment in Latin America, see also Duncan Green (1995) *Silent Revolutions: The rise of market economics in Latin America* (London: Cassell/Latin America Bureau). See also Michel Chossudovsky (1997) *The Globalization of Poverty: Impacts of IMF and World Bank reforms* (London: Zed).

9. On this point, see Green, *Silent Revolutions*; William I. Robinson (1999) 'Latin America in the Age of Inequality: Confronting the new utopia', *International Studies Review*, vol. 1, no. 3, pp41–67.

10. See James A. Wilkie (ed.) (1995) *Statistical Abstracts for Latin America* (SALA) (Los Angeles: UCLA Latin American Center Publications, vol. 31).

11. World Bank, *World Development Indicators 2001*, Table 6.1, p322.

12. World Bank, *World Development Report* (Washington, DC and New York: World Bank and Oxford University Press), 1991 and 1992 reports, and 2001 and 2002 reports.

13. Compiled from ECLAC (2000), *Preliminary Overview of the Economies of Latin America and the Caribbean*, Table A-18, p104, and *Economic Survey for Latin America and the Caribbean, 2000–01*, Table IV.1, p80, and *Preliminary Overview*, 2002, Table A-18, p122.

14. For example, of $91 billion that flowed into Mexico between 1990 and 1993, $61 billion was in such financial portfolio investment and only $16.6 billion was in direct investment. See Carlos Marichal (1997) 'The Vicious Cycles of Mexican Debt', *NACLA Report on the Americas* (vol. xxxi, no. 3, Nov/Dec., p28). For discussion, see also Valpy Fitzgerald (1998) 'Asia's Financial Crisis: What it can teach us', *ENVIO* (vol. 17, No. 200, March, pp33–38); Henry Veltmeyer (1997) 'Latin America in

the New World Order', *The Canadian Journal of Sociology* (vol. 22, no. 2, pp197–242).

15. ECLAC, *Preliminary Overview*, Tables A-13, p99, A-14, p100, and ECLAC, 1998–1999, Table III.1, p50.

16. See ECLAC, *Preliminary Overview*, 2002, Table A-2, p108.

17. ECLAC, as cited in 'Wanted: A new regional agenda for economic growth', *The Economist*, 26 April 2003, p27 (article on pp27–9).

18. ECLAC, *Preliminary Overview*, Table A-1, p85.

19. For this data, see ECLAC, *Economic Survey, 1998–1999*, Table VII.11, p114.

20. Space constraints limit discussion, but note that the principal contradiction among dominant classes worldwide under globalisation is between national-based fractions of capital and transnational fractions. This contradiction has in fact become politicised in many countries of Latin America and the world, and helps to explain many visible conjunctural disputes among ruling classes and states within and between countries. See William I. Robinson and Jerry Harris (2000), 'Towards a Global Ruling Class?: Globalization and the transnational capitalist class', *Science and Society*, vol. 64, no. 1, pp11–54; Robinson, 'Social Theory and Globalization'.

21. See World Bank (1997), *Poverty and Income Distribution in Latin America: The Story of the 1980s* (Washington, DC: World Bank).

22. See Comision Economica para America Latina (CEPAL), *Panorama Social de America Latina* (Santiago, Chile: CEPAL/United Nations, various reports).

23. World Bank, *World Development Indicators* (1998), Table 2.7.

24. ECLAC, *Social Panorama*, various years.

25. For detailed discussion on the informalisation of work in Central America, see Robinson, *Transnational Conflicts: Central America, social change and globalization*.

26. 'Great reforms, nice growth, but where are the jobs?', *The Economist*, 21 March 1998, pp37–8.

27. 'Study Shows Significant Growth in Informal Economy Since Early 2001', *Sourcemex*, Latin America Data Base, University of New Mexico, vol. 13, no. 10, 13 March 2002.

28. World Bank (1997), *Poverty*.

29. See ECLAC, *Social Panorama of Latin America 1998*, Table 17.

30. World Bank (1997), *Poverty*.

31. United Nations Development Programme (UNDP) (1995), *Human Development Report 1995* (New York: Oxford University Press/UNDP).

32. World Bank (1997), *Poverty*.

33. See David Barkin, Irene Ortiz and Fred Rosen (1997), 'Globalization and Resistance: The remaking of Mexico', *NACLA Report on the Americas* (vol. XXX, no. 4, Jan/Feb., pp14–27).

34. See Carlos Gabetta (2002) 'Argentina: IMF show state revolts', *Le Monde Diplomatique*, 12 January, retrieved on 16 January 2002 from www. mondediplo.com/2002/01/12argentina.

35. See UN *Human Development Report, 2000*, Table 1, p7.

36. For detailed discussion of the issued raised in this section, see William I. Robinson, *Promoting Polyarchy: Globalization, U.S. intervention, and hegemony*; Robinson, 'Promoting Capitalist Polyarchy: The case of Latin America', in Michael Cox, G. John Ikenberry and Takashi Inoguchi (2000), *American Democracy Promotion: Impulses, strategies, and impacts* (New York: Oxford University Press).

37. See Green, *Silent Revolutions*; John Walton and David Seddon (1994), *Free Markets and Food Riots: The politics of global adjustment* (Oxford: Blackwell).

38. See, *inter alia*, various contributions in *NACLA Report on the Americas*, vol. XXXVI, no. 1, July/August 2002, issue titled 'Crisis in the Americas'.

39. For discussion, see Janette Habel (2002) 'U.S. Demands a Secure, Compliant Hemisphere', *Le Monde Diplomatique*,' 16 January retrieved on 18 January 2002 from english@monde-diplomatique.fr.

40. Ibid.

41. On Brazil, see 'Make or Break: A Survey of Brazil', special section, pp1–16, after p54, in *The Economist*, 22 February 2003.

42. Frederic Clairmont (2001) 'USA: The making of the crisis', *Third World Resurgence*, Jan.–Feb., p46.

43. For discussion, see, *inter alia*, Jan Nederveen Pieterse (2002) 'Global Inequality: Bringing politics back in', *Third World Quarterly*, vol. 23, no. 6, pp1023–46; Sanjay G. Reddy and Thomas W. Pogge (2002) 'How *Not* to Count The Poor', retrieved from the Internet, at www.socialanalysis.org, on 15 July 2002; Giovanni Andrea Cornia and Julius Court (2001), 'Inequality, Growth and Poverty in the Era of Liberalization and Globalization', *Policy Brief No. 4* (Helsinki: The United Nations University, World Institute for Development Economics Research).

44. UNDP, as cited in Peter Stalker (2000) *Workers Without Frontiers: The impact of globalization on international migration* (Boulder: Lynne Rienner), p139.

45. Roberto Patricio Korzeniewicz and Timothy Patrick Moran (1997) 'World Economic Trends in the Distribution of Income, 1965–1992', *American Journal of Sociology*, vol. 102, no. 4, January.

46. Branko Milanovic 'True World Income Distribution, 1988 and 1993: First calculation based on household surveys alone', World Bank Research Paper, reproduced in Marc Lee (2002) 'The Global Divide: Inequality in the world economy,' *Behind the Numbers: Economic Facts, Figures and Analysis*, vol. 4, no. 2, 18 April, Canadian Centre for Policy Alternatives.

47. Sklair, *The Transnational Capitalist Class*, p57.

48. Joseph Halevi (2002) 'The Argentine Crisis', *Monthly Review*, vol. 53, no. 11, April, pp18, 21.

49. See, *inter alia*, on US gated communities, Edward J. Blakely and Mary Gail Snyder (1997) *Fortress America: Gated Communities in the United States* (Washington, DC: Brookings and Cambridge, MA: Lincoln Institute of Land Policy) [citation from p30]. On the phenomenon in Istanbul, see A. Bartu (1999) 'Redefining the Public Sphere through Fortified Enclaves: A view from Istanbul', WALD International Conference, Istanbul, 1999; in Bangalore, see A. King (1999) 'Suburb/Ethnoburb/Globurg: Framing transnational urban space in Asia', WALD International Conference,

Istanbul, 1999; on Los Angeles, Mike Davis (1999) *Ecology of Fear: Los Angeles and the imagination of disaster* (New York: Metropolitan Books).

50. Giovanni Arrighi, 'Workers of the World at Century's End', *Review*, vol. 19, no. 3, p348.

51. See, e.g., Robin Broad and Richard Cavanagh (2003) 'The Death of the Washington Consensus?,' in Broad (ed.), *Global Backlash: Citizen initiatives for a just world economy* (Lanham: Rowman and Littlefield). Revealingly, John Williamson, who had first coined the term 'Washington Consensus' (see note 3), and former Peruvian economy minister Pedro-Pablo Kuczynksi co-authored a report in 2003, 'After the Washington Consensus: Restarting growth and reform in Latin America' (Washington, DC: Institute for International Economics), in which he argued that the way forward was to 'complete, correct, and complement the reforms of a decade ago' (as cited in *The Economist*, 'Wanted: a New Regional Agenda', p29). He and Kuczynksi went on to recommend a series of 'crisis proofing' measures, which could be taken as the transnational elite's blueprint for a new phase of adjustment in the region. Among these measures were further trade liberalisation, selective controls on capital inflows (but not outflows), new fiscal reforms, further flexibilisation of the labour market (including 'reforms to severance pay and ancillary benefits, to reduce payroll taxes'), a set of institutional reforms (including improved bank supervision, bankruptcy laws, and tax reforms to close loopholes).

# 7
# Facing Global Apartheid

*Patrick Bond*

'South Africa is what she is today because, driven by the spirit of human and international solidarity, you, the peoples of the world, took a stand and said that apartheid in South Africa will not pass!' With these words, Thabo Mbeki welcomed dignitaries to the World Summit on Sustainable Development in August 2002: 'Our common and decisive victory against domestic apartheid confirms that you, the peoples of the world, have both the responsibility and the possibility to achieve a decisive victory against global apartheid.'[1]

In this chapter, I address some perpetual tasks to help assure that at least my own compass is pointing to the left: renewing an analysis of the problem of imperialism that is broadly consistent with Freeman (this volume); tracking indicators of growing momentum and ideological maturity within, specifically, the African left; enquiring into the most appropriate scale politics for resistance; and updating the ways in which new opportunities are opening in constructive areas of struggle. The people I turn to for encouragement are not only the usual suspects – independent leftist activists, organisers and intellectuals – but also veterans of conservative institutions: Cape Town's Anglican Archbishop Njongonkulu Ndungane and even former World Bankers who have seen the light. More durably, to root the work in political-economic theory, I mainly rely upon Rosa Luxemburg and contemporary writers in her tradition. Though best known as a German revolutionary killed by social-democratic competitors in 1919, Luxemburg's intellectual work was stellar (even if flawed in some areas). She played a central role in interpreting an earlier version of global apartheid – which she and her contemporaries (Lenin, Trotsky, Bukharin, Hilferding, Bernstein, Bauer) simply called 'imperialism'.[2]

To begin, however, consider the array of global forces that we are presented with. At least five categories that describe ideological positions have emerged and solidified since the late 1990s, and their beliefs, contradictions, institutions and leading personalities remain relatively coherent. I summarise them in the tables at the end of this chapter. They are:

- global justice movements
- Third World nationalism
- the post-Washington Consensus
- the Washington Consensus, and
- the resurgent right wing.

The five currents are recognisable by:

- their political-economic *agenda*
- leading *institutions*
- internal *disputes*, and
- some exemplary public *proponents*.

The tables are self-explanatory, although several obvious caveats apply, not least of which is the highly subjective snapshot nature of such an exercise. The ideological currents are rough approximations, sometimes proudly worn as labels, sometimes not. Many individuals move not merely rhetorically, but also substantively, from one camp to another (e.g. Joe Stiglitz has moved left over time; Lula has moved right). Some, like Thabo Mbeki, are in more than one camp at once, and their posture depends in part upon their 'scale' of politics (international, continental, national or local).

### A NEW POLITICAL ECONOMY AND GEOPOLITICS OF IMPERIALISM?

How might we come to grips with the profound challenge of theorising and resisting global economic oppression, based in part upon this sort of snapshot mapping of ideology? What other tools are required to assess the deeper processes that structure the power relations that systematically generate inequality? Luxemburg considered the polarisation intrinsic within global development to be uneven and combined, in the first instance, *functional*. Yet it was also ultimately contradictory, as she insisted in her book *Accumulation of Capital*, because of

the deep and fundamental antagonism between the capacity to consume and the capacity to produce in a capitalist society, a conflict resulting from the very accumulation of capital which periodically bursts out in crises and spurs capital on to a continual extension of the market.[3]

Luxemburg's thesis regarding the power relationships responsible for global uneven development was straightforward.

> Capital cannot accumulate without the aid of non-capitalist organisations, nor, on the other hand, can it tolerate their continued existence side by side with itself. Only the continuous and progressive disintegration of non-capitalist organisations makes accumulation of capital possible. The relations between capitalism and the non-capitalist modes of production start making their appearance on the international stage. Its predominant methods are colonial policy, an international loan system – a policy of spheres of interest – and war. Force, fraud, oppression, looting are openly displayed without any attempt at concealment, and it requires an effort to discover within this tangle of political violence and contests of power the stern laws of the economic process.[4]

This is a fine description, and immediately alerts us to similarities between early twentieth and early twenty-first-century global apartheid. Today, the international stage offers us views of a new colonial policy (HIPC, PRSPs, the New Partnership for Africa's Development, donor aid, the Pentagon and all the other means Washington and its allies deploy to maintain control). Today, we still suffer an international loan system that corresponds to spheres of interest writ large (not merely through banking relations on colonial-geographical lines). Today, there are persistent, periodic wars, in Africa and around the world, which reflect the tensions associated with capitalist crisis, inter-imperialist rivalry and barbarism.

We need continual reminding of earlier debates in the same spirit, prior to reviewing opportunities at the global scale, and finally returning to local ways that people can make a difference in the fight against global apartheid. A grassroots 'anti-capitalism' is indeed emerging and linking across countries and continents, to change power relations and more successfully fight a mode of capital accumulation that has degenerated into untenable capital accumulation via, in Luxemburg's word, 'appropriation'. For Luxemburg, as for many contemporary critics, capitalist crisis tendencies were translated into an aggressive, systematic geopolitical process, characterised by 'oppressive taxation, war, or squandering and monopolisation of the nation's land, and thus belongs to the spheres of political power and criminal law no less than with economics'.[5]

If diverse forms of underdevelopment are integrated within the mode of production and reproduction, how is this condition managed by international economic managers? David Harvey's answer has much that applies to Africa today:

> A closer look at Marx's description of primitive accumulation reveals a wide range of processes. These include the commodification and privatisation of land and the forceful expulsion of peasant populations; conversion of various forms of property rights (common, collective, state, etc.) into exclusive private property rights; suppression of rights to the commons; commodification of labor power and the suppression of alternative (indigenous) forms of production and consumption; colonial, neocolonial and imperial processes of appropriation of assets (including natural resources); monetisation of exchange and taxation (particularly of land); slave trade; and usury, the national debt and ultimately the credit system as radical means of primitive accumulation.[6]

For Harvey, some of the most effective vehicles for capital accumulation via appropriation (or his phrase, 'dispossession') are financial:

> The credit system and finance capital have, as Lenin, Hilferding and Luxemburg all remarked, been major levers of predation, fraud and thievery. Stock promotions, Ponzi schemes, structured asset destruction through inflation, asset stripping through mergers and acquisitions, the promotion of levels of debt encumbrancy that reduce whole populations, even in the advanced capitalist countries, to debt peonage, to say nothing of corporate fraud, dispossession of assets (the raiding of pension funds and their decimation by stock and corporate collapses) by credit and stock manipulations – all of these are central features of what contemporary capitalism is about.[7]

The financial markets are amplifying traditional forms of 'primitive accumulation',[8] which remain highly relevant to Africa given the spread of the commodity form, amid the continent's crippling debt and capital flight. Moreover, trade and investment relationships also soon turn into systems of dispossession, Harvey notes, and have also disproportionately impoverished Africa:

> The emphasis upon intellectual property rights in the WTO negotiations (the so-called TRIPS agreement) points to ways in which the patenting and licensing of genetic materials, seed plasmas, and all manner of other products, can now be used against whole populations whose management practices have played a crucial role in the development of those materials. Biopiracy is rampant and the pillaging of the world's stockpile of genetic resources is well under way to the benefit of a few large multinational companies. The escalating depletion of the global environmental commons (land, air, water) and proliferating habitat degradations that preclude anything but capital intensive modes of agricultural production have likewise resulted from the wholesale commodification of nature in all its forms. The commodification of cultural forms, histories and intellectual creativity entails wholesale dispossessions (the music industry is notorious for the appropriation and exploitation of grassroots culture and creativity). The corporatisation and privatisation of hitherto public assets (like universities) to say nothing of the wave of privatisation (of water, public utilities of all kinds) that has swept the world indicate a new wave of 'enclosing the commons.' As in the past, the power of the state is frequently used to force such processes through – even against popular will.[9]

Samir Amin describes this process with a less polite, but no less accurate, idea, namely theft:

> The US programme is certainly imperialist in the most brutal sense of that word, but it is not 'imperial' in the sense that Antonio Negri has given the term, since it does not aim to manage the societies of the planet in order better to integrate them into a coherent capitalist system. Instead, it aims only at looting their resources.[10]

Since all of these points are obvious in South Africa and across the continent, the next step is to work through how capital accumulation through appropriation – that is, the commodification of everything – entails a specific system of geopolitics. *Socialist Register* editors Leo Panitch and Sam Gindin have been tracing the post-1945 development of the US state. They explain why Washington today represents such an enormous concentration and centralisation of the powers of trade, finance and warmaking:

> Most important here was the immense attention the Treasury and State Department paid during World War II to planning for relaunching a coordinated liberal trading regime and a rule-based financial order via manipulating its main allies' debtor status, the complete domination of the dollar as world currency and the fact that 50% of world production was now accounted for by the US economy.

> The Bretton Woods conference confirmed as nothing else had yet done the immense managerial capacity the American state had developed. With the IMF and World Bank headquarters established at American insistence in Washington, DC, a pattern was set for international economic management among all the leading capitalist countries that also continues to this day, one in which even when it is European or Japanese finance ministries and central banks who propose, it is the US Treasury and Federal Reserve that dispose.

> Yet the new integral relationship that developed between American empire and global capitalism could not be reduced to a one-way (let alone solely coercive) imposition. The relationship was often more properly characterised by the phrase 'imperialism by invitation.' But while this often meant the active consent of the citizenry of a country, the notion of US state (as opposed to cultural or economic) hegemony only adequately captured the relationship that developed among states and ruling classes. Active mass consent to even informal imperial rule was always mediated by the legitimacy that each state integrated within the American imperium could retain for itself and muster for any particular American state project; just as the American state itself did not take as its own responsibility the incorporation of the needs of the subordinate classes or other states within its own construction of informal imperial rule.[11]

Here we find the main hint of the emerging contradiction within the politics of contemporary imperialism, certainly as applied to Africa. For one, Panitch and Gindin allow, the liberalisation of finance enormously strengthened Wall Street through the 1970s and proved crucial to the broader changes that followed [in a] belated recognition on the part of American capital generally that the strengthening of finance was an essential, if sometimes painful, cost of reconstituting American economic power.[12]

However, here we find not only the strength of finance capital but also its vulnerabilities. For example, more than $7 trillion was wiped off the value of the New York Stock Exchange in 2000–02, and the Bush regime faced enormous problems in maintaining the hegemony of the US dollar during a period of such sustained deficits: trade, payments and the government budget.

Amin points out a variety of other areas where US imperialism will meet its match:

Competition between Ariane rockets and those of NASA, as well as between Airbus and Boeing, testifies to the vulnerability of present American advantages. Faced by European and Japanese competition in high-technology products, and by Chinese, Korean and other Asian and Latin American industrialised countries in competition for manufactured products, as well as by Europe and the southern cone of Latin America in agriculture, the United States probably would not be able to win were it not for the recourse to 'extra-economic' means, violating the principles of liberalism imposed on its competitors. In fact, the US only benefits from comparative advantages in the armaments sector, precisely because this sector largely operates outside the rules of the market and benefits from state support.[13]

The point, Amin continues, is that the US

lives parasitically to the detriment of its partners in the world system. The world produces, and the United States, which has practically no funds in reserve, consumes. The 'advantage' of the US is that of a predator whose deficit is covered by loans from others, whether consenting or forced. The US cannot give up the asymmetric practice of liberalism, since this is the only way that it can compensate for its deficiencies. American 'prosperity' comes at the price of others' stagnation.[14]

By 2002, the predation was accounted for in a $503 billion annual trade account deficit (5 per cent of GDP), a $6.4 trillion dollar accumulated state debt (60 per cent of GDP), and hundreds of billions of dollars in annual government deficits for the foreseeable future. Even though the dollar itself crashed by 27 per cent against the euro (possibly an ascendant hegemonic currency) between late 2001 and mid-2003, there was much further to fall as a result of these chronic imbalances.

In addition to economic crisis management, there are equally serious problems for the US in maintaining control over those parts of the interstate system which may be experiencing an involuntary 'deglobalisation' process. Outside the 'functioning core' of global capital, Panitch and Gindin cite a website publication of the US Naval War College which, under the title 'The Pentagon's New Map', lists countries considered danger zones for imperialism: Argentina, Brazil, Colombia and Venezuela, along with smaller Latin American states not coping with social protest; most of the Arab regimes; Afghanistan, Pakistan, India, China and North Korea; Russia; and in Africa, the hotspots of Angola, Burundi, the DRC, Rwanda, Somalia, but also the Western 'success story' of South Africa.[15]

Together, these diverse potential rebels against US empire represent the majority of the world. They not only can 'incubate the next generation of global terrorists' – to the dismay of the Naval War College – but also fall prey themselves, as host to failed states, to interminable poverty, to disease and to routine mass murder. More optimistically, Panitch and Gindin conclude, 'an American imperialism that is so blatantly imperialistic risks losing the very appearance that historically made it plausible and attractive'.[16]

There are few, if any, serious anti-imperialists among Africa's elites, including in Pretoria, notwithstanding the heady rhetoric cited at the outset of this chapter. If the politicians are not willing to take advantage of contradictions in relation to the US empire – and to capital accumulation by appropriation and dispossession, more generally – are the African people?

## AFRICAN ANTI-CAPITALISMS

Since we have asked the question of Thabo Mbeki and his fellow African National Congress leaders – will you polish or abolish global apartheid? – and arrived at an unsatisfactory answer,[17] it is time to look to more radical traditions and more realistic vehicles of social change in Africa. A leading radical sociologist, Jimi Adesina, reminds us of

> Amilcar Cabral's injunction that for the African petit bourgeois class to become one with the people, it must commit class suicide. In other words, it must turn its back on its natural instinct to realise its class potential of becoming a bourgeois class and share in the aspiration of the people – not only in nation building, widening of social access, but in the area of resource accumulation and control.[18]

Of course, the potential for a revolutionary civil service cadreship in Africa was never realised for more than a brief, romantic moment (unlike, for example, in Cuba). In part, this reflected the nature and power of the imperial project already described. In part it reflected, as Adesina laments, the ascendancy 'of a petty bourgeoisie with bourgeois aspirations. This shift has been both at the level of the state and the civil society (or societies), voluntary and compelled.' He continues:

> The sociological effect was to (a) shift the balance of forces within the State itself in favour of neoliberal fellow-travellers, and (b) to establish neoliberal principles as the underlining framework of policy discussions. In many cases this involved personnel changes. In other cases, it was a matter of a dominant ideology becoming hegemonic. Government unites with economic mandates: Ministries of Finance, central banks, bureaux with oversight mandate for privatisation and commercialisation, often became the first line soldiers for the emergent neoliberal orthodoxy. 'Capacity building' projects by the Bretton Woods Institutions and similarly oriented western agencies focused on reinforcing this ideological commitment.[19]

Under the circumstances, a progressive future will be forged not from good ideas, technicist interventions and insider persuasion tactics, but rather in the crucible of anti-capitalist struggles from the grassroots and shopfloors.[20] Across Africa, there is increasing evidence to allow us to move from inspiring historical examples to a diverse set of ecological, community, women's and labour struggles.

Africa was and remains, after all, the world's leading example of accumulation by appropriation and dispossession. But there have been, too, waves of resistance. The anti-slavery and anti-colonial tribal-based uprisings of the eighteenth and nineteenth centuries were only suppressed by the Europeans' brutal military superiority, ultimately requiring automatic weaponry. Twentieth-century settler-capitalism could only take hold through coercive mechanisms that dragged Africans out of traditional modes of production into the mines, fields and factories. Many rural women had the added burden, then, of subsidising capitalism with an infrastructure that reproduced cheap labour, since schools, medical insurance and pensions for urban families were largely non-existent.

Against such superexploitation, Africa's interrelated radical traditions grew and intermingled. They included vibrant nationalist liberation insurgencies, political parties that claimed one or another variants of socialism, mass movements (sometimes peasant-based, sometimes emerging from degraded urban ghettoes), and powerful unions. Religious protesters, women's groups, students and youths also played catalytic roles that changed history in given locales. If Luxemburg's critique of imperialism was based upon pressures building up throughout the world system, then these were some of the most important anti-capitalist campaigns ever. For example, the 1885 meeting in Berlin that carved up Africa between the main colonial powers reflected pressures directly related to the capitalist crises of the 1870s to 1890s, particularly in the London and Paris financial centres. Soon, the stock markets would react as badly to news of, for example, Ndebele raids on Cecil John Rhodes's mine surveyors in Zimbabwe, as modern brokers did to the Zapatista uprising and the failure of WTO negotiations in Seattle a century later.[21]

What kinds of globalised resistance can be retraced? Anti-slavery was among the most important international solidarity movements ever. African nationalist movements exiled in London and Paris established even greater Pan-Africanist visions, as well as solidarity relations with Northern critics of colonialism, apartheid and racism. The combined anti-colonial/imperialist phase, from the 1960s to the liberation of South Africa in 1994, gave leftists and anti-racists (from militants like Malcolm X and Stokely Carmichael to church-basement activists) inspiration – although as Che Guevara found out during a hellish year (1965) organising and occasionally fighting in what was then Mobutu's Zaire, not all peasant societies proved ripe for the struggle.

To update to contemporary times, we must first note the continent's increasingly desperate and militant labour movement.[22] Labour and indeed much of African civil society were, by the turn of the present century, civilised, tamed and channeled into serving neoliberalism. Meanwhile, the potentially anti-capitalist remnants of the 'old left' were prevaricating about the new movements, when not actively trying to discredit, demobilise and repress their left challengers.

In recent years, Egypt, Ghana, Kenya, Mauritius, Nigeria, Senegal, South Africa, Zambia and Zimbabwe have been among the most intense recent sites of conflicts between anti-capitalists and ruling parties (some of which played out over differential resistance to the Iraq War). But across the continent, the contradictions between global justice movements and Third World nationalism are endemic, and the continuation of 'IMF riots' described earlier suggests that the leftist critique of neoliberalism remains intact.

The micro-developmental and ecological damage done through neoliberal policies is also widely recognised. Some of the most impressive recent upsurges of protest have been in areas of what can be termed 'environmental justice'. Several examples are illustrative, including from the Nigerian oil Delta region. In mid-2002, women conducted sit-ins at the local offices of multinationals just prior to the World Summit on Sustainable Development, and in early 2003, oil workers revolted at several Delta platforms over wages and broader community demands, and took hostage numerous multinational corporate managers

In Botswana, indigenous-rights campaigners, aided by Survival International, began targeting the De Beers diamond corporation, the World Bank and the Botswana government for the displacement of Basarwa/San Bushmen from the central Kalahari in 2002, following vigorous efforts by London-based Global Witness and Fatal Transactions to delegitimise conflict diamonds. Removals from the central Kalahari were allegedly coerced, as the World Bank invested $2 million in explorations. According to the *Guardian*, the San targeted for relocation away from diamond mining areas 'had their water supplies cut off before being dumped in bleak settlements with derisory compensation'.[23] According to University of Botswana political scientists Ian Taylor and Gladys Mokhawa, 'The success of this campaign might be seen in the ability to give birth to an issue and to determine its agenda at both a national and global level to change policy.' The impact was so great that by August 2002, the *Botswana Gazette* described the government as a 'disease-ridden international polecat'. A San activist explained, 'Basarwa in this country are ill-treated and looked down upon. We want the world to know that.'

Predictably, the immediate response from government officials was that San organisers were 'highly seditious' for drawing in 'fringe, lunatic and racist' allies in Britain.[24] The International Rivers Network has received similar nationalist, xenophobic insults for supporting those resisting large dams that threaten mass displacement in Namibia, Lesotho and Uganda.[25]

As capital globalised, so too were these kinds of struggles finding increasingly effective international supporters. South Africans in the Environmental Justice Networking Forum and far-sighted NGOs like groundWork began working more closely with counterparts elsewhere over environmental racism, dumping of toxics, compensation for asbestos, anti-incinerator campaigns and air pollution. Movements against privatisation of Africa's basic services – mainly water and electricity – began in Accra and Johannesburg in 2000 and have attracted great international support. Their influence is spawning similar campaigns across Southern and West Africa. The Soweto Electricity Crisis Committee's Operation Khanyisa ('Switch On') illegally reconnects people whose supplies were cut because of poverty and rising prices associated with services commercialisation. Similar community-based protests in Durban and Cape Town against disconnections, evictions and landlessness have won recognition from across the world.[26]

The question arises, can such specific protests and campaigns graduate to a more generalised programme and mature anti-capitalist ideology? If so, it is likely – though not certain – that the African Social Forum will be the site. In January 2002, dozens of African social movements met in Bamako, Mali, in preparation for the Porto Alegre World Social Forum. It was one of the first substantial conferences since the era of liberation to combine progressive NGOs and social movements from all parts of the continent, and was followed by African Social Forum sessions in Johannesburg (August 2002) and Addis Ababa (January 2003). The Bamako Declaration included the following paragraphs:

A strong consensus emerged at the Bamako Forum that the values, practices, structures and institutions of the currently dominant neoliberal order are inimical to and incompatible with the realisation of Africa's dignity, values and aspirations.

The Forum rejected neo-liberal globalisation and further integration of Africa into an unjust system as a basis for its growth and development. In this context, there was a strong consensus that initiatives such as Nepad that are inspired by the IMF–WB strategies of Structural Adjustment Programmes, trade liberalisation that continues to subject Africa to an unequal exchange, and strictures on governance borrowed from the practices of Western countries and not rooted in the culture and history of the peoples of Africa.[27]

African groups began networking more actively in 2002 when the New Partnership for Africa's Development (Nepad) was introduced by Mbeki and a handful of other African leaders. The main point to make here, is not merely that these and other progressive African movement networks (e.g., labour-related, economic justice practitioners in churches, health equity specialists, numerous types of environmentalists, and so on) are advancing strong, mature, ideological statements about the debt, trade and related economic oppression they face. What is perhaps of greater interest is that instead of working merely through NGO-type circuits, they are increasingly tying their work to militant street action, as was evident at the Durban World Conference Against Racism in August 2001 and the Johannesburg World Summit on Sustainable Development a year later.

A major challenge remains, though, in weeding out Africa's 'homegrown' (but really alien and systematically imported) neoliberal philosophy and institutions. According to Adesina, the realm of ideas was of crucial importance in the 1980s dominance of the Washington Consensus over Africa:

At the level of civil society, concerted efforts were put in place to develop a new generation, committed to the neoliberal vision. The African Economic Research Consortium is such an initiative. The neoliberal counter-revolution took to mind the Maoist principle on revolutionary insurgency – burrow deep within the population. The collapse in public sector wages and the secular decline in formal sector employment stimulated the growth of the NGO sector and the drift into the informal sector. The emergence of the governance argument, initiated the campaign to extend and deepen the 'civil society', of a neoliberal hue.[28]

Ideas will be just as important as the embryonic anti-capitalist movement expands and deepens. My own sense is that African intellectuals are hungry once again for each others' contributions to a more open (thoroughly destalinised) brand of socialism, although that remains to be seen. A re-emerging interest in historical materialism – i.e., for theoretically grounded explanation and for political–strategic guidance – was evident at the April 2002 Accra meeting of the Council for Development and Social Research in Africa and Third World Network-Africa. Codesria/TWN-Africa called upon 'Africa's scholars and activist intellectuals within African and in the Diaspora, to join forces with social groups whose interests and needs are central to the development of Africa'.[29]

Aside from Marxism, what are some of the more popular themes that are resonating in such intellectual centres, in Africa and elsewhere? To take one example, Samir Amin famously argues for a 'delinking' strategy that 'is not synonymous with autarky, but rather with the subordination of external relations to the logic of internal development ... permeated with the multiplicity of divergent interests'.[30] In 2002, a restatement of Amin's delinking theme came from Focus on the Global South director Walden Bello, in his book *Deglobalization*: 'I am not talking about withdrawing from the international economy. I am speaking about reorienting our economies from production for export to production for the local market.'[31]

There was no question, at this stage, of overthrowing the capitalist mode of production, merely the scale at which it operated. The implicit possibility of attracting potential allies among a (mainly mythical) 'national patriotic bourgeoisie' still exists in some formulations of delinking, which coincides with reformist tendencies among the African intelligentsia and some currents of anti-capitalism (especially trade unions). The challenge, as ever, is to establish what kinds of reforms – capital controls, inward-oriented industrial strategies, generous social policies, and the like – are 'reformist', versus those which could potentially be 'non-reformist reforms'. The latter open the door to a stronger contestation of capitalism itself. A first step towards an effective deglobalisation – and here we obviously do not mean the autarchic experiences of Albania, Burma or North Korea, or the corrupt chaos of contemporary Zimbabwe – is to disempower Washington.

The strategic formula that the South African left has broadly adopted (which I have elsewhere termed 'internationalism plus the nation-state'[32]) could begin by removing the boot of the World Bank from Third World necks, as a key example of what can and must be done. At the same time, if uneven development is amplified by a scale shift from national to global determination of political economy, part of the anti-capitalist project must be to wrest control of the nation-state away from current ruling elites. As Marx advocated, each working class must first settle accounts with their own (national) bourgeoisies. Both must occur simultaneously, otherwise no matter the calibre of leadership – Aristide, Lula, Mandela or anyone else – the hand of Washington will prop up the comprador elements in a given state, and in turn those will empower Washington.

Of course, even were policies adopted designed to 'lock capital down',[33] a series of national capitalist strategies in a society like South Africa would be insufficient to halt and reverse uneven global development in its current form: overaccumulation crisis, displacement via hyperactive financial and trade circuits, increased accumulation by dispossession, intensified destruction of the environment, reduction of the social wage and community, the shift of the burden of failed states especially to women, the rise of dubious NGO activities, and the accompanying geopolitical rearrangements. Foremost among the problems that must be addressed, simultaneously, is the rescaling of many political-economic responsibilities. These are now handled by embryonic world-state institutions overly influenced by the gun-toting, neoliberal US administrations. To make any progress, deglobalisation and delinking from the most destructive circuits of global capital will also be necessary.

## THE LIMITS OF ELITE OPINION

Below, we consider the political challenges and the approaches to alliance-building that are beginning to emerge. In terms of more directly economic problems, it is useful to contextualise the damage being done from Washington by quoting some disillusioned insiders. Among several well-meaning economists who have tried to change the Bank from the inside, David Ellerman saw more than his share of gambits, from a vantage point in the chief economist's office during the late 1990s and early 2000s. Finally in 2003, Ellerman threw up his hands:

Agencies such as the World Bank and the IMF are now almost entirely motivated now by big power politics and their own internal organisational imperatives. All their energies are consumed in doing whatever is necessary to perpetuate their global status. Intellectual and political energies spent trying to 'reform' these agencies are largely a waste of time and a misdirection of energies. Dominant global institutions, like monopolies or dominant oligopolies in the private sector, can be counted on to use the power to maintain their dominance—and yet that dominance or monopolistic power is the root of the problem.[34]

Abuse of power and dogmatic ideology were long-standing complaints of Joseph Stiglitz, and justified his August 2002 call to consider abolition of the IMF:

> I used to say that since we are going to need these institutions it is better to reform them than to start from scratch. I'm beginning to have second thoughts. I'm beginning to ask, has the credibility of the IMF been so eroded that maybe it's better to start from scratch? Is the institution so resistant to learning to change, to becoming a more democratic institution, that maybe it is time to think about creating some new institutions that really reflect today's reality, today's greater sense of democracy. It is really time to re-ask the question: should we reform or should we build from start?[35]

At the same time, a Columbia University colleague of Stiglitz, Jeffrey Sachs, began arguing that low-income countries should simply not repay World Bank and IMF loans, and should instead redirect the debt repayments towards health and education. After all, he insisted, no-one

> in the creditor world, including the White House, believes that those countries can service these debts without extreme human cost. The money should instead be rerouted as grants to be spent on more demanding social needs at home. Poor countries should take the first step by demanding that all outstanding debt service payments to official creditors be reprocessed as grants for the fight against HIV/AIDS.[36]

Notwithstanding opposition from Northern and Southern elites, the idea was not as outlandish as it appeared at first blush, according to the *Boston Globe*, for during the 1980s Bolivia and Poland both got away with this strategy: 'Because the two countries used that money for social causes both were later able to win debt forgiveness.'[37]

Simultaneously, George Soros complained about inadequate debt cancellation on offer from the Bretton Woods institutions, whose failure to bring the required relief indicates that there is something fundamentally wrong with the international financial system as currently constituted. In recent years, the so-called Washington Consensus has put its faith in the self-correcting nature of financial markets. That faith has been misplaced.[38]

### BREAKING THE CHAINS OF GLOBAL FINANCIAL APARTHEID

Archbishop Ndungane lays out the threat from the global justice movements in no uncertain terms:

[If] we must release ourselves from debt peonage – by demanding the repudiation and cancellation of debt – we will campaign to that end. And if the World Bank and IMF continue to stand in the way of social progress, movements like Jubilee South Africa will have no regrets about calling for their abolition. To that end, the World Bank Bonds Boycott movement is gaining even great momentum. Even a money centre city like San Francisco decided to redirect funds away from Bank bonds into other investments, on the moral grounds that taking profits from World Bank operations contributes to poverty, misery and ecological degradation. More and more investors are realising that profiting from poverty through World Bank bonds is not only immoral, but will not make good financial sense as the market shrinks.[39]

To be sure, some global justice movement activists and strategists still hold out hope for the kinds of reforms that South African finance minister Trevor Manuel also claims to support: transparency, more participation by affected people, a shift towards a post-Washington Consensus approach, gender equity and a stronger environmental consciousness. Since 2001, however, there have been virtually no successes on the reform front, and considerable backsliding.

Aside from the Extractive Industries Review (hotly contested at the time of writing), the two major recent processes in which well-meaning civil society advocates went inside the Bank led to failure: the World Commission on Dams (chaired by then South African water minister Kader Asmal) and the Structural Adjustment Participatory Review Initiative (Sapri). In the first instance, a South Africa Bank water expert, John Briscoe, actively lobbied Southern governments to reject the findings of a vast, multi-stakeholder research team in 2001.[40] According to Patrick McCully of International Rivers Network,

'The World Bank's singularly negative and non-committal response to the WCD Report means that the Bank will no longer be accepted as an honest broker in any further multi-stakeholder dialogues.'[41]

As for Sapri, hundreds of organisations and scholars in nine countries – Bangladesh, Ecuador, El Salvador, Ghana, Hungary, Mexico, the Philippines, Uganda and Zimbabwe – engaged in detailed analysis from 1997 to 2002, often alongside local Bank and IMF officials. Bank staff withdrew from the process in August 2001, once the incontrovertible conclusions were becoming obvious.[42] At the point in April 2002 when the research – a 188-page report, 'The Policy Roots of Economic Crisis and Poverty' – was tabled for action, the civil society groups found that Washington gave them only a deaf ear:

> The Bank's continual calls to street protesters to seek change from the Bank through dialogue were denounced as disingenuous, and increased public pressure was encouraged to make the institution more open, democratic and responsive to the people of the Global South. 'This Sapri investigation has shown that the same policies are being applied everywhere, with very similar results,' said Lidy Nacpil of the Freedom from Debt Coalition, Sapri's lead organisation in the Philippines. 'The Bank may claim that it has changed, but these policies remain firmly entrenched. It is imperative that we maintain the pressure on the Bank and the IMF.'[43]

Richard Peet, author of a recent book on the Bank, interpreted:

> In 2000, the World Bank published a report entitled 'Voices of the Poor: Can Anyone Hear Us?' with an introduction by Clare Short, UK Secretary of State for International Development and James Wolfensohn, President of the World Bank. The report reached safe, moralistic conclusions like 'poverty is multidimensional' and 'households are crumbling under the stresses of poverty'. The last sentence of the introduction reads: 'Our hope is that the voices in this book will call you to action as they have us.'
>
> But in the case of Sapri, where thousands of civil society movements called on the World Bank to listen, its own action was simply to leave the discussion. Why might this be? What these social movements were telling the Bank was that the poverty they sought to 'alleviate' had been produced by the structural adjustments they themselves had imposed – that they were merely rectifying a small part of their own massive mistakes. This made

everything they had done in the way of structural adjustment over the previous 20 years ... not meaningless (if only we were dealing with mere existential angst!), but pernicious, even malevolent, given that thousands of people active in development had been telling them for years to stop 'structurally adjusting' desperate countries. So the President of the World Bank did not listen to Sapri, because he could not. For he would hear, and he even might learn, that his finest, most splendid ideas had produced the worst, most harmful effects.[44]

As a result of such experiences, it has become clear that weakening the Bretton Woods component of global apartheid is an extremely important strategy for South African, Southern African and African justice movements. This insight generated at least one potentially critical tactic, worth mentioning now. In addition to the unifying work against Nepad, many Africans especially in the Jubilee movement have long argued the merits of closing ('nixing' not 'fixing') the key Washington institutions, the IMF and World Bank, because they are:

- global neoliberalism's 'brain' and policeman;
- active across the African continent, in nearly every country;
- reliant upon unreformed neoliberal logic, ranging from macroeconomics to micro development policy;
- responsible for even project-level conditionality;
- capable of commodifying even the most vital public services; and
- already subject to periodic IMF riots and other activism, and suffering a severe legitimacy crisis.

Already, campaigning against the IMF and World Bank is quite sophisticated:

- several international and local lobbies aim to force the WB/IMF and WTO to stop commodifying water, health, education and other services;
- global justice movement components such as Anti-Privatisation Forums and environmental justice groups exist in many Southern African cities;
- the Southern African People's Solidarity Network links progressive activists, churches, etc. in an explicit ideological challenge to the Washington Consensus;

- Jubilee movements continue fighting for debt repudiation;
- the African Social Forum is developing tough positions on debt and development;
- most Southern African progressive movements demand that IMF and Bank quit their countries; and
- reparations protests and lawsuits are under way against financiers – including, potentially, the Bank and IMF – that supported apartheid and African dictatorships.

In mid-2003, South African activists began considering how to bring the Bretton Woods institutions directly into court cases, given the difficulty that the institutions give their staff diplomatic immunity. Whether or not suing the World Bank and IMF to compensate South African society for their generous 1951–82 loans to the apartheid regime will recoup money, it at least provides a good education.

So too does the most intriguing tactic against global apartheid: the World Bank Bonds Boycott, as mentioned above by Ndungane.[45] US groups like Center for Economic Justice and Global Exchange continued to work with Jubilee South Africa and Brazil's Movement of the Landless, among others, to demand of their Northern comrades: is it ethical for socially conscious people to invest in the World Bank by buying its bonds (responsible for 80 per cent of the institution's resources), hence drawing out dividends that represent the fruits of enormous suffering? The boycott impressed a London *Evening Standard* financial markets commentator during the IMF/Bank spring 2002 meetings: 'The growing sophistication of radical activists increases the likelihood that once-accepted fixed-income investment practices can no longer be taken as off limits from the threat of moral suasion.'[46]

In the short term, the boycott campaign sends a clear signal to the Bank: end anti-social, environmentally destructive activities, and cancel the debt! When enough investors endorse the campaign, the Bank will suffer a declining bond rating, making it also fiduciarily irresponsible to invest – a real threat. In turn, some of the organisers hope, this lays the basis for a 'run on the Bank', to defund the institution entirely, initially through a collapsed bond market and then through taxpayer revolt. The World Bank Bonds Boycott is only one of a variety of campaigns that could become more explicitly anti-capitalist, or that instead could rest at a comfortable populist, moral level.

The anti-capitalist component of the global justice movements understands best of all that the World Bank and IMF may have changed their rhetorics but not their structural adjustment programmes. Perhaps most crucially, the rhetorics of 'pro-poor' development do not quite cover up the fact that, virtually everywhere, the Bretton Woods institutions maintain their commitment to accumulation by appropriation and dispossession, that is, the privatisation of everything.

The institutions' legitimacy is the only target that the African social movements can aim at. That they do with an increasing militancy that now targets not the World Bank's 'failure to consult' or 'lack of transparency' or 'undemocratic governance' – all easy populist critiques. Now, most of the attention that leading Africans pay to the Washington Consensus ideology is to the core content: commodification, whether in relation to water, electricity, housing, land, anti-retroviral medicines and health services, education, basic income grant support or other social services, or ideally, all at once.

With the anti-capitalist focus on neoliberalism in general, and institutions like the Bank, IMF, WTO and others in particular, the next issue is one of positionality. The most fierce debates that I see in the progressive African movements tend to be over the extent to which co-option is a threat, e.g. in the African Social Forum's potential work within the African Union structures, or in social movements being sucked into World Bank/IMF PRSP processes. At the end of the day, the highest stakes are bound up in maintaining the momentum of these movements, momentum that can be crushed by the repression so commonly deployed by African elites, or which can ebb away after victories. Who, to conclude, are their allies?

## WHO IS FOR AND AGAINST GLOBAL APARTHEID?

The fight against global apartheid will continue to come primarily and most forcefully from below: from the social, labour, women's, community, environmental, youth, disabled, indigenous and similar movements aggrieved by neoliberalism and its parallel oppressions. Unfortunately, that means that the most likely near-future realignment of the global forces discussed in the appendix appears deeply unsatisfying, if radical social and ecological change is desired in the short to medium term.

Under the circumstances, it is likely that, as in the 1930s, the right-wing resurgence will continue growing, and will increasingly fuse with economic interests of the Washington Consensus (and its US/UK corporate/banking backers), notwithstanding the obvious ideological contradictions. Meanwhile, it is likely that supporters of the post-Washington Consensus will seek closer alignment with more 'responsible' Third World nationalists (e.g. Lula), and that both will fight against the more principled, radical forces within the global justice movements.

Is there any chance that the three rows at the top might unite against the right-wing resurgence and Washington neoliberals? Samir Amin contends the necessity of such a political project. Beginning with the global justice movements and Third World nationalists, he calls for

> The reconstruction of a Southern Front capable of giving the peoples of Asia and Africa, together with their solidarity across three continents, the capacity to make their voices heard will also come about by liberating ourselves from the illusions of a 'non-asymmetric' globalised liberal system that will allow the nations of the Third World to make up their 'backwardness'.[47]

Drawing some inspiration from the February 2003 Kuala Lumpur meeting of the Non-Aligned Movement, at which Mbeki turned over the chair to Mahathir, Amin heard a wake-up call:

> The Southern countries are becoming aware of the fact that the neoliberal globalised management has nothing to offer to them and that being the case, the neo-liberal system had to use military violence in order to be established, thereby playing the game enshrined in the American project. The [Non-Aligned] Movement is becoming – as suggested – that of 'non-alignment with liberal globalisation and US hegemony'.

Moreover, Amin argues that in early 2003, the 'Franco-African Summit strengthened the eventual alliance taking shape between Europe and the South'.[48] Post-Washington Consensus advocates in a 'social Europe' would, in this scenario, join the Southern Front:

> There exist conditions capable of promoting closer relations between at least all the peoples of the ancient world. This union could be given concrete expression at the international diplomatic level by thickening the Paris–Berlin–Moscow–Peking axis, that

could be strengthened by developing friendly relations between this axis and the reconstituted Afro-Asian front.[49]

On the surface, it appears that Bush's mid-2003 diplomacy with Putin and the Evian meeting – which stitched back together G8 unity and showed no signs of European solidarity to Africa – negates that option.

Nevertheless Amin's is an attractive scenario: a global popular front against the United States:

[With] an authentic cohesion between Europe, Russia, China, the whole of Asia and the entire Africa will constitute the foundation on which will be constructed a multi-centrist, democratic and pacific world.[50]

From a traditional Trotskyist position, University of Natal researcher Peter Dwyer articulates a usefully sceptical reaction:

Are we to seriously believe that we can enter into (or rely upon for more than a nano-second) some sort of alliance with 'some members of the military,' intelligence political and business elites? Even if some of the above were against the war, their reasons for doing so are rarely if ever progressive ones. Whilst we must always exploit contradictions, tensions and differences amongst the ruling classes, this should not mean entering into alliances with them – they should not be part of the global peace movement. France *et al.* were never going to be reliable allies for the global peace movement.[51]

Amin has conceded this point:

The political regimes set up in many of the Southern countries are not democratic, to say the least, and are sometimes really odious. These authoritarian power structures favour comprador groups whose interests consist in expanding the global imperialist capitalism. The alternative – construction of a front comprising peoples of the South – can materialise through democratisation. This necessary democratisation will be a difficult and long process but it certainly cannot be realised by establishing puppet regimes to open their countries' resources to plunder by North American multinational companies, regimes that will consequently be even more fragile, less credible and less legitimate than those they succeeded under protection by the American invader.[52]

A stronger case for the global popular anti-US front comes from Jeremy Brecher:

> If the Bush program is regarded as little but the continuation of US imperialism as usual, then I understand the logic of saying that popular movements require no new alliances with national elites and governments. But if it represents a greatly augmented threat to the peace and future well-being of the world – as the (very different) phenomenon of Nazism represented something far more threatening than traditional German capitalism and militarism – then one must consider all the forces that could possibly be brought to bear to defeat it.
>
> Let me add immediately that I entirely agree that various governments and elites I discuss as potential coalition partners 'should not be part of the global peace movement' and that they are 'never going to be reliable allies'. Indeed, there were other errors of the left in the 1930s and 1940s that grew in part from subservience to the state interests of one or another power (the capitalist powers for the Social Democrats; the USSR for the Communists). I emphasise the need for the new global peace movement to remain independent of the dominance of any of the various forces with whom alliances need to be constructed. The movement's independence from elites and governments should go hand in hand with its effort to move them toward collective resistance to US dictation and aggression.[53]

Any one of these formulations, pro or con, requires very close attention to the dynamics of state power. Is that, though, the direction in which most of the global justice movements are actually heading?

## SHOULD MOVEMENTS TAKE THE STATE, OR LOCALISE?

World systems theorist William Martin points out that:

> for at least several hundred years there have been successive waves of movements which have attacked and destabilised the capitalist world-economy, its hegemonic powers, and yet, at the same time,

come to provide the foundation for a new ordering of accumulation and political rule on a world scale. Seen from this perspective, present movements take on a very distinctive meaning, and pose for us quite different possible futures.[54]

Martin and his Binghamton University colleagues have identified four time periods that qualify as 'waves of movements': 1760–1848, 1848–1917, 1917–1968 and 1968–2001.[55]
The most recent left movements have

a solid understanding that capturing national power could not be equated with capturing control over economic or cultural lives that were embedded in the much deeper and wider domains of the capitalist world-economy. This strategic advance presented a dilemma, however, that remained unresolved: how does one organise and attack capital and inequality, if even the capture of state power leaves its global foundations unchecked? Inability to resolve this dilemma was considerably complicated by faltering attempts to bridge the differences of race and gender across the core–periphery divide.[56]

The answer lies in the actual grassroots struggles of what Hardt/Negri termed the 'multitudes', namely – as Martin puts it – in

the demands for the decommodification of land, labour, and cultural life, demands so prominent in the local, but increasingly globally-integrated, struggles against the privatisation of basic human needs (land, water, education, health). In this regard, late-capitalist antisystemic movements may find much to learn from earlier movements against incorporation into the capitalist world – movements which have often been dismissed as attempts to retain 'pre-capitalist' modes of life and production.

In addition to their new perspective on the state, for Martin, the 'very different' nature of the contemporary global justice movements is that they are based upon 'attempts to construct a new strategy suited precisely to the fundamental structures of governance within a single, expanding, capitalist world-economy'.

In opposition to uneven global capitalist development, this point is indisputable, and reflected not only in the big protests from Seattle onwards, but also in the surgical campaigning against international targets, as exemplified by the World Bank Bonds Boycott. But we might begin to part company with Martin (and Hardt/Negri) when he asserts the merits of understanding 'the problem as one of democratically embedding society in a world-economy, as opposed to the liberal's fictitious, mid-twentieth century, national economies, [which] poses a much sharper challenge to the structures and central powers of the capitalist world-economy'. Hence, 'there can be no return to the nationalist programs of the twentieth century'.[57]

Elsewhere, I have provided much evidence to support a different interpretation of the probable trajectory of global justice movements, based upon nixing the embryonic global economic state, making intensifying demands upon nation-states and capital (the only conceivable targets) for the decommodification of basic goods, services and labour power. Yet we must all acknowledge frankly, that political scale remains a point of great contention

While a formula of 'internationalism plus the nation-state' is probably most appropriate for the short term, there are potentially important experiments that continue in local settings, such as the neighbourhood assemblies and factory occupations of crisis-ridden Argentina. Amory Starr and Jason Adams are North American academic-activists who promote a localist 'autonomism' that explicitly endorses Amin, so as to extend the logic of delinking and deglobalisation to the very local level:

> The most resolute of these are the now-famous indigenous movements, such as the U'wa and the Ogoni, who expel 'development' from their lands. They affirm the possibility and necessity of collaboration among autonomous communities when necessary. These movements don't just want 'another world' but 'a world in which many worlds fit' (a phrase of the Zapatistas).
>
> Drawing on Rousseau, Gandhian development, anarchism, indigenous culture, and village anthropology, a diverse range of scholars emphasise the benefits of 'decentralised political institutions' which would protect people from exploitation, alleviate unemployment through 'complementary small-scale industry,' prioritise 'solving the problems of poverty' rather than 'compatibility with the world market,' and 'protect the local globally.'[58]

Amin himself, though, has turned back to global-scale coalition-building, as described above. Indeed, to be as formidable an opponent as is required, the global justice movements will have to more profoundly deconstruct global apartheid from the top down.

One reason is the failure of early-twenty-first-century reformism, as documented above. The Washington Consensus neoliberals and their Washington neighbours who adhere to the right-wing resurgence remain too powerful a bloc. Post-Washington reformers have had a desperately unsuccessful recent period, in virtually all spheres of activity: preventing the Iraq War; making the bureaucratised and increasingly neoliberal United Nations relevant and constructive; reforming governance and economic policy at the international financial institutions; solving environment problems with Kyoto-style market mechanisms; establishing genuine anti-poverty programmes; and even protecting traditional bourgeois-liberal civil rights. Neither can success be claimed by Third World nationalists, who are terribly uneven, with some – like Lula of Brazil and, to some degree, Mbeki – ascendant but only at the cost of their core constituencies. However, most such leaders, especially African elites like Mbeki and Obasanjo, cannot be taken terribly seriously, and are, even on their own limited terms, unable to move a decisive agenda.

Usually, the global justice movements stand resolutely against both exhausted Third Worldist state elites and unimaginative global-scale post-Washington Consensus reformers. And they remain a uniquely surgical force when confronting the international power elite. As Fidel Castro explained to a May 2003 Havana conference of Marxist economists,

> These are FIGHTERS, and that's what we must call them. They won at Seattle. At Quebec, they forced the elites into a fortified position. It was more than a demonstration, it was an insurgency. The leaders of the world must now meet inside a bunker. They had to meet on a ship in Italy, and on a mountain in Canada. They needed police barriers in Davos, in peaceful Switzerland. The most important thing is that the fighters have created a real fear. The IMF and World Bank cannot meet properly.[59]

In short, it is easy to predict a period ahead of continuing militancy and independent honing of strategies and tactics for the left. Already, to this end, the popular and intellectual literatures on the global justice movements are overwhelming.[60] Are there any easy ways to establish a typology of the different tendencies? Alex Callinicos breaks up the global justice movement into 'localist', 'reformist', 'autonomist' and 'socialist' ideologies. Christophe Aguiton cites three currents: 'radical internationalist', 'nationalist' and 'neo-reformist'. Peter Waterman argues against these categories, by

> surpassing traditional left internationalism. 'Emancipation' might seem a more appropriate term than 'left' when discussing today the transformation of society, nature, culture, work and psychology – as well as, of course, that increasingly important but placeless place, cyberspace.[61]

What all this means in terms of political mapping (with reference to the appendix) is that there would appear diminishing patience between at least three blocs – global justice movements, Third World nationalists and post-Washington Consensus reformers – and the two most obdurate status quo blocs, the Washington Consensus and resurgent right wing. The latter two appear to be working in harmony, with only the Washington institutions' adoption of somewhat more 'sustainable' rhetoric distinguishing its main implementing institutions (World Bank, IMF and WTO) from prior years. The resurgent right wing often continues to express rhetorical support for both 'sustainability' and free markets, yet adopted a post-September 11 movement towards protectionism, racism, xenophobia, bailouts, and unilateralism on most eco-social grounds. The combination of the Washington Consensus and resurgent right wing is intimidating.

For the sake of future political strategy, therefore, the major question is whether the global justice movements will provide not only delegitimisation of the Washington Consensus and resurgent right wing, but also continue to express hostility to the post-Washington Consensus and fight Third World nationalists on home turf. Presently, this configuration of forces applies to South Africa, Nigeria and Zimbabwe, and to other strategically important countries in Asia and Latin America. If proponents of a strengthened WSSD-type gathering aim to continue holding summits of this type, it is unlikely that they will have an easier time of it in countries characterised by conflicts between the global justice movements and Third World nationalists.

## NEXT STEPS: TOWARDS A 'FIFTH INTERNATIONAL'?

The rise of the global justice movements as the world's first-ever multi-issue political convergence was profoundly important, and

South Africa has been a site of crucial, productive conflicts for these movements' development. The time may well arise for a formalisation of the movement's character in explicitly political terms, such as within the traditions of international socialism – for which the first four 'internationals' provide a host of lessons, largely negative, about world-scale co-ordination.[62]

The recent period has witnessed impressive alliances, no matter how brief, between the various global justice movements in fighting for both economic progress and peace. The merits of various related causes coming together, as they did in the WSSD, will be reflected to some extent in wide-ranging protests at such coming events at the time of writing as the Cancun WTO and, in Latin America, campaigning against the Free Trade Area of the Americas. Similar linkage on eco-social issues – water, global warming, biodiversity, land, health – are evident in various other sectoral processes. The strength of the linkages depends, in future, in part upon more national-level civil societies having the chance to learn and experience the sorts of political dynamics that were on display, in many ways, at the WSSD.

Even with progressive civil society writ large, there remain, without doubt, a good many post-Washington Consensus-type development NGOs, labour movements and environmentalists who have ambitions for making an impact upon global apartheid, in the same spirit as Pretoria has attempted. By and large they have been terribly disappointed by the weak outcomes of their endeavours. In contrast, international global justice movements organisations and individuals have been, by and large, delighted with the power and vision of South Africa's social movements, and especially how undaunted they have become when combating neoliberalism more broadly.

Hence the best terms to describe the various components of international civil society are probably no longer based on 'North' and 'South' geographic standpoints, and not even 'Global North' and 'Global South' (to make allowance for uneven development within societies). Instead, the two main competing ideologies of civil society – global justice movements and post-Washington Consensus – seem to have settled in as the more permanent and important divisions. (There are also some NGOs that work closely with Third World nationalists, and also some NGOs that advocate specifically Washington Consensus policies, but it is likely that neither group will profoundly influence future relationships between civil societies of the North and South.)

The differences between the global justice movements and the post-Washington Consensus approaches are getting stronger in some regards (as noted, the global justice movements often advocating more forceful 'nixing' of institutions which the post-Washington Consensus would rather 'fix'). It is not inconceivable that a 'global-Keynesian' approach emphasising national sovereignty, genuine wealth/income transfers to poor people, and ecologically sound industrialisation may emerge as a philosophy that unites the post-Washington Consensus, Third World nationalists and global justice movements approaches in future.[63] (I remain sceptical, however, that the 'global' part can be realised at a time of such exceptionally unequal power relations.)

As Amin and Brecher (among others) argue, opposition to US unilateralism in the military/diplomatic, economic and environmental spheres would be an important basis for pulling such a broad-based alliance together (much as it was during the Second World War against the Axis powers). However, the WSSD suggests that there are debilitating differences between, especially, the global justice movements on the one hand, and the Third World nationalists and post-Washington Consensus advocates on the other. As a result, our final word must be one of caution.

The importance of empowering the local/national 'affiliates' of the global justice movements, such as the South African social movements and their regional allies, cannot be emphasised enough. My sense is that this process will occur unevenly in coming years via the World Social Forum decentralisation initiatives now being established. In South Africa, given the split between the trade union grouping Cosatu and most social movements, it is not likely that a 'social forum' branding exercise will be successful until a wider-ranging challenge to the ruling party occurs (perhaps along the lines of precedents from trade unions in Zambia and Zimbabwe over recent years). Instead, South African social movements will help lead a Southern African Social Forum (in 2004, headquartered at the Lusaka NGO Women for Change). In late 2003, Zimbabwe and Niger were the first countries in Africa to establish genuine national Social Forums.

More generally, the rise of national and regional Social Forums in most parts of the world bodes well for more co-ordinated civil society inputs into global governance. My sense is that nation-state priorities will be seen as overriding, because the balance of forces at the international scale simply does not offer progressive social movements any real scope for satisfying reforms, as efforts on debt, trade, environment, militarism and so many other examples continually prove. Quite intense protests will continue at not only WTO, World Bank, IMF, G8, Davos and similar elite meetings, but also at UN events, if the WSSD is a precedent.

However, all optimistic outcomes depends upon an obvious prerequisite: the hard work of local, then national, then regional and finally global-scale organising. Skipping any of these steps through enlightened top-down interventions will never make more than a momentary dent, and may divert these new and enthusiastic forms of organising into a technicist cul-de-sac. Hence, in sum, the approach of the South African social movements – thinking globally and acting locally first, while changing the balance of forces nationally and internationally, so that acting globally might one day generate something meaningful – is a wise route towards a final attack on global apartheid, and capitalism itself.

In sum, notwithstanding the enormous progress in identifying the source of their problems in the capitalist mode of production, South African (and African and Third World) anti-capitalists must not merely reject the international character of neoliberalism. They must also confront both its local champions (including state agents) no matter how much the Third World nationalist camp confuses matters by Talking Left Acting Right, and also its internal logic. I tend to think that this negates prospects for alliances between global justice movements and Third World nationalists, unless more radically left-leaning governments (e.g. Cuba, Venezuela) eventually invent a model that convinces anti-capitalists that the state won't necessarily repress or co-opt their initiatives.

No matter the continual reversals, the opportunities to take up these challenges, and link them across countries and sectors of struggle, is now greater than at any time in memory. This is partly because global apartheid – uneven development and accumulation by dispossession – is still omnipresent, and the purveyors of neoliberal ideology and the strategists of imperialism continue expressing their breathtaking arrogance with such resolve.

Still, if the bulk of work lies in activism, that does not mean the intellectual project can be set aside. Even if the theory of uneven development is explored from many angles,[64] it will still be necessary to expand our case studies of concrete forms of unevenness, and in the process to demonstrate in both intellectual and political terms that the theory can easily jump scale from local to global and back; that it can transcend political-economic enquiries into investment and labour relations by reaching ever further into the sphere of social reproduction; and, most importantly, that it can inform activists intent on reversing unevenness and ultimately defeating imperialism.

# APPENDIX

## FIVE IDEOLOGICAL REACTIONS TO 'GLOBAL APARTHEID'

### Global justice movements

*Main agenda*
'Deglobalisation' of capital (not people) and 'globalisation-from-below'; anti-war; anti-racism; indigenous rights; women's liberation; ecology; 'decommodified' state services; participatory democracy

*Internal disputes*
Role of nation-state; party politics; fix-it v nix-it strategies for international agencies; gender and racial power relations; divergent interests (e.g. Northern labour and environment against Southern sovereignty); and tactics (especially merits of symbolic property destruction)

*Leading institutions*
Social movements; environmental justice activists; indigenous peoples and autonomist groups; radical activist networks; some left labour movements; left-wing think-tanks (Focus on the Global South, FoodFirst, Global Exchange, IBASE, IFG, IPS, Nader centres, TNI); leftist media and websites (e.g. Indymedia, Pacifica, www.zmag.org); a few semi-liberated zones (Porto Alegre, Kerala); and sectoral or local coalitions allied to World Social Forum

*Exemplary proponents*
M. Albert T. Ali S. Amin
C. Augiton M. Barlow
D. Barsamian H. Belafonte
W. Bello A. Bendana F. Betto
J. Bove J. Brecher R. Brenner
D. Brutus N. Bullard A. Buzgalin
L. Cagan A. Callinicos L. Cassarini
J. Cavanagh C. Chalmers
N. Chomsky A. Choudry
T. Clarke A. Cockburn K. Danaher
A. Escobar E. Galeano S. George
D. Glover A. Grubacic M. Hardt
D. Harvey D. Henwood
J. Holloway B. Kagarlitsky
P. Kingsnorth N. Klein M. Lowy
Marcos A. Mittal G. Monbiot
M. Moore E. Morales R. Nader
V. Navarro A. Negri T. Ngwane
N. Njehu G. Palast M. Patkar
J. Pilger A. Roy E. Said J. Sen
V. Shiva J. Singh B. Sousa Santos
A. Starr J. Stedile T. Teivainen,
V. Vargas G. Vidal H. Wainwright
L. Wallach M. Weisbrot
R. Weissman H. Zinn

## Third World nationalism

*Main agenda*
Increased (but fairer) global
integration via reform – not
transformation – of interstate
system, based on debt relief
and expanded market access;
democratised global governance;
regionalism; anti-imperialism

*Internal disputes*
Degree of militancy against
North; divergent regional
interests; religion; egos and
internecine rivalries

*Leading institutions*
Non-Aligned Movement, G77
and South Centre; self-selecting
regimes (often authoritarian):
Argentina, Chile, China, Egypt,
India, Iraq, Libya, Malaysia,
Nigeria, Pakistan, Palestine,
Russia, South Africa, Turkey,
Zimbabwe with a few – like
Brazil, Cuba and Venezuela
– that lean left (but others
soft on imperialism, e.g. East
Timor, Ecuador and Eritrea); and
supportive NGOs (e.g. Third
World Network, Seatini)

*Exemplary proponents*
Y. Arafat F. Castro H. Chavez
M. Gaddafi H. Jintao M. Khor
N. Kirshner R. Lagos Lula
M. Mahathir N. Mandela T. Mbeki
R. Mugabe O. Obasanjo D. Ortega
V. Putin Y. Tandon

## Post-Washington Consensus

*Main agenda*
Fix 'imperfect markets'; add
'sustainable development' to
existing capitalist framework via
global state-building; promote
global Keynesianism; oppose US
unilateralism and militarism

*Internal disputes*
Some look leftward (for broader
alliances) while others look
right to Washington Consensus
(resources, legitimacy)

*Leading institutions*
WSSD; some UN agencies (e.g. UNCTAD, UNICEF, UNRISD); some international NGOs (e.g. Care, Civicus, IUCN, Oxfam, TI); large enviromental groups (e.g. Sierra and WWF); big labour (e.g., ICFTU and AFL-CIO); liberal foundations (e.g. Carnegie, Ford, MacArthur, Mott, Open Society, Rockefeller); Columbia University economics department; and Canadian and Scandinavian governments

*Exemplary proponents*
Y. Akyuz K. Annan L. Axworthy Bono G. Brundtland S. Byers B. Cassen J. Chretien P. Eigen J. Fischer A. Giddens W. Hutton P. Krugman W. Maathai P. Martin T. Mkandawire M. Moody-Stuart K. Naidoo T. Palley J. Persson John Paul II M. Robinson D. Rodrik J. Sachs W. Sachs A. Sen G. Soros J. Stiglitz P. Sweeney G. Verhofstadt E. von Weizaecher K. Watkins

## Washington Consensus

*Main agenda*
Rename neoliberalism (PRSPs, HIPC and PPPs) but with some provisions for 'transparency' and self-regulation; more effective bail-out mechanisms; general support for US-led empire

*Internal disputes*
Differing reactions to US empire owing to divergent national-capitalist interests and domestic political dynamics

*Leading institutions*
US state (Fed, Treasury, USAid); corporate media and big business; World Bank, IMF, WTO; elite clubs (Bilderburgers, Trilateral Commission, World Economic Forum); UN agencies (UNDP, Global Compact); universities and think-tanks (University of Chicago economics department, Council on Foreign Relations, Institute of International Finance, Brookings); most EU governments and Japan

*Exemplary proponents*
T. Blair G. Brown M. Camdessus J. Chirac B. Clinton A. Erwin S. Fischer M. Friedman T. Friedman A. Greenspan S. Harbinson A. Krueger P. Lamy M. Malloch Brown T. Manuel R. Prodi K. Rogoff R. Rubin G. Schroeder Supachai P. J. Snow L. Summers J. Taylor J. Wolfensohn E. Zedillo R. Zoellick

## Resurgent right wing

*Main agenda*
Unilateral petro-military imperialism; protectionism, tariffs, subsidies, bailouts and other crony deals; reverse globalisation of people via racism and xenophobia; intensified social control

*Internal disputes*
Conflict over extent of US imperial reach and over how to protect national sovereignty, cultural traditions and patriarchy

*Leading institutions*
Republican Party populist and libertarian wings; Project for New American Century; right-wing think-tanks (AEI, Cato, CSIS, Heritage, Manhattan); the Christian Right; petro-military complex; Pentagon; right-wing media (Fox, *National Interest*, *Weekly Standard*, *Washington Times*); and proto-fascist European parties – but also Israel's Likud and perhaps Islamic extremism

*Exemplary proponents*
E. Abrams J. Aznar S. Berlusconi O. bin Laden C. Black P. Buchanan G. Bush D. Cheney N. Gingrich J. Haider R. Kagan H. Kissinger W. Kristol J. M. le Pen R. Limbaugh R. Murdoch J. Negroponte M. Peretz R. Perle N. Podhoretz O. Reich C. Rice D. Rumsfeld A. Scalia A. Sharon P. Wolfowitz J. Woolsey

### NOTES

1. Mbeki, T. (2002), 'Address by President Mbeki at the Welcome Ceremony of the WSSD', Johannesburg, 25 August.
2. A useful survey is found in A. Brewer (1980), *Marxist Theories of Imperialism: A critical survey* (London: Routledge and Kegan Paul). Original texts include N. Bukharin (1972) [1917], *Imperialism and the World Economy* (New York: Monthly Review Press); H. Grossmann (1992) [1929], *The Law of Accumulation and Breakdown of the Capitalist System* (London: Pluto Press); R. Hilferding (1981) [1910], *Finance Capital* (London: Routledge and Kegan Paul); and V. Lenin (1986) [1917], *Imperialism* (Moscow: Progress Publishers).
3. R. Luxemburg (1968) [1923], *The Accumulation of Capital* (New York: Monthly Review Press), p347.
4. Ibid., pp396, 452–3.

5. Ibid., p370. Updates of the theme that capitalism requires pre-capitalist 'articulations' are found in D. Seddon (ed.) (1998), *Relations of Production: Marxist approaches to economic anthropology* (London: Frank Cass); and H. Wolpe (ed.) (1980), *The Articulations of Modes of Production* (London: Routledge and Kegan Paul).

6. D. Harvey, (2003), 'The "New" Imperialism: On spatio-temporal fixes and accumulation by dispossession', in L. Panitch and C. Leys, *Socialist Register 2004* (London: Merlin Press and New York: Monthly Review Press).

7. Ibid.

8. For more theoretical and empirical information on primitive accumulation, see D. Moore (2002), 'Zimbabwe's Triple Crisis: Primitive accumulation, nation-state formation and democratisation in the age of neoliberal globalisation', Paper presented to the conference on Transition and Crisis in Zimbabwe, Centre of African Studies, University of Florida, Gainesville, 2 March; M. Perelman (2000), *The Invention of Capitalism: Classical political economy and the secret history of primitive accumulation* (Durham: Duke University Press); C. von Werlhof (2000), 'Globalization and the Permanent Process of Primitive Accumulation: The example of the MAI, the Multilateral Agreement on Investment', *Journal of World Systems Research*, vol. 6, no. 3; P. Zarembka (2000), 'Accumulation of Capital, Its Definition: A century after Lenin and Luxemburg', in P. Zarembka (ed.), *Value, Capitalist Dynamics and Money: Research in political economy, Volume 18* (Stamford and Amsterdam: JAI/Elsevier); and P. Zarembka (2002), 'Primitive Accumulation in Marxism: Historical or trans-historical separation from means of production?', *The Commoner*, http://www.thecommoner.org, March.

9. Harvey, 'The "New" Imperialism'.

10. S. Amin (2003), 'Confronting the Empire', paper presented to the conference on The Work of Karl Marx and the Challenges of the 21st Century, Institute of Philosophy of the Ministry of Science, Technology and the Environment, the National Association of Economists of Cuba, the Cuban Trade Union Federation and the Centre for the Study of Economy and Planning, Havana, 5–8 May.

11. L. Panitch and S. Gindin (2003), 'Global Capitalism and American Empire', in Panitch and Leys, *Socialist Register 2004*.

12. Ibid.

13. Amin, 'Confronting the Empire'.

14. Ibid.

15. United States Naval War College (2003), 'The Pentagon's New Map', http://www.nwc.navy.mil/newrules/ ThePentagonsNewMap.htm.

16. Panitch and Gindin, 'Global Capitalism and American Empire'.

17. P. Bond (2003) [2001], *Against Global Apartheid: South Africa meets the World Bank, IMF and International Finance* (Cape Town: University of Cape Town Press and London: Zed Books); (2004), *Talk Left, Walk Right: South Africa's frustrated global reforms* (Pietermaritzburg: University of KwaZulu-Natal Press).

18. J. Adesina (2002), 'Nepad and the Challenge of Africa's Development: Towards the political economy of a discourse', Unpublished paper, Rhodes University Department of Sociology, Grahamstown.

19. Ibid.
20. This is a perpetual theme in P. Bond (2002), *Unsustainable South Africa: Environment, development and social protest* (London: Merlin Press and Pietermaritzburg: University of Natal Press).
21. Bond, *Against Global Apartheid*, Ch. 12.
22. These are covered well elsewhere, and don't bear repetition: J. Fisher (2002), 'Africa', in E. Bircham and J. Charlton (eds) (2002), *Anti-Capitalism: A guide to the movement* (London: Bookmarks); L. Zeilig (ed.) (2002), *Class Struggle and Resistance in Africa* (Cheltenham: New Clarion).
23. *Guardian*, 20 February 2003.
24. I. Taylor and G. Mokhawa (2003), 'Not Forever: Botswana, conflict diamonds and the Bushmen', *African Affairs*, vol. 102. The UN Committee on the Elimination of Racial Discrimination also condemned Botswana. On the other side, the permanent secretary in Botswana's Ministry of Mineral Resources and Water Affairs (and deputy Chairman of Debswana) called Survival a 'terrorist organisation' in 2003.
25. http://www.irn.org.
26. Many such community campaigns are covered thoroughly on the South African Indymedia website, which is one of several – Nigeria and Zimbabwe were also active by the end of 2002, with more planned – that periodically report on anti-capitalist activism.
27. Cited in P. Bond (ed.) (2002), *Fanon's Warning: A civil society reader on the New Partnership for Africa's Development* (Trenton: Africa World Press and Cape Town: AIDC), p48.
28. Adesina, 'Nepad and the Challenge of Africa's Development'.
29. Report of the Codesria/TWN Conference on Africa and the Challenge of the 21st Century, Accra, 23–26 April, excerpted from Bond, *Fanon's Warning*. Such a revival would have to be, in my own opinion, grounded in classical theories of commodity-form and value, accumulation and overaccumulation, spatio-temporal crisis and crisis displacement, accumulation by dispossession, and the untenable rise of finance/commerce, augmented for better incorporation of the reproductive aspects and gender dynamics of capitalism, systemic environmental degradation, aspects of social resistance, and many other ethnic and cultural factors that have been used by critics illegitimately to denounce Marxism as a holistic theory of social relations.
30. S. Amin (1985), *Delinking: Towards a polycentric world* (London: Zed Books).
31. W. Bello (2002), *Deglobalization: Ideas for a new world economy* (London: Zed Press).
32. Bond, *Against Global Apartheid*, Part Four.
33. Ibid., Ch. 12.
34. D. Ellerman (2004), *Helping People Help Themselves: From the World Bank to an alternative philosophy of development* (Ann Arbor: University of Michigan Press). Persuasion by reformists within the chief economist's office simply did not affect the institution, agreed William Easterly, a former senior staffer: 'There's a big disconnect between World Bank operations and World Bank research. There's almost an organisational feud between the research wing and the rest of the Bank. The rest of

the Bank thinks research people are just talking about irrelevant things and don't know the reality of what's going on on the ground' (*New York Times*, 7 June 2003).

35. *Financial Times*, 21 August 2002. Stiglitz was interviewed by Doug Henwood on WBAI in New York. Because the idea is such an important one and the social forces of the global justice movements are mobilising, it is not surprising that the mainstream press, and the South African media in particular, have been so wary about allowing this idea to spread.

36. Interpress Service, 2 August 2002.

37. Not surprisingly (because his prior job was public relations director for the World Bank), the UNDP's Mark Malloch Brown insisted, 'It would be an absurdity for countries that are so dependent on financial assistance to go unilaterally and poke the donors in the eye.' Mozambican Prime Minister Pascoal Mocumbi agreed: 'If I stopped paying debt service, all my poverty-reduction money would stop from the World Bank and IMF. Fifty percent of our budget is from donors. I can't not pay. The country would stop.' UN special AIDS envoy Stephen Lewis retorted, 'There are some donors who would be privately pleased, although they would never publicly take this stand' (*Boston Globe*, 4 August 2002).

38. *Financial Times*, 13 August 2002.

39. N. Ndungane (2003), *A World with a Human Face: A voice from Africa* (Cape Town: David Philip), p31.

40. *Mail and Guardian*, 27 April–3 May 2001.

41. P. McCully (2002), 'Avoiding Solutions, Worsening Problems', San Francisco, International Rivers Network, http://www.irn.org, p40. For more on the background and South African politics associated with the Commission, see Bond, *Unsustainable South Africa*, Chs 3 and 7.

42. Sapri provided six conclusions from the studies:

    (1) Trade liberalisation, financial sector liberalisation, the weakening of state support and reduction of demand for local goods and services have devastated local industries especially small and medium-sized enterprises providing most national employment.

    (2) Structural and sectoral policy reforms in agriculture and mining have undermined the viability of small farms, weakened food security and damaged the natural environment.

    (3) A combination of labour market reforms, lay-offs resulting from privatisation and the shrinking of labour-intensive productive sectors have undermined the position of workers, causing employment to drop, real wages to fall and workers' rights to weaken.

    (4) Privatisation of public utilities and the application of user fees to healthcare and education have disproportionately reduced the poor's access to affordable services.

    (5) Increased impoverishment caused by structural adjustment has affected women more than men.

    (6) Many of the anticipated gains in efficiency, competitiveness, savings and revenues from privatisation have failed to materialise. Trade liberalisation has increased rather than decreased current account deficits and external debt, while transnational corporations have become more powerful in the structurally adjusted countries.

43. http://www.saprin.org/.

44. R. Peet (2003), *The World Bank, IMF and WTO* (London: Zed Press), Ch. 4.

45. http://www.worldbankboycott.org. Note that the organisations that had endorsed the WBBB included major religious orders (the Conference of Major Superiors of Men, Pax Christi USA, the Unitarian Universalist General Assembly, and dozens of others); the most important social responsibility funds (Calvert Group, Global Greengrants Fund, Ben and Jerry's Foundation, and Trillium Assets Management); the University of New Mexico endowment fund; other US cities (including Milwaukee and Cambridge); and major trade union pension/investment funds (e.g. Teamsters, Postal Workers, Service Employees Int'l, American Federation of Government Employees, Longshoremen, Communication Workers of America, United Electrical Workers).

46. *Evening Standard*, 17 April 2002.

47. Amin, 'Confronting the Empire'.

48. S. Amin (2003), 'Laying New Foundations for Solidarity Among Peoples of the South', paper presented to the conference on The Work of Karl Marx and the Challenges of the 21st Century, Institute of Philosophy of the Ministry of Science, Technology and the Environment, the National Association of Economists of Cuba, the Cuban Trade Union Federation and the Centre for the Study of Economy and Planning, Havana, 5–8 May.

49. Ibid.

50. Ibid.

51. P. Dwyer (2003), 'The New Global Peace Movement vs. the Bush Juggernaut', http://www.lists.kabissa.org/ mailman/listinfo/debate, 26 May.

52. Amin, 'Laying New Foundations for Solidarity Among Peoples of the South'.

53. J. Brecher (2003), 'The New Global Peace Movement vs. the Bush Juggernaut', http://www.lists.kabissa.org/ mailman/listinfo/debate, 6 June. See also Brecher's longer analysis: http://www.foreignpolicy-infocus. org/ papers/juggernaut/index.html.

54. W. Martin (2003), 'Three Hundred Years of World Movements: Towards the end of the capitalist world-economy?', presented at the Sociology Seminar, Rand Afrikaans University, Johannesburg, 13 June. See also A.G. Frank and M. Fuentes (1990), 'Civil Democracy: Social movements in recent world history', in S. Amin, G. Arrighi, A.G. Frank and I. Wallerstein, *Transforming the Revolution: Social movements and the world-system* (New York: Monthly Review Press).

55. Going back to the Habsburg and Ottoman Empires, Martin continues, 'It is possible to trace transnational networks of not only ideological opposition to older imperial networks, but also increasingly interconnected revolt against core agents of the rising capitalist world-economy. Merchants, mariners and diasporic networks, integrally tied to global economic processes and political struggles, began to fuel nationalist and revivalist revolts' that reached as far as Indonesia. In the eighteenth century, 'a rising tide of revolts against the central, proletarian base of the eighteenth

century existed, leading to the destruction of a world-wide system of enslavement and slave-based commodity production'. This entailed 'extensive networking and clustering of emancipatory struggles across colonial boundaries prior to, rather than derived from, the French (and American) Revolution', of which Haiti was a crucial example. The mid-nineteenth century was the period of state-oriented party-building, and from 1917 national independence revolutions were common, all based upon the 'expectation that state power would bring emancipation' (Martin, 'Three Hundred Years of World Movements').

56. Ibid.
57. Ibid.
58. A. Starr and J. Adams (2003), 'Anti-globalisation: The global fight for local autonomy', *New Political Science*, vol. 25, no. 1.
59. Transcribed by the author and cited in P. Bond (2003), 'Cuba Dares', ZNet Commentary, http://www.zmag.org, 29 May.
60. There are numerous books that analyse the global justice movements. Aside from Naomi Klein's *NoLogo*, the one broad overview that has sold the most copies in English is E. Bircham and J. Charlton (eds) (2002), *Anti-Capitalism: A guide to the movement* (London: Bookmarks). Some of the numerous other recent English-language movement analyses include C. Aguiton (2003), *The World Belongs to Us!* (London: Verso); S. Alvarez, E. Dagnino and A. Escobar (eds) (1998), *Cultures of Politics; Politics of Cultures: Re-visioning Latin American social movements* (Boulder: Westview); S. Amin and F. Houtart (eds) (2003), *The Globalisation of Resistance: The state of the struggles* (London: Zed); A. Anand, A. Escobar, J. Sen and P. Waterman (eds) (2003), *Are Other Worlds Possible? The past, present, and futures of the World Social Forum* (New Delhi: Viveka); A. Callinicos (2003), *An Anti-Capitalist Manifesto* (Cambridge: Polity); W. Fisher and T. Ponniah (eds) (2003), *Another World is Possible: Popular Alternatives to Globalization at the World Social Forum* (London: Zed); Kingsnorth, *One No, Many Yesses*; J. Smith and H. Johnston (eds) (2002), *Globalization and Resistance: Transnational dimensions of social movements* (Lanham: Rowman and Littlefield); A. Starr (2000), *Naming the Enemy: Anti-corporate movements confront globalisation* (London: Zed); P. Waterman (2001), *Globalization, Social Movements and the New Internationalisms* (London: Continuum).
61. P. Waterman (2003), 'The Global Justice and Solidarity Movement', http://groups.yahoo.com/group/GloSoDia/.
62. The first international was the International Working Men's (*sic*) Association, which Marx and Engels helped kickstart with the *Communist Manifesto* in 1848. The second was a social democratic flop, which did not prevent workers from turning nationalistic at the time of the First World War. The third was a Stalinist merger of Soviet defensiveness and nationalist liberation, which exhausted itself long before the Berlin Wall fell. The fourth represented one key strand of the Trotskyist tradition, which surveyed Stalin's murder of Leon, but faded by the 1990s (though still alive in Mbeki's nightmares and the laudable journal *International Viewpoint*). A fifth international would have to innovate in terms of avoiding sectarianism, vanguardism, dogmatism, patriarchy, anthropocentrism, and other classic sins of the 'groupuscule' left.

63. For more on the concept, see, e.g., P. Mosley,(1997), 'The World Bank, "Global Keynesianism" and the Distribution of the Gains from Growth', *World Development*, vol. 25, no. 11; G. Koehler (1999), 'Global Keynesianism and Beyond', *Journal of World-Systems Research*, no. 5, http://csf.colorado.edu/wsystems/jwsr.html; G. Koehler and A. Tausch (2002), *Global Keynesianism: Unequal exchange and global exploitation* (Huntington, USA: Nova Science).

64. See, e.g., M. Aglietta (1976), *A Theory of Capitalist Regulation* (London: New Left Books); P. Bond (1998), *Uneven Zimbabwe: A study of finance, development and underdevelopment* (Trenton: Africa World Press), and (1999), 'Uneven Development', in P. O'Hara (ed.), *Encyclopaedia of Political Economy* (London: Routledge); Harvey, *The Limits to Capital*; E. Mandel (1962), *Marxist Economic Theory*, Vol. 1 (London: Merlin Press); N. Smith (1990), *Uneven Development* (Oxford: Basil Blackwell).

# 8

# Unity, Diversity and International Co-operation: The US War Drive and the Anti-war Movement

*Kate Hudson*[1]

The US/UK war against Iraq has provoked one of the largest anti-war campaigns that the world has ever seen. In Britain we have seen an unprecedented level of opposition to the government's support for that war, and the scale of the opposition – which on 15 February 2003 moved towards a mobilisation of 2 million – surprised even the anti-war campaigners. We are striving towards an understanding of the factors that have led both to the war itself, and to the scale of opposition to it, not least because we are aware that there is a strong likelihood of future wars, and we need to sustain this great movement to pressurise our government against participation in further illegal wars.

The war against Iraq has shifted the balance of power, both in the Middle East, and in the world as a whole, further in the direction of the United States, and it is clear that this is neither the beginning nor the end of US incursions. This is only the latest stage in a process of US wars, which is part of a conscious US strategy. The recent war against Afghanistan has already consolidated bases in Central Asia for the US; the war against Yugoslavia in the 1990s had already consolidated US influence in the Balkans. In fact, in military terms there has been an enormous advance for the US since the end of the Soviet Union and the Cold War in 1991.

Yet although the US is in some senses at the height of its powers, there are contradictions within the situation that we should consider in order to understand the overall situation. The first issue is that while the US is militarily very powerful it has some fundamental economic problems, as evidenced by its massive balance of payments deficit. Between the Second World War and 1974, the US economically subsidised the non-socialist world, so it had real hegemony – the consent of peoples to its domination. Since the economic crisis of

1974, the situation has reversed. The US has subsidised itself at the expense of the rest of the world, which has given rise to increasing antagonisms. Of course, the US has had the advantage of supposedly winning the Cold War, and facing no great rival superpower. So the US has a pre-eminence in the world that is real, but it is sustained by sucking in wealth from the rest of the world. On that basis the UK is not going to get the kind of consent to domination it got in the postwar decades, from Germany say, or from Japan, whom it basically funded and ran.

Now US domination has to be established by force, and the major factor in this is to ensure the economic wherewithal for the US economy. Thus domination of the Middle East is a crucial factor, because of the importance of oil to the US economy. So while the US appears to be at the peak of its global hegemony, in reality it is losing its hegemony, because the consent of peoples and even nations that have traditionally backed the US is being withdrawn.

Over this war against Iraq, the US faced enormous popular protests on a worldwide basis. This opposition built on and consolidated opposition that already existed against neoliberalism and globalisation in many parts of the world. More people than ever before, in Britain, and in the rest of the world, have realised what the real agenda of the war was, and are not taken in by pretexts such as supposed weapons of mass destruction or arguments about humanitarian war. But the war also led to an unprecedented development that is of great significance – the deep divisions in the advanced industrialised countries, leading to a split within the European Union and NATO; division between those countries that have opted to try and stay in the US framework, either through close economic links, like the UK, or in the hope of economic support and security guarantees, like Poland, and between those who have tried to draw the line at further US economic and military domination, which will negatively affect their own economies and interests, like France, Germany, Russia and so on. Obviously the peace movement does not take sides between rival economic interests, but nevertheless the fact that the Western powers were divided over the war gave hope to countless people that it would actually be possible to prevent the illegal war against Iraq from happening.

So the US has gained increasing military dominance in the world, to advance its economic interests and subsidise its economy, but in becoming an economic parasite on the rest of the world, it has lost the consent of peoples and states, as so clearly shown recently. But of course this does not mean that the US is about to roll over and give up. On the contrary, its level of military power is such that it can just go ahead. The example of the Iraq War shows that it just doesn't care about global opposition either from peoples or states. There are indications that the US has its sights on Iran, and it seems likely that if it can't bring about a regime change through interfering in the political framework, it may well resort to war. Much of the rhetoric used against Iran, since the war on Iraq, is very similar to that used against Iraq in the build-up towards war.

This overall approach has been clearly articulated by the US administration, and one can point to many policy and strategy areas that make the US trajectory totally explicit. Three of these are particularly worthy of note. First, the Project for the New American Century, which was established in spring 1997, supposedly as a non-profit, educational organisation whose goal is to ensure American global leadership. It is actually a neo-conservative think-tank with Cheney, Rumsfeld and Wolfowitz in its leadership. Its origins date back to the early 1990s, when the Defense Secretary, Dick Cheney, was setting out his 'peace through strength' policy, based on an aggressive and unilateral approach to securing US domination. Taking a very positive attitude towards the foreign policy approach of the Reagan administration, it argued some fundamental propositions: that American leadership is good for both America and the world; that such leadership requires military strength, diplomatic energy and commitment to moral principle; and that too few American political leaders today are making the case for global leadership. The Project clearly articulated the foreign policy aims of the Bush camp prior to his election, and was strongly oriented towards winning people over within the US political arena. Having secured the presidency, Bush has subsequently been able to push forward the agenda outlined by the Project.

Two specific military strategies fit very clearly within this overall framework. First is the notion of full-spectrum dominance. In May 2000, the Department of Defense issued Joint Vision 2020, a document that spells out how the US will achieve full-spectrum military dominance on land, sea, air and space by the year 2020. With it comes the grave danger of the militarisation of space. Indeed, US Space Command former commander in chief General Joseph W. Ashy stated, 'Some people don't want to hear this ... but – absolutely – we're going to fight in space. We're going to fight from space and we're going to fight into space' (www.cnduk.org). Full-spectrum dominance is defined as 'the ability of US forces, operating unilaterally or in combination with multinational or interagency partners, to defeat any adversary and control any situation across the full range of military operations'. This will be secured by investing in and developing new military capabilities. The four capabilities deemed to be at the heart of full-spectrum dominance are 'dominant maneuver, precision engagement, focused logistics and full-dimensional protection' (www.defenselink.mil/news/Jun2000). Joint Vision 2020 addresses full-spectrum dominance across a range of conflicts from nuclear war to major theatre wars, to smaller-scale contingencies. The US National Missile Defense Program, which is an update of Reagan's Star Wars policy, is clearly a facet of this. It is a system that will allow the US to hide behind a defensive shield of sensors that would detect any incoming missiles and shoot them down. Thus, it will allow the US to make pre-emptive nuclear attacks on other countries and is already leading to a new nuclear arms race. It has also already led to the withdrawal of the US from the Anti-Ballistic Missile Treaty, against the wishes of the overwhelming majority of the UN – a further sign of US unilateralism and, according to John Pilger, 'the first time in the nuclear era that Washington had renounced a major arms control accord' (*Morning Star*, 16 August 2003, p9). The British government has already given the go-ahead for use of British facilities at Fylingdales and Menwith Hill in Yorkshire for NMD, which will put Britain in the firing line in the event of any future conflict. It would seem that in spite of considerable rhetoric about 'new threats' in the post 9/11 world, the logic of NMD is primarily against nuclear powers or major state actors, such as Russia and – potentially – China. So indeed is NATO expansion into Eastern Europe, especially with its newly defined remit for out-of-area operations.

Secondly, the Nuclear Posture Review, submitted to the US Congress in December 2001, which lays out the direction of US nuclear forces for the next five to ten years, and indicates a major change in approach. The Review establishes a so-called New Triad, comprising offensive strike systems (both nuclear and non-nuclear); defences (active and passive); and a revitalised defence infrastructure to provide new capabilities in a timely fashion to meet emerging threats. Basically the approach of the Review is to abandon the deterrent notion of mutually assured destruction and to introduce the concept of the offensive strike system and reinforce the policy of nuclear first use. It also speaks of the 'need' for 'low-yield nuclear weapons for possible attacks on a shopping list of 'enemies of the

United States' – Libya, Syria, Iran, Iraq and North Korea' (ibid.). The overall policy approach is totally overt about pre-emption, nuclear first strike and unilateralism.

In the face of this approach by the US, clearly the largest and most effective anti-war movement is essential on a worldwide basis. We have seen the development of a real mass movement over the last two years, which focused on the prevention of the war on Iraq. It is most likely that there will be further challenges facing anti-war movements in the next months and years, so an understanding of how this movement has evolved is essential.

I would like to consider three key factors: the unity of the movement, the diversity of the movement, and the importance of the international co-operation that has made it possible to co-ordinate worldwide activity in an effective way. The first two will make specific reference to the anti-war movement in Britain, but it is clear from discussion with anti-war leaders and activists from across the world that this general pattern is valid internationally.

First, the unity of the movement. Following the attacks on the US on September 11, 2001, the Campaign for Nuclear Disarmament (CND) condemned the terrorist atrocities and demanded that those responsible be brought to justice. At the same time we made it clear that we equally condemned all killings of innocent civilians, whether perpetrated by state or non-state actors, and that we were not prepared to stand by and watch the US attack Afghanistan in order to take revenge. We wanted to see the guilty brought to justice, not the killing of innocent civilians. This simple position proved to be a basis for building opposition to the war on Afghanistan.

At the same time, as well as the opposition voiced by CND as a peace organisation, there was also the development of a more directly politically based organisation, the Stop the War Coalition, the position of which was to campaign against the US's so-called 'war on terrorism'. The leadership of this organisation originated in the ultra-left section of British politics, but it soon became a much broader and genuinely mass movement, which was able to attract not only political activists but ordinary citizens, trade unions, faith groups and a range of different political parties – in short, people from every walk of life. As the focus moved during 2002 towards the threat of war against Iraq, another significant organisation became a part of the broader movement against the war. This was the Muslim Association of Britain. Britain has a significant Muslim community, primarily based on immigration from former British colonies over the last few decades. In the period after September 11, Muslims have often been under attack in a racist backlash – often being seen as potential terrorists. The British government has done little to challenge this absurd caricature, and some observers consider that the government has taken advantage of this portrayal to introduce more draconian treatment of asylum seekers. The Muslim community opposed the attacks on Afghanistan, but also became increasingly involved in the campaign against war on Iraq. This culminated in a tripartite alliance from the end of 2002 between CND, the Stop the War Coalition and the Muslim Association of Britain.

It was this alliance that led the mobilisations against the war on Iraq in the early months of 2003. A key factor in the maintenance of this unity was the insistence on a simple uniting theme – No War on Iraq. While the organisations were at liberty to develop their own issues in their own publicity materials, the common position was clear. We specifically rejected any attempts to integrate political positions about the Saddam Hussein regime, or about the Kurds, or any other issue that – while serious and important in its own right – could lead to a fracturing of unity. Since the end of the main phase of the war on Iraq and the lessening of anti-war activity that has followed, we have been aware of a number of political attacks on the anti-war movement, both by disaffected elements within it and by pro-war forces outside the movement. These have tended to take two forms: first, attacks on the left elements within the Stop the War Coalition who have been accused of sectarianism and manipulation of the movement; and secondly, attacks on the Muslim Association for supposed fundamentalism. These transparent attempts to split the movement have been rejected by the three organisations, and we continue to work together. To secure the future effectiveness of the anti-war movement, unity is essential, and further joint activities are being planned.

Secondly, the diversity of the movement. The three key organisations together bring diverse communities to the movement, but there are other features of the diversity of the movement that are worth exploring. Going back to 2001, the first big demonstration against the war on Afghanistan, with around 50,000 participants, took place in October. Our second demo, which was planned for November, actually took place about a week after the fall of Kabul. There were many who said at the time that no-one would come on this second demonstration, but in the event, it was larger than the first, with around 80,000 participants. There was a quite extraordinary and noticeable change at this second demonstration, because there was for the first time a huge diversity on the march. Whereas the first demonstration had been primarily pacifists and anti-war demonstrators, this demonstration included campaigners against globalisation, against oppression in the occupied territories, against debt, against the arms trade and much more. It was as if a sudden realisation had occurred, on the part of many people, of how all these events and problems in the world are actually linked together and that it is in some way part of a huge process. Many long-standing peace activists commented on the diverse nature of the movement at this point, and profoundly welcomed it.

It is important to analyse this development, and it is helpful to understand it in the context of the developments of the last decade. With the end of the Cold War after the events of 1989 and 1991, the conventional wisdom was that a new world order of peace, prosperity and security would be ushered in, and some even spoke of 'the end of history' in the sense of the end of the great conflicts of the modern age based around class. Clearly, with hindsight this was not the case, and the years since then have seen the rise of popular protest. This was firstly in response to neoliberal economic reforms, which have led in Western Europe to a strengthening of the left, and more broadly to anti-capitalist and anti-neoliberal globalisation tendencies.

After 1991, neoliberalism – free market economics pioneered in the 1980s by Reagan and Thatcher – swept across the world. As the 1990s progressed, country after country was opened up, not only to the free movement of goods, but also to the free movement of capital. In this process the main beneficiary overall was the US, and the trend of capital flows was from the poorest countries in the world to the richest. National protections for economies, tariffs and so on, were systematically broken down, barriers to market entry were demolished, often as conditions of economic aid to the Third World – such as structural adjustment policies. This was also the time of the beginning of the great attacks on the welfare states. In the US, Newt Gingrich, leader of the Republicans in the US Congress, claimed that extensive welfare provision and progressive taxation had been artefacts of the Cold War. He argued that with the external threat of Communism banished, these internal concessions to the socialist threat should be dismantled. This type of approach was welcomed by many politicians in Western Europe who sought to make European capitalism more competitive, and the Treaty of Maastricht in the European Union indicated a move towards the breaking down of welfare provision, huge reductions in government spending and so on. Politically this drive towards neoliberalism and the breaking down of Keynesian welfare economics was welcomed by many – not only from the right, but also from social democracy. Tony Blair, for example, was typical of social democratic leaders who opted for neoliberalism, embracing policies of privatisation and public spending cuts. The so-called 'Third Way' politics was an attempt to give a social-friendly gloss to neoliberalism.

Thus the 1990s was a time of the extension of neoliberalism worldwide – this was the globalisation that so many have experienced, with such negative consequences. But of course this process has not gone unchallenged. From the early 1990s there has been increasing opposition to neoliberalism, in particular in Latin America, where its consequences have been devastating. But there has also been considerable campaigning in Western Europe against it – in opposition to the implementation of the Maastricht criteria, for example. There have been big public sector strikes in France against government spending cuts, and big demonstrations in Italy against attacks on pensions. These campaigns have strengthened the left in parts of Western Europe. In Eastern Europe and the former Soviet Union, countries have been severely affected by privatisation and government spending cuts, and there has been a massive increase in poverty since 1989, with not so much mass organised opposition.

The development of the anti-globalisation movement has been a powerful process in recent years. It is not a socially marginalised phenomenon as some people like to portray, but involves many movements from civil society, non-governmental organisations, trade unions and progressive governments. The impetus for the shaping of this broad range of forces into a more cohesive entity has come through the World Social Forum, first held in Porto Alegre in Brazil, giving rise to the slogan 'Another World is Possible', and now expanded into other continents.

Secondly, there has been a mass radicalisation against war, which has increasingly – perhaps because of the former politicisation around globalisation – had an anti-imperialist element to it. What has particularly brought these two movements into greater alignment is the increasingly transparent linking factor: US economic policies opening up the world not only to globalisation of trade but also to globalisation of capital flows; and US military policies driving towards a pre-emptive unilateralism and a push for full-spectrum dominance primarily for strategic and resource reasons. There has been widespread opposition to the concrete manifestations of both of these policy areas: in the economic field there has been mass campaigning against attacks on welfare states, for the cancellation of debt and even for taxation on capital movement; in the military field there has been mass anti-war campaigning, primarily against the war on Iraq, but also against the US national missile defence system and the new nuclear arms race that it is beginning.

The overall context of these policies is now completely clear, because US policies are totally explicit, as has been outlined above. These factors also play a role, not only in the reasons for the scale of the popular opposition to the war internationally, but also to the unprecedented split within NATO over the war on Iraq, and also the division within the European Union. At the moment of its greatest military dominance, the US actually has serious problems – in its economy and within its traditional alliances. So, the new movements and campaigns against all these assaults have contributed to the diversity of the anti-war movement, and their interrelated nature is increasingly understood.

Thirdly, then, the importance of international links in the development of the anti-war movement. On 15 February 2003, demonstrations against the war took place simultaneously in many countries across the world leading to the mobilisation of many millions of people. Such a level of co-ordination had a massive impact. This initiative grew out of the establishment of an International Anti-War Coordination at the European Social Forum meeting in Florence in November 2002. The Social Forum movement, stemming from the World Social Forums in Porto Alegre, is an important factor in both the diversity of the anti-war movement and in its international dimensions. As mentioned, the Social Forums bring together an incredibly wide range of social movements and civil society organisations for progressive discussion and debate. The European Social Forum in Florence in November 2002, organised on the theme 'Against neo-liberalism, racism and war', was attended by around 50,000 to 60,000 people from all over Europe and culminated in a demonstration of a million people against war. The International Anti-War Coordination has continued to meet, sometimes in the context of the Social Forum and sometimes separately. The second European Social Forum took place in Paris in November 2003, and CND had a strong presence there, working with Mouvement de la Paix from France and other European peace movements to raise the profile of peace and anti-nuclear campaigning with a huge audience that is open to our ideas. The fourth World Social Forum – the first outside Latin America – took place in Mumbai, India in January 2004. From a meeting of the Global Anti-War Assembly at that event came the call for an international day of action against war on 20 March 2004 – the anniversary of the beginning of the war against Iraq. Through these initiatives and new alliances, the peace movement is presented with many new opportunities for campaigning and broadening its outreach through working with these new radicalised forces.

Thus one can conclude that the development and strength of the anti-war movement is the result of a complex interplay of factors, both on the world stage and in our nationally specific situations. What is sure is that the world is a very different place, not only since the end of the Cold War but now also since September 11. Understanding the new global situation is vital to the maintenance and further development of the peace and anti-war movements, to ensure that our movements are not merely responsive to US initiatives, but can also plan and develop effective strategies to exploit the contradictions within the global situation, and thereby prevent further illegal and immoral wars and prevent the use of nuclear weapons.

### NOTE

1. London South Bank University and Chair, Campaign for Nuclear Disarmament.

# 9

# From Global Crisis to Neo-imperialism: The Case for a Radical Alternative

*Boris Kagarlitsky*

Neoliberal economic policies have dominated the world for more than two decades. 'Globalisation' has become not just the slogan of the day, but also the justification for all sorts of outrages, occurring before the gaze of all and sundry. Opponents of the system have been branded as dinosaurs or Luddites resisting technological progress. Neoliberal policies were proclaimed as the only way to bring prosperity everywhere and upgrade the less developed world to the levels of the West. These promises were absurd and at best utopian. By the end of 1990s most of the world's population was actually worse off than before the beginning of neoliberal experiment (economic success could be seen only in the countries that, like China, refused to follow 'orthodox' economic policies). However, that all didn't matter as long as global financial elites and transnational corporations felt good. Unfortunately, it was not the case anymore in the 2000s. A warning that should have been heeded was the Asian crisis of 1997–98, the consequences of which were overcome only at vast cost.

Globalisation was never about the 'global village'. If a massive increase of information flows happened, it was mostly a side effect of the process (and though praised in press, this side effect was in many ways an unwanted one). The real key to neoliberal globalisation was global mobility of capital. This new global mobility was not completely new. Discussing the history of financial markets *The Economist* magazine called the late nineteenth century a 'golden age' of financial globalisation, which unfortunately was 'interrupted' by the First World War and other social and political catastrophes.[1] Interrupted by – or led to?

## GLOBAL MOBILITY OF CAPITAL

In the 1990s globalisation was often presented as a mere result of technological change. In fact, even a brief glance at the question shows that the liberalisation of capital markets began long before the appearance of personal computers or the Internet. Neoliberal strategies were formulated in the 1970s. The globalisation that took place during the 1980s and 1990s represented the victory of financial over industrial capital. By the mid-1990s, a bloc had been consolidated on this basis between financial capital, the energy corporations and high-tech firms. The representatives of financial capital were trying to lower inflation to the maximum extent possible, even at the cost of reducing economic growth.

It was not technology that gave birth to the mobility of capital, but the mobility of capital that sharply increased the demand for the introduction of new technology. The speed with which information is transmitted does not in the least indicate that the possibilities for financial control have weakened; quite the reverse. The same mechanisms that can be used to shift capital can also be used to detect this process. With electronic transactions, the state is theoretically able to obtain complete information on what is occurring, and the legal financial market can thus be controlled without difficulty. The countries of Scandinavia, which had been less consistent in carrying out this liberalisation, did not encounter more massive violations than countries that had adhered to a more 'orthodox' market approach.

The mobility of capital has become a vital principle. Trade can be conducted on a world scale, information knows no borders, and even in ancient times money travelled about the globe. Production, by contrast, ties capital down, fixing it to a particular spot. The late twentieth century witnessed the triumph of finance capital. The new technologies were meant to service the economy that was being established, and the corresponding sector of business thus entered readily into an alliance with the ruling group, embracing its ideology. In their turn, the new technologies became attractive to finance capital. In the high-tech sector, rapid growth combined with small investments created the ideal preconditions for a speculative boom. The growth of stock market quotations (the American NASDAQ index) amounted to a redistribution of wealth between the 'traditional' and 'new' sectors of the economy. Industrial capital found this situation acceptable so long as the economy as a whole, and corporate profits along with it, continued to expand. The industrial capitalists made up for their losses by shifting their production to countries with cheap labour power, and by intensifying exploitation. In the process, however, the entire model of consumer society that had grown up since the Second World War came under threat.

The new model not only required a massive shift of industry to poorer countries, but, by condemning workers in the West to take part in a 'race to the bottom', undermined the rules of Western consumer society as established in the 1950s and 1960s. The new equilibrium can be sustained only while the middle layers remain relatively numerous, and the growth of their incomes ensures that consumer demand is pumped steadily through the market mechanisms. But in the late 1990s the middle classes started feeling the pressure. The less stable the position of the working population as a whole, the more vulnerable will be the white-collar layers and the labour aristocracy. For a certain time this trend may be counteracted by two factors: the growth of new technologies, creating well-paid jobs in a few 'fashionable' sectors, and increases in the debts owed by the middle layers, who can no longer permit themselves their accustomed standard of living, but cannot renounce it either.

The high-tech sector expanded owing to demand for its products from the rapidly growing commercial–financial sector. The rate at which information can be transmitted has risen dramatically. However, this does not mean that the processes this information is supposed to describe have accelerated at the same rate. Furthermore, the mechanisms through which decisions are taken, and the speed with which the decision-making process operates, did not change rapidly during the 1990s. The more rapid the turnover of financial capital has become, the greater the gap between stock market speculations and the processes taking place in the 'real sector'.

Production takes time. After the initial investments have been made, time is needed for new means of production to be assimilated. First buildings have to be constructed; only then can equipment be purchased and installed, and only after this can workers be hired. Goods on sale also have to find purchasers, which needs a certain time. Customers can reject commodities, or buy less of them than expected. Meanwhile, the speculative market promises instant profits. The rate of turnover of capital is greater here by whole orders of magnitude, and in this regard, speculation is far more attractive.

Fictitious capital, of course, cannot exist without some real, working economy. It was the combination of speculative capital and high technology that created the effect of the 'new economy', which lay behind the explosive increase of stock prices first in the US and then throughout the world. These peculiarities of the financial market led inevitably to the desynchronisation of investment processes in various sectors. As always happens in the market, the sectors that promised less in the way of profit suffered a shortage of investment. In distinction from classical capitalism, however, investment flowed not only to the sectors where profits were higher, but also to those from which money could be extracted more quickly. In this respect even a highly profitable productive enterprise lost out to a thoroughly dubious – and from the point of view of the real economy, quite meaningless – stock market operation. Trillions of dollars were withdrawn from the real economy to be put in circulation on the stock market. The industrial sector had thus to bear a double burden: it had to ensure the profitability of enterprises, and at the same time subsidise an orgy of financial speculation. The result was an inevitable shortage of capital investment in industry, especially in the Third World, in Russia and a few other countries of Eastern Europe. Meanwhile the countries of East Asia, which were protecting their capital markets and hence did not experience a shortage of investment, encountered the opposite problem. The maturing crisis of consumer society limited demand for their goods. By the late 1990s East Asia was stricken by a classic crisis of overcapacity, at the same time as other parts of the world lacked funds for modernising industry, and wages were falling.

Liberal theory assumes that processes occurring in parallel will be synchronised spontaneously by the market mechanism. In principle, the liberals are right. But one should not forget that there is little joy for entrepreneurs in the means through which the market resolves the dilemma – a global economic crisis.

## HIGH PROFITS AND AFTER

The expansion that lasted from 1992 to 2000 was among the most prolonged in the history of capitalism. This period was also remarkable for high profits and the rapid growth of stock prices, against a background of economic growth that was nowhere near so robust. Marx noted the tendency, inherent to capitalism, for the rate of profit to decline. On the whole, history bears out this conclusion, but there are certain periods when profits start growing rapidly. The reason for this paradox is that the structure of a capitalist economy is not unchanging. New sectors and new markets rise up. Profit rates in these areas are at first extremely high, and it is only later that they start to decline in accordance with the general principles inherent to the system. The 'information economy' was subject to the same market cycles as the traditional economy, but in this case the cycles operated with a certain delay. After the potential for expansion in these sectors was exhausted, the 'new economy' itself became a decisive factor in the downturn.

The 1990s saw both the rapid growth of new sectors – this was the period when the infrastructure of the 'information society' was set in place – and at the same time the conquest of 'new markets' by capital. It was not only the installing of a neoliberal economic regime in the countries of the former 'Communist bloc' and 'Third World', but also the 'marketisation' of a whole series of areas of life in the West. Those areas which had earlier been excluded from the sphere of market relations, like health, education, public transport, and so forth were placed on a commercial basis. The need to increase profits by appropriating new sectors also explains the irresistible desire of neoliberal decision makers to implant private enterprise in ever new areas of life (this was the reason why, for example, the General Agreement on Trade and Services (GATS) was drawn up in 2000–01). Every time anything went wrong with privatisation or marketisation, they explained that the only reason for this was that we didn't privatise enough, marketise enough or liberalise enough. But this advice, when followed, led to even more trouble – to be cured with even greater doses of free market economics. This is like a fire brigade that tries to extinguish fire by pouring gasoline on it and then explains its failures by saying it just didn't have enough gasoline.

As new sectors and markets arise, their own cycles form within them; these may not coincide with the cycles of the 'old' markets and sectors. In Eastern Europe the transition to capitalism was accompanied by prolonged depression, which gave way to economic growth only in the late 1990s, when the potential for growth in the West was already petering out. This was particularly obvious in the case of Russia, where output began to increase only in 1999–2000, after the Asian economic crisis. For capitalism, the unevenness of development between sectors and countries is both a cause of growth and a cause of destabilisation.

It is a myth that free markets lead to homogenisation. In fact they lead to polarisation – between social classes, between countries, between regions.[2]

In the global economy of the 1990s, the US became a sort of magnet attracting capital from the entire world. This was due not so much to the dynamism of the American economy as to the exceptional position occupied by the US in the world system. It was not simply that the US represented an enormous market, and that the US dollar acted as the world currency. The more open the economies of other countries, the greater became the flow of capital into the US. America was the leading global centre of accumulation. The larger the American capital market, the more attractive it was to investors. By drawing capital out of other parts of the world, the US destabilised the situation in these regions, but at the same time the growth of the US economy acted as a sort of shock-absorber, staving off a world depression.

Throughout the decade, the increase in stock prices substantially exceeded the growth of profits, but as long as profits also grew noticeably this was not of great importance. From the moment when profits began to fall, maintaining the stock market bubble became impossible.

## BACK TO THE OIL

During periods of economic growth, raw materials prices also grow. This cannot fail to have an effect on oil prices. The shock of the Asian economic crisis drove down oil prices, but once production revived in Asia, they were driven back up again dramatically. When oil prices began increasing in the autumn of 1999, it seemed quite natural to expect that a sharp rise would be followed by a fall in demand and by stabilisation of the market, after which prices would decline. Moreover, oil producers themselves were taking fright at the excessively rapid rise in fuel prices, and had begun raising their output. The market, however, seemed to have run wild. To the increase in supply, it reacted with an even greater rise in prices.

Why did it happen? Over some 15 years, vast sums had been taken out of the 'real economy' throughout the world, and had moved over into the sphere of financial speculation. Monetarist economists had convinced the world that the only sources of inflation were state spending and the printing of paper money. Meanwhile, the rapid rise of share prices in the US, at the same time as almost all central banks were applying harsh policies, led to a curious form of inflation in which paper money was not devalued, but speculative financial capital grew at a rate totally out of step with the increase of production. The economies of the West came to feature a sort of 'inflationary overhang'. This 'superfluous' money eventually burst on to the oil market. The inflationary potential accumulated in the

Western economies could not be realised owing to the harsh policies of the central banks, but as time passed, the greater this potential became. All that was needed was for some channel to appear, and this excess money would burst onto the market. After the Organisation of Petroleum Exporting Countries (OPEC) had reviewed the situation and sharply reduced quotas, oil prices leapt upward. Under the pressure of the new oil prices, the financial 'overhang' collapsed, and inflation was destined sooner or later to fly out of control, with the 'superfluous' money breaking free and spreading throughout all sectors of the world economy. It is one of the ironies of history that the first oil shock, in 1973, disorganised the system of state regulation and undermined the 'socialism of redistribution' that held sway in the West; by contrast, the second oil shock is disorganising the system of market-corporative regulation, and is striking a blow against neoliberal capitalism. The wheel has turned full circle.

It was not the oil prices that caused world economy's recession. On the contrary, the contradictions of the neoliberal model, accumulated throughout the 1980s and 1990s, created a crisis that expressed itself, among other things, in oil prices. However, that led to a set of new developments. First, a struggle for resources between major centres of capitalist production and accumulation intensified. Second, this new oil shock created an illusion that controlling the price of oil would be the key to resolving the crisis. How illusory this thinking was we would be able to see throughout the early years of the new century. But this line of thinking was very natural for bourgeois politicians and decisionmakers who refuse to see structural problems of the system as the cause of current illness. And this thinking inevitably resulted in the whole new complex of strategies adopted both by the conservative US leadership under President George Bush and his critics among the European establishment.

The international financial crisis of 1997–98 started in Asia and its shock waves knocked down economies in Russia and Latin America, spreading panic on Western financial markets. This crisis came as a surprise for global elites, which fooled themselves with promises of market prosperity and expansion without recessions. The answer was spontaneous and not at all strategic. The English economist John Ross called it 'a drunken orgy of Keynesianism', meaning that inflationist measures were introduced in most countries massively, unexpectedly and completely unsystematically. This stabilised Japan, worked in Russia, and saved Brazil from total chaos (unlike Argentina where these measures were not taken and chaos erupted). But after

1999 elites more or less regained confidence and tried to formulate new strategic projects.

These new projects in many ways remind us of the imperialist strategies of the late nineteenth century, when long-term depression starting in 1870 provoked a massive wave of colonial expansion, increased competition between the main powers and turned relatively peaceful Europe into a very dangerous place.

Many analysts saw the US military expansion after September 11 as an attempt to pull the economy out of crisis by throwing money into the war machine. But unlike the 1980s, when Ronald Reagan practised 'military Keynesianism', this approach couldn't work in the 2000s. The US economy in the late 1980s and 1990s became deeply deindustrialised. Unlike 1930, 1960 and even 1980, when industrial expansion in the military sector pulled other sectors out of recession, the military-industrial complex in 'post-modern' America became an enclave, in many ways disconnected from the rest of the economy. Weapons produced for the US military in the early twenty-first century are also different. It is not true that traditional warfare is over. But the strategy adopted by the US army (for political rather than strategic reasons) is based on avoiding conventional warfare as much as possible. This also means that industry is less involved in mass production and more interested in high-cost high-tech gadgets that give less and less stimulus for civilian industries.

This military expansion is much closer to the imperialist arms expansion of the late nineteenth century, which was very costly and not so stimulating for other branches of industry. Also, like the nineteenth-century imperialism and unlike Keynesianism it is combined with low taxes and growing pressure on the budgets where less and less money is left for welfare. If Keynesianism promised to bring butter and guns together (or rather to earn butter through producing guns), this imperialist approach is forcing upon societies a choice between guns and butter.

Neo-imperialism is more than just a strategy adopted by the extreme conservatives who managed to come to power in the US. It is a way through the which global free market capitalist system tries to adapt itself to the crisis.

## EURO-AMBITIONS

Financial capital in the US was able to exploit the specific advantages of the dollar. At the same time a national currency and a worldwide monetary unit, the dollar attracted investors; the surplus mass of dollars spread throughout the world, lowering the risk of inflation in the US, and in the process making the dollar even more attractive. The European finance markets lacked such advantages. It is this, and not an imaginary lag by Europe in the development of advanced technologies, which explains the fact that the 'new economy' has not developed as rapidly on the eastern side of the Atlantic. Stock prices rose, but not at the same rate as in the US. For one thing, European companies could not build a financial pyramid since they did not have the financial resources to maintain it, and for another, it was impossible to expand the indebtedness of companies and the population to the same extent as in the US. In principle, this could be regarded as a sign of healthier and more stable development, but from the point of view of the finance capital that held sway in Europe just as in America, it represented the main problem, the source of the weakness of the European economy. The ambitious project of introducing a single currency, a project undertaken by the ruling classes of the European Union in the late 1990s, amounted to an attempt to even up the situation and attract speculative capital to the European financial markets.

Becoming a second or alternative world currency, the euro was meant to equalise the chances for competitors, thus infecting the European economy with all the maladies afflicting the US. The population spontaneously sensed the threat and put up resistance, but the mainstream press and politicians, naturally, ascribed this to 'conservatism' and the emotional or cultural attachment of Europeans to their old national currencies.

The project of the euro was as ambitious as it was adventurous, and most importantly, very badly thought-out. In the late 1990s the leadership of the European Union imposed common rules on all the member countries, rules that presumed a lowering of inflation to a uniform level of less than 3 per cent. What followed had the character of a one-off campaign, in the best Soviet tradition, with the countries rushing to report on time the results they had achieved.

The trouble was that in such circumstances, a uniform rate of inflation is impossible unless all the other parameters of economic development are equalised. Unless there is a policy of redistribution, in fact, market disproportions tend to increase. The European Union adopted some redistributive measures, but the leaders, in line with their common neoliberal ideology, staked on the elemental forces of the market. Paradoxically, it was this that undermined the chances of a stable future for the euro.

With the help of administrative and political pressure, inflation was lowered simultaneously in all the countries involved. Then it started growing with still greater force in those countries that had artificially reduced its level for the sake of entering the euro-zone. Only now, this was no longer a problem of one or another particular country, but a destabilising factor for the entire European project. The euro was supposed to replace the national currencies on 1 January 2002. It would have been hard to imagine a less opportune moment. By the time the new currency was supposed to enter circulation, the world and European economies were already in recession. This meant that supporting growth, or even mitigating the crisis, required a lowering of central bank interest rates. But this was something the EU could not permit itself without at the same time dashing the hopes of turning the euro into a real rival to the dollar – that is, without defeating the whole purpose of the project. Still worse, the various countries entered the crisis in different condition. Effective management of the situation required fundamentally different approaches in Germany, in Scandinavia, and in the countries of Southern Europe. This, however, proved technically impossible. The single European Central Bank had been established precisely in order to implement a common policy. Assembling ships into a single convoy requires the observance of definite rules. The whole convoy has to move at the speed of the slowest ship. If this rule is not followed, the remaining ships fall behind, and the convoy is dispersed.

The paradox was that the European Union could not allow itself to slow down and keep to a single rhythm of movement. The countries of Southern Europe could not keep pace with Germany. The transition to a single currency coincided with the process of integration into the EU of the countries of the former Eastern Bloc; the Czech Republic, Poland and Hungary already stood in the first rank, expecting a final decision. However, there was not the slightest hope that the newcomers would manage to cope in the long term with tasks that even countries that had been integrated into the EU for many years were finding beyond them. The European 'convoy' was becoming even more heterogeneous.

In the spring of 2001 the European Central Bank again refused to lower its interest rates, so affirming its commitment to a strong euro – at any price. This approach seemed to work. After a period of relative instability in 2003 the euro started to grow. Naturally, this growth of the euro was a result of a weakening US dollar rather than of a strengthening European economy. American private and public debt crisis, hidden inflation and a passive trade balance made maintaining a strong dollar impossible. In fact, however, a strong euro failed to become good news for Europeans. It meant deepening economic depression in the EU. More, weaker European countries had to suffer additionally. In the pre-euro situation, the decline of the dollar resulted in the US currency falling unevenly vis-à-vis different EU currencies. For example, the Spanish peseta or Italian lira could remain rather cheap relative to the dollar, while the German mark was rising more rapidly. Italian and Spanish exports as well as their tourist industries were able to enjoy competitive advantages. Nothing like this was possible this time.

Russia was to suffer additionally, though this time its misfortune, contrary to the tradition, wasn't of its own making. Selling oil for US dollars, it imported goods and technologies for euros. Most of its debt was also nominated in euros. Each increase of the euro exchange rate vis-à-vis the US currency meant additional losses for the Russian state and companies, including those operating on the domestic market. Though as an 'oil currency' the rouble got stronger against the dollar that wasn't causing much satisfaction in Russia. People's savings were devalued because they were kept mostly in dollars, and domestic inflation was on the rise because of the 'euro factor'.

European decision-makers were ready to pay a high price to make the euro an international reserve currency, competing with the American dollar. Unfortunately, this price might well become the destruction of the common economic space, and ultimately, the collapse of the euro. The sole hope for the European project was that the crisis would bring about a spontaneous fall in the price of the dollar, and inflation in the US. This, however, did not portend a happy future for the euro either. The European Central Bank would be able to lower interest rates and unleash inflation, thus slowing the convoy and allowing the laggards to catch up, but this would be very remote from the original ambitious plans of the European elites. Instead of nearing their strategic goals, they would now have to concentrate exclusively on minimising the damage caused by their own past decisions.

## EUROPE AND THE NEW IMPERIALISM

Though the euro was proclaimed to be among other things a 'political project' designed to strengthen 'European unity' in purely economic terms it risks producing a completely opposite effect. Contrary to the mainstream theories, united markets don't automatically lead to homogenisation. They rather produce an opposite effect – polarisation. As well as social polarisation, they create a polarisation between poor and rich regions, core and periphery and so on. The market is a mighty mechanism of redistribution, which favours those already more rich, more powerful and, in bourgeois terms, more effective.

In fact, money is not only a means of payment (as political economists would have us believe), but also a cultural symbol of sorts. It should have a history. The euro, however, is the handiwork of bureaucrats and technocrats. Even the appearance of the notes attests to the lack of culture and impoverished imagination of its creators.

Each denomination is adorned with nondescript walls and doors. And there is not a single human face. European Union bureaucrats explained that any historical figure who is popular in one country may arouse negative emotions in neighbouring countries. However, if these gentlemen are speaking of pan-European traditions and of shared history, then there should be some historical figures that embody this.

I, for one, do not understand who in Europe could be irritated by portraits of Aristotle, Leonardo da Vinci, Molière, Mozart, Goethe or Einstein. Even Columbus might be OK, though some of us on the left will remember his connection with colonialism. But therein lies the tragedy – the eurocrats themselves probably can't remember a single one of these names. Literature, philosophy, science, exploration and art have little if any, meaning for them. Out of the whole of European history, they have only learned about Napoleon and Bismarck, and even then only superficially.

Moreover, the euro has another failing that is even more serious. The intention of the project's initiators was that a single currency would assist and facilitate European integration. In practice, it is likely to have the opposite effect.

The stability of a currency depends, at the end of the day, on the state of a country's economy. And the economies and levels of development of different EU member states differ considerably. While Northern European member states, by and large, have few problems in achieving low inflation, Mediterranean countries have difficulty.

If the European Central Bank chooses to support a high exchange rate, the result will be that 'backward' countries will find that they are no longer competitive (as the unfortunate example of Argentina shows). If, on the other hand, the decision is made to meet the 'backward' countries halfway, then Italy, Portugal, Spain and Greece will export inflation to Germany and Finland.

The paradox was that the European Union could not allow itself to slow down and keep to a single rhythm of movement. The countries of Southern Europe could not keep pace with Germany. The transition to a single currency coincided with the process of integration into the European Union of the countries of the former Eastern Bloc; the Czech Republic, Poland and Hungary already stood in the first rank, expecting a final decision. Unlike Western EU members, who had a choice of joining the euro or not, Eastern applicants were obliged to switch their currencies to the euro as part of the deal to enter the Union. The reason for that decision was clear: euro-zone needed to grow in order to compete with the dollar. Obligatory 'euroisation' of Eastern Europe will lead to its automatic de-dollarisation.

However, the price of this decision is also extremely high. There was not the slightest hope that the newcomers would manage to cope in the long term with tasks that even countries that had been integrated into the European Union for many years were finding beyond them. More, if the positive results of euro-zone growth are consumed by Western financial elites, the price will be paid by the local economies of Eastern countries. Unlike Portugal and Greece, which in the earlier times received generous help to come closer to their more advanced partners in United Europe, new Eastern members can't expect anything similar. Help packages for new members are much smaller now than those of the early 1980s. And the reason for that is not that EU can't afford now to be as generous as in the past. Eastern new members are bigger than Greece and Portugal, the costs of enlargement are higher. But most important of all is the euro phenomenon itself. Haying high subsidies means potentially weakening the single currency. So, the European 'convoy' has to become even more heterogeneous. In the meantime, national governments are deprived of the usual monetary instruments to influence the economy and social development. At the European level there will inevitably be serious conflicts over monetary policy. These conflicts will not be easy to resolve, as the interests of the member states are diametrically opposed.

In the spring of 2001 the European Central Bank again refused to lower its interest rates, so affirming its commitment to a strong euro – at any price. The trouble was that this price might well become the destruction of the common economic space, and ultimately, the collapse of the euro. The sole hope for the European project was that the crisis would bring about a spontaneous fall in the price of the dollar, and inflation in the US. This, however, did not portend a happy future for the euro either. The European Central Bank would be able to lower interest rates and unleash inflation, thus slowing the convoy and allowing the laggards to catch up, but this would be very remote from the original ambitious plans of the European elites. Instead of nearing their strategic goals, they would now have to concentrate exclusively on minimising the damage caused by their own past decisions. Decision-making inevitably becomes political. In theory, those countries that objectively have weaker economies are interested in a looser approach to the budget and higher inflation.

Everything ends in some kind of bureaucratic, fudged solution that will make things worse for everyone. Inflation will be too high for the north and too low for the south. Ironically, not the Southern EU members but Germany and France came under pressure in 2002–03. When Germans had their national currency balancing the budget was easy and Berlin put excessive pressure on other EU members in order to do the same. Once the euro came into being, Germany suddenly discovered itself in trouble. The budget deficit was increasing at a scary speed. The reason for that was the stagnation of the German economy. But this stagnation itself had causes in the financial sphere. On the one hand, with the euro, Germany and France imported inflationist pressures from their Southern neighbours. On the other hand, keeping the price of the currency high at any cost meant slowing down the economy.

Interestingly enough, the German social democratic government discovered the answer in pension and tax reform. This was a standard neoliberal approach of blaming the victim. Germans suffering from the ambitions of their own financial capital had to abandon 'excessive' social gains. While neoliberalism was the source of the problem, this problem itself became a source for justification of even harsher neoliberal measures.

No matter how problematic the euro-project, it would be wrong to predict that its failures will lead to weakening of the European Union. On the contrary, the more problems there are with the euro, the more there will be a pressure to strengthen the EU as a quasi-state. Or at least, to single out a kind of consolidated 'neo-imperial core', which can act as a new political and economic hegemon imposing its will on weaker members and allies.

The contradictions between Western EU members and Central European countries entering the Union were already visible in

2003, when the US administration decided to attack Iraq. France and Germany, traditional leaders of European integration, strongly opposed the US move, while Poland, Hungary and other former Communist countries sided with Washington. The US administration itself tried to use this quarrel as much as possible, exposing the difference between the 'Old' and the 'New' (pro-American) Europe. Naturally, political elites of the 'new' Europe emerging out of the disintegration of the Communist system were quite reactionary and, indeed, corrupt. Civil society was much weaker than that in the West (as a result public opposition for reactionary policies of domestic governments were much weaker than, say, in Italy or Spain). However, contradictions between 'Old' and 'New' Europe were quite deep and, in fact, getting deeper. Siding with the US against French and German European leadership was, for reactionary, corrupt and backward Central European elites the only way to compensate their economic weakness.

In history we see many examples of economic problems being compensated by political consolidation. But hitherto it had not happened on the basis of a free market approach. Political integration is the only means to compensate disproportions and contradictions produced by the united market and single currency. In that sense European political integration follows the creation of nation-states in the sixteenth to the eighteenth centuries. United markets by themselves do not produce unified states but they create a need to form integrated political bodies precisely because markets don't work. Or rather, they work differently as described in the liberal theory.

Increasing regional and social polarisation, provoked by market development, forces the ruling elites to use political instruments. But this political integration doesn't lead to social and interregional homogenisation either. The state compensates disproportions and contradiction through a combination of redistribution and repression.

The state is also essential to make a united currency work. True, historically there have been currencies without a state. Early medieval monetary systems were international currencies without a stable link to a concrete state. In the sixteenth and seventeenth centuries a taler (or Ricksdaler) was used with the same value not only in different German states but also in the Swedish provinces and under the name of 'efimok' in Russia. So, Europe already had a kind of single currency long before modern times. However, it was precisely the need to guarantee the stability and protection of the currency that stimulated the formation of a stronger state.

To be able to redistribute and repress effectively, the state needs to be as centralised as possible. Unification and integration of markets at the national level in early modern Europe was not achieved through lose confederations and democratic citizen participation but through authoritarian absolutist monarchies. In this sense the democratic deficit of EU structures in Brussels, so often mentioned by Euro-sceptics, is exactly adequate to the economic and social sides of the European project. More, there is clearly too much democracy and citizens' participation in a united Europe to make it work successfully and to realise the ambitions of its 'grand design'. If the process of neoliberal and market-driven integration is to be carried out successfully, it will bring about not a European Federation and even less 'a Europe of regions' but a centralised European Empire.

Whether this will this happen in practice is a different question. The EU provides us with a classical case of combined and uneven development. As long as the continent remains politically disunited and retains the form of a union of independent states, there is always a chance that some countries will get more integrated than others. Some risk falling out. Some break ranks. Some elites are rapidly merging into a new European ruling class, others remain at the national level and can't change without completely losing legitimacy and the ability to rule. Many companies go global, others turn continental, but a lot of them remain national or even regional and local. While the core of the newly emerging euro-bourgeoisie can't repress their 'nationally rooted' partners, it can lead them. And having a common enemy is the way to assemble forces and exercise a successful hegemony.

The logic of European integration makes the conflict with the US not only inevitable but also more and more structural, even institutional. The new empire will not emerge without challenging the old one. The crisis of the neoliberal order demonstrates that resources of the global market are limited as well as the market itself. Overproduction and excess capacity, overaccumulation and the need for cheap resources to stimulate slowing down growth, all provoke stronger competition at every level from companies to international institutions. Competing capitalist projects could 'peacefully co-exist' as long as the system provided them all with enough resources. Now times change. Competition becomes rivalry.

This is why the forces of European integration started engaging the US on several fronts. Already in 1999 the collapse of the Seattle Ministerial meeting was brought about not only by the protests on the streets but also by an open confrontation between the US delegation and EU bureaucrats led by the French.

Later the EU bureaucracy continued to use the WTO as a battleground against the US, culminating in May 2003 when it managed to pass though the WTO system a resolution that allowed EU countries to impose trade sanctions on US companies using export subsidies directly or indirectly. The US was forced to promise to reconsider its export policies. Earlier, in March 2003 EU bureaucrats gained another victory by forcing the US administration to remove trade barriers, which were used to prevent European steel and other metal products from reaching the American market.

This was a very important achievement because earlier it was always the US that used the WTO to impose its rules on competing countries. As late as in 1999 the WTO gave its blessing to a set of sanctions against European goods imposed by the US.

The conflict in the United Nations in March 2003 when France and Germany backed by their Russian satellites acted against Washington on the issue of Iraq was not just a result of these governments reacting to the pressure of global and domestic public opinion. Neither was the decision to set up their own military force, taken by France, Germany, Belgium and Luxembourg, a mere result of political ambitions, frustration and anger against Washington. All these events demonstrate a consistent logic. At the centre of this logic we see the single currency project.

## GLOBAL COMPETITION

No global money will work without a global power. And the euro as would-be global money needs a new imperial force. There is no chance it can win against the dollar without this. More, it makes no sense financially or economically, if the new imperialist project isn't carried far enough. People investing in euros, and even risking the strangulation of the European economies in order to challenge the dollar as an international reserve currency, are not just ambitious central bankers who badly miscalculated. Naturally, there may be some element of miscalculation or bureaucratic mistakes, but this doesn't explain much. Representing the ascendancy of European financial capital, the euro is much more than just a monetary unit or a payment instrument. It is an incorporation of global financial competition or, as earlier Marxists would have put it, of inter-imperialist contradictions.

The wars in Kosovo and Iraq were widely seen as representative of American expansionism. But that was only partly true. US expansion was aimed not only against the victim countries but it was also a defence against the new economic project emerging in Europe. The era of Euro-Atlantic wars[3] began when some analysts called the bombing of Kosovo an attack on the euro.[4] Clearly, EU leaders backed Washington's policy on Kosovo but they were less happy with the decision to use military force by NATO. In 1999 they had no escape and had to follow the leader. The Euro-project was not yet ripe and the global crisis far from its culmination. The euro launched at the value of $1.2 declined to less than one dollar in a few months and it took the single currency more than two years to recover its value to $1.1.

If Kosovo was a contradictory event, which can be interpreted in different ways, the war in Iraq produced an open confrontation. This confrontation involved not only EU member states but also candidate states and Russia. It also revealed the weaknesses and contradictions in the Euro-imperial project itself.

No European unity was demonstrated when in 2003 it became clear that the US was going to attack Iraq. While the US administration's war drive was strongly resisted by governments of France and Germany, later joined by Russia, Britain followed the Washington line, together with Spain and Italy and with enthusiastic support from the Eastern European 'applicant states', most notably Poland. This divide didn't follow party lines. Social Democrats in most countries were anti-war, but that didn't impress the British Labour government. Conservatives tended to be more pro-American but right-wing French President Jacques Chirac became one of the leading opponents of war, joined by the Austrian conservative government, which even threatened to shoot down American warplanes if they passed through its territory. Public opinion was equally anti-war in England and France or Spain, Italy, Germany. Even in Poland, which remains by far the most pro-American society in Europe, there was no unanimous support for George Bush and his war plans. Was it only because some governments were more prepared to listen to public opinion? Not exactly. Most European governments showed no interest in public opinion on most other issues, including most important domestic problems. No doubt, public opinion played a role but it worked so well exactly because there were (as in Seattle) other factors and interests involved as well.

The role of Britain needs here special examination. The neoliberal project developed by Margaret Thatcher and the British right in the late 1970s was presented as a tough but necessary cure for a country that had started lagging behind the rest of Europe, suffering a 'post-imperial syndrome' and spoiled by 'excessive social protection'. After Maggie Thatcher's neo-Conservatives and Tony Blair's New Labour had run the country for more than two decades, English capitalism failed to become stronger. The modernisation of Britain was no faster than the development of other EU countries, indeed in technological terms it was by far slower than those of the social-democratic Nordic countries (most notably Finland, which managed to become a major European high-tech power retaining a strong welfare state and impressive public sector). After two decades of neoliberal pseudo-modernisation British capitalism, in fact, became less modern, more backward, demonstrating very little potential for innovation. As a result Britain as an EU member failed to get its voice properly heard. Though English politicians kept praising Europe (and especially the neoliberal aspects of the integration project), in fact it was not moving closer to the Franco-German 'continental core'. The strategy of British elites became based on the need to cultivate its 'special relations' with the US as a way of compensating for its increasing weakness and isolation within United Europe.

In that respect it is not surprising that the approach of the British government was so close to the attitude of Poland (as the biggest Eastern 'applicant country', also with old and failed imperial ambitions). This line was openly formulated by the Polish social-democratic Foreign Minister Wlodzimierz Cimoszewicz. Explaining the importance of future Polish entrance into the EU, he declared in 2002 that Poland's role inside the Union would be to represent American interests there. This role of Poland was rewarded after the Iraq War when Washington gave Poland its own zone to administer in conquered Iraq.

Even before the war broke out George Bush called applicant countries from the former Soviet Bloc a 'New Europe'. This term makes very little historical sense. Eastern 'applicant countries' in fact were not alone in supporting America. They were joined by Italy, Portugal and Spain. In fact, here we see a very clear divide between what can be called a 'continental core' (France, Germany, Austria, Belgium and Luxembourg) and the countries that in one way or another were becoming marginalised in the new European project. They are the ones that face more serious structural problems and need to increase their political weight in order to use it as a bargaining tool within the Union. Naturally, political division around the issue of war isn't perfect. Holland, which clearly belongs to the 'euro-core', is missing from the 'anti-war' list. On the other hand, the 'anti-war' bloc was supported by Greece, which economically and historically belongs to the same group as Spain and Portugal. In both cases politics and public opinion played a role. But the crisis over Iraq is just the starting point of a long process.

What George Bush with his geo-historical illiteracy presented as a division between 'Old' and 'New' Europe was in reality a contradiction between the 'euro-core' and the 'euro-marginals' emerging as a result of market-driven integration. The political aspect of this division is also very important. While the 'euro-core' (as a geo-political and geo-economic reality) becomes more consolidated and capable of developing a common interest, those marginalised within the European project find it much less easy to establish a common ground. It is symbolic that Italy or Spain, discussing their possible contribution to the occupation force in Iraq, resolutely refused to put it under Polish command (only British command was acceptable).

'Euro-marginal' countries can have something in common only as long as they remain part of a United Europe. Their elites are also much more consolidated and remain divided between transnational, national and European factions. That makes domestic politics more unstable and in the long run creates new opportunities to the anti-bourgeois forces. It is no accident that the more backward European capitalist classes are also most pro-American. They are scared that there will be no good role for them in the Euro-Empire. Their ambitions are not satisfied. These elites find it more difficult to integrate systematically into the European project than to develop spontaneous relations with transnational corporations, often based in the US. But they can't disengage from the European project either. First, it is too late. Second, US friendship doesn't produce a clear alternative to the EU. So for the time being they are doomed to the role of internal trouble-makers and American Trojan horses within a united imperialist Europe. They need US friendship precisely to stay within the EU and to have their voice there heard.

Britain, as a former empire, naturally had to become Europe's top trouble-maker. But this also guarantees totally insurmountable contradictions, which Blair's government has to face. In choosing the pro-Atlantic orientation, Blair and his Tory friends in the British parliament have to encourage stronger integration into the EU exactly because of that. Britain's importance for the US is exactly that it is an insider in the EU, with an important voice. Unlike more naïve conservatives who keep emotional ties to the pound, New Labour knows that it cannot escape getting closer to the euro-zone if it wants to counterpose itself to it. Tony Blair has expressed this clearly several times. This logic of 'internal subversion' of Europe explains why, after successfully defeating public opinion on the war issue, Blair's government immediately started a new unpopular adventure – trying to integrate the country into the euro-zone.

The strength of the City of London lies very much in its capacity to serve as an extension in Europe. It is not true that in the globalised world geography doesn't matter. Political and economic geography matter because globalisation is realised not on the moon, but in a real world, where no economic process, no matter how advanced, can disconnect itself from time and space.

Of course, Blair's policy on the euro also reflects the political and ideological inertia natural for every government. But this inertia itself represents the weaknesses and contradictions of British capitalism vis-à-vis the 'euro-core'. Britain is still in the initial stage of European financial integration. Initially the ruling classes around the continent needed the euro as a tool against organised labour. It was needed to contain the social demands of the working classes and erode the welfare state ('which we no longer can afford'). However, the welfare state in Britain is so eroded after Thatcher and New Labour, and the workers' movement was so massively defeated, that the local elite didn't need the euro for that purpose. The British ruling elites foresaw the problems associated with the euro, and found very few advantages for themselves. As a result, Britain was stuck outside the euro-zone, but incorporated into the decision-making mechanism and involved in the process of financial integration.

Again we see here a strange similarity between Britain and the Eastern European 'applicant states'. They also declare entering the euro-zone as a political goal but in practice tend to postpone the decision (the Czech Republic declared in May 2002 that it could enter no earlier than 2009–10).

Among other things, unlocking this situation for Blair became a matter of political prestige. Like Cimoszewicz, Blair's administration saw British membership in the euro-zone as a way to continue the policy of defending American interests. But this attitude is just simply too obvious for the 'euro-core' leaders. Blair is faced with the dilemma: either he has to integrate totally or disengage completely, thus dropping both the special relationship with the US and British special ambitions. Neither answer is acceptable for Washington or the City of London.

Unlike the war, where Blair could gamble and win, economics is a tough game, which, in the long run, leaves no chance to gamblers. The European contradictions of Blair's government will inevitably wreck it, sooner or later. And this is, probably, good news for the British left.

Another country that is becoming a playground of competing imperialist forces and tendencies is Russia.

### THE STRUGGLE FOR RUSSIA

Russia's role in the diplomatic struggle around Iraq was very important. Not a superpower any more, Russia not only inherited a permanent membership on the Security Council and a right to veto its decisions but the huge debt that Iraq owed the Soviet Union. This is why the diplomatic struggle around the war in Iraq was very much the struggle between Washington and Berlin for Russia's vote in the UN. The global crisis that came to a head over the weekend of 14–15 February 2003 resulted in defeat and unprecedented humiliation for the administration of US President George Bush. Washington had been sure that France would not veto its proposed UN resolution on launching military action against Iraq. But it finally became clear that the US proposal was dead in the water even without a French veto. The weapons inspectors did not follow the script that Washington had expected, and Security Council members took the floor one after the other to state their opposition to war.

An even bigger humiliation for Bush followed in the form of huge anti-war marches around the world, including the US. The few West European governments that still support Washington came in for massive street pressure. A consensus is building around the world that Bush is a dangerous man. The leadership in Washington kept stubbornly repeating that Saddam Hussein posed a threat to humanity, but their exhortations had the opposite effect. Hussein clearly posed a threat to his own people, but millions of people around the world have reached the conclusion that Bush, not Hussein, poses a threat to the planet.

While the US leadership came under attack, Russia once more demonstrated its impotence and insignificance. Over the past decade Russia has been politically dependent on the US, and economically dependent on Germany. The US dictated Russia's political agenda, while Germany gradually became its most important business partner and source of foreign investment. This system worked quite well so long as Germany kept a low profile in international affairs and at least made a show of solidarity with the US. When disagreements between the US and Germany came to the surface, however, the Russian leadership was at a loss.

Moscow behaved like one of Ivan Pavlov's dogs. So long as the signals come one at a time, the dog's conditioned reflexes respond properly – it salivates at the sound of the bell. Then the scientist gives it two contradictory signals. The poor beast goes into a panic, spinning around in its cage. Something similar happened with the Russian leadership during the winter of 2003. Only when it became clear that France and Germany would secure a majority in the Security Council, and that no veto would be required, did Russian President Vladimir Putin demonstratively side with the victors.

For ten years Kremlin ideologues have led the public to believe that Russia must support the US or risk condemnation from the 'entire civilised world'. The events of February 2003 revealed, however, that Washington is now isolated. Russian policy-makers drew the right conclusion in the end. As was immediately obvious, however, their actions were driven not by firm principles or concern for the national interest, but sheer opportunism. The sight of Russian leaders mouthing words dictated in Berlin while never taking their eyes off of Washington was nothing short of embarrassing.

During the war in Iraq Russian government-controlled television resembled that of Soviet times, using every opportunity to condemn American aggression. However, when the military operation finished and US troops successfully took over most of Iraqi's territory, the Russian elite started panicking again. The tone of propaganda changed and reconciliation with Washington was seen as an absolute necessity. Unfortunately for Putin and his team, Russia's euro-core patrons saw things very differently. Contrary to most expectations, full-scale reconciliation between 'euro-core' countries and the US-led 'coalition of the willing' didn't happen. In this new situation Russia's importance in the global struggle is increasing. The US acquired not only control of Iraqi oil but the possibility of influencing OPEC, where the Iraqi puppet administration has a seat. In the 'euro-core' countries only France has its own oil companies, and these are much smaller in scale than their American or even British counterparts. This means that it becomes strategically important for the 'euro-core' to secure Russian resources for themselves. On the other hand, Washington doesn't really need Russian resources. But the logic of competition means that the US-led faction of transnational capital has absolutely no interest in having Russian oil and gas secured for the 'euro-core' economies. This turns Russia into a real battlefield. The 'euro-core' is interested in stabilising Russia. In fact, that becomes a necessary condition of the success of the 'euro-core' project as such. While relations within the EU become less predictable, stable and tolerant, it becomes a matter of strategic importance for the 'euro-core' to keep Russia on its side. And this is not just oil and other resources. While America can play Eastern Europe against the 'euro-core', Germany in its turn can play Russia against the Poles, Czechs and Ukrainians.

Summing up, the 'euro-core' neo-imperialist project needs Russia to be stable and secure, and needs Iraq, occupied by the Anglo-American forces, to remain an unstable and insecure place. The success of the US global project, on the contrary, depends on the ability to keep Iraq stable and destabilise Russia. This is a classical imperialist game, not very different from that experienced in the early twentieth century. The difference, however, is that imperialist blocs today cannot be seen as simply national capitalist elites, but rather as supranational formations, using nation-states in the absence of a better instrument. All supranational political instruments, designed after the Second World War, failed to perform in the new situation and, ironically, instead of being strengthened by market-driven globalisation, were undermined by it. Not only is the UN in a shambles and the EU seriously weakened, but even the WTO and the IMF face problems because of gradual American disengagement. This disengagement is more than just a result of conservative unilateralist approach of the Bush administration. Contrary to liberal theory, market integration doesn't lead to economic homogenisation. If this theory is not true for the European region, it is even less true for the global economy. After 20 years of globalisation, all contradictions increased. Inequality between states and regions is increasing exactly the same way as social polarisation. These are just two sides of the same phenomenon. Market polarisation globally is accompanied by combined and uneven development and increasing competition. Transnational corporations in their rivalry simply can't avoid forming alliances with the states, which remain strategic instruments of capitalist expansion and domination.

The struggle between imperialist powers was always much more than a rivalry of states for territory or even markets. Capitalism is a system that subordinates all human activities to the accumulation of capital. Oppressing people, gaining profits, market competition and even the exploitation of free labour were practised by human societies long before the bourgeois revolutions. But it is the bourgeois system that organises all these activities for the single purpose of capital accumulation. So the highest form of capitalist competition is the struggle between different centres of accumulation. This was exactly what predetermined so many wars, from the Anglo-Dutch conflicts of the seventeenth century to the First World War. And this conflict is very much at work now.

What is the meaning of this new situation for Eastern Europe or the Middle East? These will be the areas of most struggle in the near future. The Russian elite is already visibly divided into pro-American and pro-German factions. It is clearly easier to destabilise than to achieve stability. So, it is not difficult to predict that both in Iraq and Russia destabilisation strategies will work better than attempts to bring order to these regions. We will see an escalation of tension. Domestic contradictions will be increased by outside interference. But is this necessarily bad news? For Russia in 1905 and 1917 inter-imperialist contradictions became an essential factor to facilitate revolutionary change. These contradictions opened up new opportunities, because the ruling elites were disunited and confused. German efforts to destabilise tsarist Russia helped to bring about the revolution in 1917. That revolution was in no means a result of German conspiracy, but all these conspiracies and counter-conspiracies in Berlin, London and St Petersburg made the job of Russian revolutionaries much easier.

When bourgeois elites are split there is always a chance for the left. When they embark on projects doomed to fail because of internal contradictions there is a great opportunity for change. In that respect both Russia and some 'euro-marginal' countries like Britain, Italy or Spain can see political and social struggle erupting as an outcome of the global crisis. Are we entering a new era of revolutions or is it a beginning of the time of reforms? Or, probably, both?

## IS NEW REFORMISM AN ANSWER?

Global Keynesianism can be seen as an answer to the crisis of neoliberal order the same way as original Keynesianism became an answer to the mess of international free market capitalism of the early twentieth century. There is one problem here, however. Reforms in the twentieth century didn't happen without revolutions. And these revolutions were important because they didn't challenge the bourgeois order in their own countries but called into question the survival of the global capitalist system as such. Today we have no revolutionary movements comparable to those of the early twentieth century. Neither has the bourgeoisie its new J.M. Keynes. And though Keynes himself was no more than a progressive liberal, mass workers movement and social democratic parties were needed to put all these reforms in place. If revolutionary forces are weak now, reformist currents are even weaker. The most radical representatives of today's social democracy, like President Lula's Workers' Party in Brazil, are far to the right of the most moderate social reformers of the mid-twentieth century.

Even if the ruling groups were prepared to make a change of course, doing this is virtually impossible for them. During the 1990s they drove themselves into an institutional trap, which they could well find fatal. The key principle of the neoliberal 'reforms', on both a global and national level, is 'irreversibility'. Once the structures, rules and relationships have been set in place, it is impossible in principle to make corrections to them. Not a single one of the international documents of the neoliberals specifies procedures for overturning decisions that have been taken, or for allowing individual countries to opt out of an agreement. Once abolished, mechanisms of regulation cannot be restored. It is not enough that regulation should have been outlawed (paradoxically, at precisely the time when the capitalist class has more and more need of it); the institutions themselves have been dismantled. Mechanically restoring them is both impossible. The new level of development of the market also requires new forms of regulation. The trouble is that creating a new system of institutions from scratch is not just difficult, but presumes a far greater level of radicalism, far more acute conflicts, and most importantly, the destruction on a corresponding scale of the neoliberal order.

Even the bourgeois establishment these days understands that changes are necessary and inevitable. What was considered impossible yesterday becomes desirable today. Even *The Economist* came out with a dose of public self-criticism, recognising in an editorial that it was wrong on capital controls. 'Untidy as it may be, economic liberals should acknowledge that capital controls – of a certain restricted sort, and in certain cases – have a role.'[5]

However much it might wish to do so, the bourgeoisie will not be able to escape from its own institutional trap without help from outside. And the illness is just too severe to be treated with homeopathic doses of capital control 'of a certain restricted sort'. Just as in the 1930s, the only way this conflict can be resolved is through a dramatic strengthening and radicalisation of the left. The crisis of the early twentieth-first century is not simply the latest conjunctural decline within the context of the 'natural' market cycle. It is the result of long-term processes unfolding within the capitalist economy over at least two decades, and places in question the neoliberal model that has held sway throughout the current epoch. In other words, what is involved is a clearly expressed crisis of the system. Historically, the left has always played a dual role within the framework of capitalism. On the one hand, it has fought for a qualitatively new society, for socialism. On the other hand, it reformed capitalism, and thus, in essence, saved it. This holds true not just for reformists, but also for revolutionaries. Paradoxically, the one function of the left has been impossible without the other. Reform required that the system be subject to influences 'from outside', in both the politico-social and ideological senses. Without an alternative ideology, it would have been impossible to formulate the new ideas that lay at the basis of serious reformist programmes. The capitalist crisis of 1929–33 culminated in widespread reform. The crisis of the 1970s ended in a bourgeois counter-reformation. How will the current crisis end? The inevitability of a return by the left to the centre-stage of politics is obvious, even from the point of view of the long-term interests of the bourgeoisie itself, or at least, of a certain sector of it. Meanwhile, those left parties and politicians who accepted the rules of the game of the 1990s are becoming completely helpless in the face of the crisis. They are unable to propose anything meaningful to the working class, at the same time as they are no longer capable of effectively serving the ruling elites. More radical forces are moving to the forefront. What will they be able to propose?

Just as in earlier epochs, two currents are emerging within the left. The members of one of these are striving to overcome capitalism; the others, to improve it.

## THE PROGRAMME OF TRANSITION

Like it or not, the radicals and reformers have to cover a certain distance along the road together. Unless some kind of common programme can be worked out, revolution will be just as impossible as reform, since there is nothing so conducive to radical change as the certainty that reforms will succeed. Reformism often acts as a springboard for revolution, as happened in France in 1789 and in Russia in 1917. The drawing-up of a common platform uniting reformists and radicals does not signify by any means that this platform has to be as moderate as possible. Quite the reverse, since consistency and radicalism provide a guarantee of success in a world with an acute need for new ideas. Socialist and Marxist ideas have to be formulated and expressed through the movement, otherwise it will be paralysed by wishful thinking and the search for impossible and unnecessary compromises.

The movement that began in Seattle in 1999 showed that anti-capitalist protest is becoming a vital necessity for millions of people not only in poor, but also in so-called rich countries. It is exactly the anti-capitalist spirit of the movement, its readiness to break the rules and its desire to overcome the limits of conventional politics that made this movement effective. What needs to be placed in the forefront is not the moderate redistributive ideology of social democracy, but the ideas of public property and democratic change in power structures. The task is not only to revive the public sector, but also to radically transform it. Throughout the twentieth century, socialists were divided into supporters of workers' self-management and admirers of centralised planning, without either side recognising that neither ideology would suffice for the main task of socialisation, that is, placing the public sector at the service of all of society. It is now possible to say that the public sector will only work if real social control is guaranteed. This presupposes accountability and transparency on a scale absolutely inconceivable to liberal economists. Economic democracy has to be representative, and this means that not only the state and workers but also consumers and communities have to take part in the formation of boards of management.

The things we can use only collectively have to belong to society as a whole. This applies to energy, transport, extractive industries, utilities and the communications infrastructure just as to science and education. But a no less and perhaps even more fundamental question is that of the socialisation of credit. Unless this is implemented, even if only in part, it will be impossible to find a socially acceptable solution to the world debt crisis.

Meanwhile, the separation of the private and public interest is absolutely fundamental. If that had been in place during the years of neoliberal reform, the International Monetary Fund would not have been able to use money obtained from the governments of the West to make loans to the governments of the Third World and Eastern Europe in exchange for the privatisation of property, that is, to play in practice the role of a broker, and to exert political pressure in the interest of private investors. Public credits, to the last kopeck, cent, lira or penny have to go to the public sector, into projects aimed at carrying out public tasks. The situation in which private commercial risks (and losses) are socialised, while profits are privatised, is becoming intolerable. The supporters of capital call upon us to live by the rules of the market. Well then, they should live by these rules themselves. Not a single kopeck, cent, lira or penny of public money should go to private business. No public funds should be invested in corporate undertakings. If subsidies are a social, productive or technological necessity, enterprises should be transferred to public ownership. If a corporation approaches the state with an appeal for subsidies, this should be understood as a request for nationalisation. This will be in strict accordance with the much-loved laws behind the 'logic of the market'.

Keynes wrote that the socialisation of investment was the only socialist slogan that from his point of view was justified. The main principle of socialism is control by society over the investment process, not state ownership of buildings and machines. The left has never been opposed to co-operatives or to municipal enterprises. On the contrary, these are the forms of organisation of production that can best reflect the needs of local populations. They cannot, however, take the place of public investments in projects intended to serve collective needs. The public sector acts as the tool through which society directly fulfils its collective tasks, economic, social, ecological and cultural. The market and the private sector are only suited to fulfilling private tasks, and no amount of regulating can do away with this contradiction. The more pressing the common tasks of all society and all humanity, the greater the need for socialisation. In an epoch of global warming, the socialisation of the energy industry is becoming a question of the survival of humanity. And if socialism can operate in this sphere, why not in others? If it can save us from worldwide inundation, why should it not become the leading principle of our life as a whole?

Capital blackmails governments endlessly, threatening to flee to other countries. Governments submit cheerfully to this blackmail, since they are playing at the same game as the financial and corporate elites. As they set out to justify themselves to public opinion, they conceal a key fact: the mobility of capital is not without limits. Money can be transferred out, but this money is itself at risk of being turned into meaningless columns of figures on computer screens, or mountains of colourful paper. No enterprise consists solely of bank accounts, buildings and machines. It is also people, a collective of workers who have technological knowledge, qualifications and experience. Such a collective is formed over years, and cannot be transported across national boundaries.

With their obstinacy, the political and corporate elites could finish up doing capitalism a thorough disservice. Most revolutions have begun with society's need for reforms. The inability of the ruling groups to enact the changes whose time has come has then impelled society to even greater radicalisation. If the existing elites are incapable of doing what is required, then sooner or later they will themselves become victims of the changes. More than likely, this will be a good thing.

Sooner or later, 'network socialism' will open up a space for itself. The more ruthless the opposition from the elites, the more radical the common mood will become. The technological revolution, however, is forcing a radical rethink of the traditions of collectivism. The industrial epoch required discipline and strict centralisation, including (and perhaps, above all) in the network structures. The new epoch is allowing organisation to take a different shape. In the milieu of the Internet, networks are typically conceived of as being self-organising and self-regulating. In practice, of course, the possibilities of self-organisation are not limitless in any network, but however restricted they might be compared to the utopian ideal, they are immeasurably greater than during the industrial epoch.

The proletarian socialism of the nineteenth and twentieth centuries was permeated by the discipline of the factory, and this simply could not have been otherwise. The new epoch opens up new possibilities. The dreams of economic democracy that aroused the enthusiasm of socialists in the past may finally become reality. The idea of self-management by the producers, an idea that in the early twentieth century spread throughout Europe from Petrograd to Turin and Liverpool, first took the form of 'workers' control', of 'factory councils' of all conceivable varieties. Because this idea was in contradiction with factory discipline, it was doomed inevitably to defeat. The practice of self-management turned out to be full of romantic legends and organisational contradictions. Why should only workers, the people who carry out production, be involved in management? What about consumers, or people who simply live in the vicinity of the enterprise? What about the huge number of questions that in technical terms are unrelated to production, but which bear directly on the lives of multitudes of people? How are conflicting interests to be reconciled by administrative fiat, by voting, through the market, or through some quite new mechanism?

Co-operatives and municipal enterprises are creating the primary infrastructure for a new economic participation. But they cannot remain self-sufficient, in isolation from one another. Local control is ineffective if each 'site' operates separately from the others. A unifying network and democratic co-ordination are essential.

The discussion on the energy industry of the future provides a striking example of how the question becomes insoluble if all the various interests are not taken simultaneously into account. Environmentally clean electricity is expensive, while traditional generating methods are destructive, and lead to irreversible losses. Economising with energy is not something that can occur spontaneously, since any substantial fall in demand automatically reduces the price as well, thus doing away with the stimulus to further economies. Moreover, any solution requires long-term investments, which only make sense if there are clearly defined prospects for the future, at least seven to ten years ahead. In the 1960s, John Kenneth Galbraith wrote that long-term investments require state guarantees; subsequent experience has shown, however, that the people in power change, and that the money dispensed in order to provide such guarantees is by no means always used effectively. There is, however, something more important than guarantees from state bureaucrats, and that is collective decisions, democratically adopted. A new, environmentally based energy policy will only work if it is founded on a co-ordinated strategy that is agreed on various levels and that takes different interests into account. This will be a strategy that includes economising on fuel, encouraging technological innovations, making intelligent use of traditional energy sources, and implementing programmes to make up for the damage our planet has suffered as a result of industrial development. This will only work if the key decisions are taken not by the state but by society itself. The only remaining role for the state will be that of carrying out decisions under strict monitoring by citizens' associations. The collectively managed networks of the twenty-first century will be able to create transparent structures for decision-making. The possibility is emerging of civil society being included in management.

It has been fashionable to talk of the participation of civil society in decision-making ever since the mass upsurges in Seattle and Prague. Even the chiefs of the International Monetary Fund and the World Bank have felt obliged to utter a few fine words on this topic. Including a few representatives of non-government organisations on corporate boards, however, can provide only the appearance of democracy, while at the same time corrupting the leaders of the civil associations. The only way to change the situation is to set in place full-blooded democratic procedures at all levels, with civil society involved in decision-making at all levels from top to bottom. Added to this must be democratic control over the civil associations and their leaders.

We are already seeing that civil society is capable of radically changing its character. In place of many quite unrelated organisations, acting independently and to some degree in opposition to one another, there is the rise of coalitions, of networks of social solidarity. These coalitions have nothing in common with totalitarian 'fronts', since they are voluntary and constructed on a basis of equal rights, while the interactions that occur within them involve both collaboration and conflict simultaneously. The task is to create democratic procedures that render decision-making an open process, in which everyone involved has a chance to take part. The participatory budget that was tried out for the first time by the municipal authorities in Porto Alegre provides an example of just such a procedure. If the city chiefs, following the advice of 'progressive' representatives of international financial organisations, had shut themselves up in a room with a dozen or so hand-picked figures from 'civil society' and cooked up a 'socially responsible budget', the result would have been catastrophic both for the city, and for the organisations drawn into this procedure. But the Porto Alegre authorities made the budget process open to everyone, taking it from the hands not only of the bureaucrats but also from those of 'public figures'. Not only did the state finish up exposed to the scrutiny of civil society, but 'civil society' itself was placed under the control of the people.

Democratic procedures and open access to information create the conditions for new ways of managing investments. Industrial corporations can no longer get by without modern information technologies, but it is precisely these technologies that create the potential for collective control, and consequently for power to be taken from the corporate elite and for production to be placed under the control of society. The capitalist hierarchy has finished up under threat. In exactly the same way, the possibility is emerging of undermining the positions occupied by the cyber-lords in the area of modern technology, of opening up the networks to everyone, of abolishing 'information rents' or of directing them toward social needs. In this lies the essence of a new class struggle, of a social conflict that not only refuses to die out in the information epoch, but, on the contrary, takes on an unprecedented scale and intensity.

The idea of self-management, which met with defeat in the twentieth century, is now returning to the agenda. In the movement against corporate globalisation much is said about the need of people to control their lives. Participation is a key word alongside democracy, sovereignty and deglobalisation. But to achieve this we have to challenge the power of capital and most precisely, its two fundamental principles: the logic of accumulation and the rule of private property.

## NOTES

1. *The Economist*, 3 May 2003.
2. It is sometimes stated that the differences between regions appear only because we collect data on a regional and national basis. This argument is self-defeating. If data collected on this basis shows differences, it means precisely that these differences are real. Some US economists propose to collect the data on racial or class basis transnationally. If we take race as a global criterion, we easily come to some very strange conclusions, because race division is not the same everywhere. The living standards of most Russian whites, for example, are much closer to those of South African blacks than to South African whites. Even if we take class criteria without splitting it into regions, we will get a completely distorted picture. Global averages will look like the average temperature of patients in a hospital. But if we split average workers' wages according to regions we will immediately rediscover the differences. The point is that these regional differences in wages and welfare are one of the key elements that allow global capitalism to work as an integrated system. Without these differences it would have made very little sense for capital to move around the globe. The trick of globalisation is that capital moves faster than labour. As a result, capital markets get more or less integrated globally, while labour markets only

locally. Low wages affordable for workers in poorer countries help to gain profits after selling their products in the rich ones.

3. Note that the First World War was preceded by a few earlier conflicts that didn't look like a direct confrontation between the major powers. The Anglo-Boer War was in many ways a conflict between Britain and Germany who backed, encouraged, trained and supplied the Boers. The Russo-Japanese war was a clash between Germany (backing Russia) and England (supporting Japan).

4. See, for example, D. Johnstone (2002) *Fools' Crusade: Yugoslavia, NATO and Western delusions* (London: Pluto Press).

5. *The Economist*, 3 May 2003, p15.

# Notes on Contributors

**Walden Bello** is a professor at the University of the Philippines and executive director of the Bangkok-based Focus on the Global South. He is active in the peace and anti-corporate globalisation movements and has written some 13 books, including *Deglobalization* and *The Future in the Balance*.

**Patrick Bond** is a professor at the University of the Witwatersrand, and a member of the Centre for Economic Justice – Southern Africa. He researches and assists social, labour and environmental movements in Southern Africa and internationally. He has written numerous books and articles, including *Against Global Apartheid – South Africa Meets the World Bank, IMF and International Finance*.

**Alan Freeman** is a professional economist at the Greater London Authority and a fellow of the University of Greenwich. He is a contributor to Jubilee 2000's recent *Real World Economic Outlook* and was co-editor, with Ernest Mandel, of *Ricardo, Marx, Sraffa*.

**Jayati Ghosh** is Professor of Economics at Jawaharlal Nehru University and Secretary of International Development Economics Associates, a South-based network of heterodox development economists. She writes regularly in current affairs journals, including *Frontline* and *Businessline*. Her recent works include *The Market that Failed: Neoliberal economic reforms in India*, with co-author C.P. Chandrasekhar.

**Kate Hudson** is Chair of the British Campaign for Nuclear Disarmament and lectures at London South Bank University. She is the author of *Breaking the South Slav Dream: The rise and fall of Yugoslavia* and *European Communism since 1989: Towards a new European left?*

**Boris Kagarlitsky** is Director of the Institute of Globalisation Studies (IPROG), Moscow. Having been imprisoned for 'anti-Soviet' activities before the USSR dissolved he has since been prominent in the Russian left and workers' movements. He won the Deutscher Memorial Prize for his book, *The Thinking Reed: Intellectuals and the Soviet state*.

**Marylou Malig** is a research associate of Focus on the Global South, in which she also serves as regional trade liaison for South East Asia.

**Bill Robinson** is associate professor of sociology, global and international studies, and Latin American and Iberian studies at the University of California, Santa Barbara. His works include *Promoting Polyarchy* and the recent *Theory of Global Capitalism: Production, class, and state in a transnational world.*

**Sungur Savran** is a prominent Turkish anti-globalisation activist and Marxist theorist. He resigned his post at Istanbul University in the 1990s in protest at the actions of the military dictatorship. He was co-editor with Nesecan Balkan *of The Ravages of Neo-Liberalism: Economy, society and state in Turkey,* and is a frequent contributor to *Ozgur Politika* and other Turkish journals.

# Index

*Compiled by Sue Carlton*